Prol
Bus

Problem Solving in Business and Management

Hard, soft and creative approaches

Michael J. Hicks

Senior Lecturer
Thames University

INTERNATIONAL THOMSON BUSINESS PRESS
I ⓉP An International Thomson Publishing Company

London • Bonn • Boston • Johannesburg • Madrid • Melbourne • Mexico City • New York • Paris
Singapore • Tokyo • Toronto • Albany, NY • Belmont, CA • Cincinnati, OH • Detroit, MI

Problem Solving in Business and Management

Copyright ©1991 Michael J. Hicks

 I T P A division of International Thomson Publishing Inc.
The ITP logo is a trademark under licence

British Library Cataloguing-in-Publication Data
A catalogue record for this book is available from the British Library

First edition published by Chapman & Hall 1991
Reprinted 1993, 1994 and 1995
Reprinted by International Thomson Business Press 1997, 1998 and 1999

Typeset by Best-set Typesetter Ltd, Hong Kong
Printed in Croatia

ISBN 1-86152387 4

International Thomson Business Press
Berkshire House
168–173 High Holborn
London WC1V 7AA
UK

http://www.itbp.com

To my father, C.W.M. Hicks

Contents

Acknowledgements

I am very grateful to Professor Peter Checkland from the University of Lancaster's Department of Systems and Vincent Nolan and John Alexander from Synectics Ltd for reading through my accounts of their methodologies, making many helpful comments and giving permission to reproduce certain diagrams and materials.

I am also indebted to David McHugh of the School of Organization Studies at Lancashire Polytechnic for the useful advice he gave me during the writing of this book, and for his efforts subsequently, cutting the text back down to length!

A mention must also be made of John Sedgwick from Hamilton, Ontario, who first introduced me to CPS almost a decade ago now; my colleague and friend Martin Gandoff who cajoled me into writing this book and my many students whose ideas are contained in the illustrative examples.

I would also like to thank the staff at Chapman & Hall without whose help none of this would have been possible, in particular, Stephen Wellings for his initial support and encouragement and Jeremy Swinfen Green for the difficult and unenviable task of knocking the final manuscript into a mutually acceptable form.

And last, but of course not least, I must acknowledge my wife Teresa, who is now looking forward to her 'new' kitchen being finished after a four-year delay, and my four children who will now be seeing a little more of their less moody father.

Preface

Every day of our lives, we are faced with situations that require us to decide what to say and do. They may require us to resolve circumstances which we perceive as being unsatisfactory in some way or simply to choose between several courses of action. We want to be able to deal with these problems as efficiently as possible, but don't know how. We are unclear perhaps about what options might be available to us, how we should choose between them and what their potential consequences might be.

These problems are further compounded by the fact that change and uncertainty now seem to be an inevitable part of our lives. However, decision making has always been a problem, and this in itself is not really something new. The world around us is more 'turbulent' than it used to be: it is susceptible to rapid and often unpredictable changes. The 'one-off' trial and error approaches to problem solving that we have used in the past appear to be less satisfactory than before. We need more systematic, yet still flexible, problem solving strategies.

Although in the past we have used these *ad hoc* methods and on occasions been successful with them, this has not necessarily resulted in an enhancement of our problem solving skills. Systematic problem solving methods are useful in that, by understanding the process of applying them, we are better able to see their potential advantages and disadvantages when applying them elsewhere. The 'try it and see' approach seldom gives us any guidance on how to approach the next new situation that comes along.

An ability to think creatively, which is usually considered an asset in problem situations, is often perceived as being incompatible with the concept of systematic procedures. Creativity is frequently thought of (incorrectly) as a non-logical process that *just happens*, and which can rarely be called up at will in the middle of a methodical problem solving process. We need to find a way of stimulating and maintaining our creativity whilst adopting a more systematic approach for dealing with our problems. This is the subject matter of this book.

The modern business environment, with its emphasis on competition, building larger markets, strategic planning, team-working, performance appraisal and so on, has created the need for a range of new problem solving and decision making strategies. These strategies need to be systematic enough to enable people to be trained in them, and flexible enough to enable users to adapt them to the various situations where they could be applied. This need is often thought to become greater as we move up through everyday tactical (operational) decisions towards long-term policy (strategic) choices.

It could thus be argued that the techniques described in this book are more relevant for those who aspire to top management, where these strategic decisions are made. This assertion is not valid. Whilst it is certainly true that there is a particular need at that level – 'Since strategic problems are harder to pinpoint, they require special attention' (Ansoff, 1968) – and that at an operational level we have many quantitative techniques available to assist in the decision making process already, this is insufficient evidence. Quantitative methods, although frequently providing useful information, are equally often found to be inadequate for resolving problems. Blind reliance upon them can indeed be disastrous! They should be employed within an enlightened view of the problem situation. For example, it would be wise to ensure that we really do have an imbalance in capacity between sections of our production line causing the 'queueing' problems we have detected, rather than a machine operative who is working slowly because of his or her dissatisfaction over a recently assigned new task, before trying to use queueing theory or mathematical simulation to solve the problem. Most of the problem solving strategies described in this book (because they are intended for what we shall later call 'people' problems) are equally applicable, and just as important, at all levels of management.

Surveying what has already been written about problem solving and decision making elsewhere, there does appear to be some variation over what is thought to constitute these processes, and hence also over the meaning of phrases like 'problem solving techniques', 'decision support systems' and so on. Some people see problem solving and decision making as two separate but almost inextricably linked processes, while others see one process as a part of the other. (We shall be returning to this point briefly in Chapter 1.) Vincent Nolan (1989, p. 14) describes the first of these views as follows:

> Decision making ... consists of making the best choice from the known options, whereas problem solving is the process of creating

the options . . . and the greater the skill [we employ] in problem solving, the easier the decision making becomes.

Whether we consider them as one process or two, this book is about problem solving *and* decision making, although for convenience I shall mostly refer to these processes collectively as 'problem solving'.

A corollary of the viewpoint taken above seems to be that any significant difficulty experienced with decision making will usually be due to the options not being 'entirely satisfactory'. The position I have adopted is to devote the greater part of this book to ensuring that we are able to generate plenty of (better than) satisfactory options (that is, we are effective problem solvers), and then supplementing this with the provision of a relatively simple way of choosing between them.

In the past 50 years or so many different problem solving techniques, procedures, strategies, methodologies and systems have been devised. They have all claimed that they could help us tackle the problem situations we encounter in the real world and most of them have something to offer. They have each spawned a substantial following of devotees.

I believe that, at the present time, there is no *one* problem solving strategy or technique that is universally applicable to all the types of problem situation that we are likely to meet in this imperfect world. Some come very close to this ideal though, and are therefore more generally usable than others. In this book I am presenting a carefully selected subset of these strategies which together *will* help us tackle almost all types of problem situation.

Although I will be giving some explanation of the rationale underlying the strategies described, I will not be quoting extensively from research findings which validate them. Amongst the books listed in the Bibliography will be found the original texts where these strategies were first explained, and where full justifications can be heard first hand from the originators. These books also relate many examples of the applications cf these strategies to *real* problems. My sole aim is:

- to present the strategies which I consider to have had the greatest impact in improving our problem solving abilities (and which are also representative of others I have had to omit);
- to provide sufficient background information about them (including illustrative case studies) to provide a practical guide for their use;
- to show how the different approaches complement each other, and thus provide a complete problem solving system.

Many organizations, both commercial and non-commercial, do not recruit solely on the basis of qualifications any more, but consider also the extent to which potential employees possess certain personal and interpersonal skills; skills such as:

- problem solving
- self-confidence
- self-awareness and awareness of others
- self-esteem
- self-reliance
- self-management
- leadership and group member skills
- maturity

In particular, these organizations have realized the importance of having personnel with good problem solving abilities, and who are prepared to use them. This is not just true of opportunities/careers in business and management, but in virtually every field.

This attitude is being reflected in the guidance and training offered by educational bodies and institutions. The Business & Technician Education Council (BTEC) in the UK has been promoting the development of problem solving skills for many years now. Their current guidelines 'encourage' providers of BTEC training to incorporate the development of problem solving skills into *all* the various modules or units of *any* particular course. There are also now several innovative MBA courses placing considerable emphasis on problem solving.

The original spur to write this book was the apparent need for a general text on problem solving for students following BTEC Higher courses. I believe that problem solving skills cannot be developed by just subjecting the student to a series of progressively more complicated problems. There has to be some explicit input from the trainer on problem solving strategies and techniques and their underlying rationale. Because BTEC believe (and I would tend to agree with them) that it is undesirable to provide problem solving training as a separate entity from the rest of the course, this book has been compiled in such a way that certain aspects of problem solving can be extracted and used wherever appropriate. It is not my intention that the book should be used as a text for a separate module or unit in problem solving, although even that should be possible.

Since its original inception, however, the idea for this book has grown, and while writing it I have tried to keep in mind a much wider potential audience. I believe that this book will also provide an introductory text for students on both undergraduate and MBA courses, as well as being of general interest to people in business and management, or anyone else wishing to find out more about the intriguing process by which we resolve problems and make decisions.

In some ways it is sad that, although the problem solving methods offered here are not new but are between 10 and 50 years old, as yet very few people are aware of them. This is another reason for writing this book, for although it is primarily (but not solely) intended for students involved in higher education, it will also be another book on the shelves of the bookshops and libraries, and this means that there will be a slightly greater probability that other people will find out about these valuable ways of improving their problem solving skills.

Three main approaches to problem solving are described in this book. They are:

☐ The **Creative approach** We have a large amount of knowledge and experience locked in our minds and there is always something in there that is 'approximately relevant' to a given problem situation, but we do not always realize this. The techniques and strategies that fall under the Creative heading enable us to make the connections between this material and the problem we are tackling (for example, between an overflowing bath tub and a method for testing gold) and invariably produce innovative solutions. How often have you said something like 'That's a really clever/new/elegant idea – it's so simple! If only I could think of things like that . . .'? It is not just people like Archimedes who can do this, we all can!

☐ The **Rational (Logical) approach** When we say that we are dealing with something in a logical way, we usually mean that we are carefully and methodically proceeding from one stage to another, letting our analysis of each stage dictate where we should go next. On many occasions this is the most appropriate way of proceeding. But we often forget our starting point. Before we can apply this process we must have examined the problem situation, analysed some of its features and formulated some assumptions about it (that is, defined the problem). If these assumptions are wrong or inappropriate, so will be our solutions.

☐ The **Soft Systems approach** It was the realization that most of the real-world problem situations which we encounter, like the world we live in, are by their nature exceedingly complex, and also interrelated, that made us strive for a way of tackling the situation as a whole. If a problem is detected in some part of an organization, it is possible if not likely that we will need to look outside of that division, perhaps even wider than the organization, in order to find a way of resolving the problem. It is this that systems thinking attempts to do, that is, to 'model' the situation in all its complexity.

Traditional systems thinking tended to look at the problem situation with a view to detecting what was wrong with how things were being done, and then putting it right – which often meant patching up a basically defective set-up. The Soft Systems approach looks beyond the present implementation of the system and tries to discover its underlying essence. Asking not how something is being done, but why? It questions the original design rather than the implementation.

┌─── *Frame 0.1   Enterprise skills* ───────────────────┐

Displaying initiative
Generating and developing ideas*
Imagination*
Open-mindedness*
Inventiveness
Ingenuity
Adaptability
Problem solving*
Decision making*
A positive attitude
Self-reliance
Self-confidence
Self-awareness
Leadership
Team membership*
Amenability to change
Ability to manage change

└──┘

The logical approach on its own is seldom enough, and will always benefit from some creative thinking. There is a danger with the creative approach that we can get 'hooked' on the generation of ideas and shy away from the (logical) discipline required to develop and implement these ideas. If not carefully applied both of these approaches may fail to appreciate the problem in all its complexity. And to use the (Soft) Systems approach effectively requires some understanding of, and experience in using, various systems concepts.

These approaches should not be thought of as discrete alternatives, and in particular the importance of creative thinking in all problem solving cannot be understated. It is for this reason that the 'creative' theme runs throughout the book, even when we are apparently considering other problem solving methods. The success of applying a predominantly Rational or Soft Systems approach to a problem relies greatly on the amount of creative thinking that has gone on along the way.

Much is being said presently, both in a BTEC context and elsewhere, about the desirability of developing 'enterprise' skills. Various attempts have been made to identify precisely what constitutes enterprise, and there would appear to be a reasonable amount of agreement about this. A recurring theme in the various definitions of 'enterprise skills training' is the development of the various personal and interpersonal skills, listed in Frame 0.1.

Training in creative thinking and problem solving not only develops the skills marked with an asterisk, but is also believed by many people (those working in commerce and industry as well as academics) to develop and improve *all* these skills. This is because, if we actively assimilate these 'new' approaches to tackling problems, it is highly probable that they will change our outlook on, and attitudes to, many aspects of our personal and working lives for the better. But like most skills, if they are not practised regularly, our ability to apply them will become less effective. This is why it is important for us to find out as much as we can about them, so as to understand them well enough to employ them frequently and in a variety of situations. In this way we can avert any tendency to neglect these skills which might occur during our 'socialization' into new 'home' or working environments.

The unique feature of this book is the portrayal of these three approaches collectively. I believe that studying them as a set will not only reveal their innate inter-reliance but may also instil a comprehensive problem solving approach to life and thus help to rectify the unbalanced learning that is believed to have taken place on many education courses.

The idea is to build on and enhance the problem solving skills that the reader already possesses, and my starting point will be to assume that everyone reading this book has already 'endured' many years of full-time secondary education. This should have given the reader at least some 'grounding' in logical thinking, and the way we apply this to solving problems which are well defined and which often have only one desired answer. Some readers will have a good deal of work experience as well, and this may have given them a chance to develop their creative thinking skills in addition to this.

It is because of the quite widespread belief that the educational process and the society we were brought up in have often been responsible for a reduction of our ability to think creatively, and that only the fortunate few will, through their subsequent working and personal lives, have had the opportunity to 'reawaken' their latent creativity, that I will start off with a discussion on creative thinking.

After a brief discussion of what constitutes a problem (Chapter 1) and how we usually go about tackling one (Chapters 2, 3), I will explain why and how the attenuation of the creativity we were born with has taken place, and then show how we can reawaken or restore these creative abilities (Chapter 4). Since most Creative Problem Solving (CPS) techniques work best in a group environment, we will go on from there to look at some of the 'dynamics' of group problem solving (Chapter 5), before considering several CPS strategies (Chapters 6, 7).

Having discussed the creative approach, we will then return to what has been described as the 'rational', 'logical' or 'analytical' approach – the common-sense guide to thinking (Chapters 8, 9, 10) – and having covered what I consider to be all the 'ground work' progress via an introduction to systems concepts (Chapter 11) to the so-called Soft Systems approach (Chapter 12).

Having completed our look at the various problem solving strategies and techniques, we shall attempt to tackle rather more complex problems using the Synectics (a highly developed and sophisticated form of CPS) and the Soft Systems approaches, noting any similarities and/or differences between the two 'philosophies', and discuss how they may be used in conjunction to good effect (Chapter 13). Finally we shall conclude with a discussion of the problems of managing change (Chapter 14).

To provide a programme which gradually develops problem solving skills is difficult, because there is no obvious intellectual progression in the ideas presented here. Vincent Nolan (1989, p. 84) has described many of these techniques as 'mostly "common sense", in that there are sound reasons for using them where appropriate, which will be readily accepted when explained simply'. The Soft Systems approach needs to be prefaced by an explanation of 'systems' and 'systems thinking' concepts, but that is all. Success in the exploitation of the techniques described here depends more on the relative maturity of the practitioners and their experience of life.

The best that can be done is to present increasingly more and more complex problems, running from those for which there is a relatively obvious approach, to those where a combination of approaches may be the best ploy. This is what I have generally tried to do. To me the Soft Systems and Synectics approaches are the 'ultimate' states of the art, however I have chosen to group Synectics along with the rest of the discussion on the Creative approach to problem solving as the culmination of that section, as this seemed more appropriate.

In Peter Checkland's book (1981) the author insisted on the idea that any problem solving 'system' should be a flexible, modifiable and continuously evolving thing. And so, instead of a highly prescriptive 'flow chart' approach which says, 'Right. Here are the techniques. If this, this and this are so, then use method x, etc . . .', my intention is to offer what I believe to be the most useful subset of these tools which the reader can then use in any permutation he or she thinks is appropriate.

The strategies and techniques offered here are described (to my best belief) in a way that the originators would both recognize and approve of, despite the fact that other authors have adapted and modified some of them since – often to good effect. It is not that I am being pedantic or adopting a 'Luddite' outlook. I firmly believe that these techniques *should* be continuously evolving so as to be always relevant and that this end is best served by presenting the reader with the 'original' version, and then supporting this with some suggestions as to how they have or could be modified. The hope is that readers will then have a firm grounding from which they will be able to adapt and develop the techniques and strategies offered here to their own ends.

Most of the illustrations, cases, etc. given in this book are fictitious or semi-fictitious. I make no apologies for this, as they have been specifically designed to show the reader the various facets and intricacies of the methods described.

Problems, problems, problems!

1.1 What is a problem?

Before we look at how to solve real-world problems, we should agree on what actually constitutes a problem. Listed in Frame 1.1 are some descriptions of what a problem is. There are four things implicit in most of these descriptions:

- [ ] *We* have *recognized* that there is a problem.
- [ ] *We do not know* how to resolve this problem.
- [ ] *We want* to resolve it.
- [ ] *We* (perceive that we) *are able* to implement a solution when we find it.

1.2 Do I have a problem?

A problem situation must be perceived by someone; otherewise there is not a problem. But who needs to perceive the problem? Someone may think that *we* have a problem; but if we do not perceive it as a problem for *us*, we may not feel the need to do anything about it. But does that mean we can deny the existence of this problem? We may not realize that we have a problem, but that does not stop us from having one.

> Managing director to sales manager: 'The performance of your salesmen in our South-East region was pretty poor last month, you had better do something about it!'

As sales manager, we thought that things were fine. We didn't have any problems ... But we certainly have now! Whether the problem is our salesmen not reaching their targets, or the managing director thinking that we are not doing our job properly, we are now in a situation which is no longer how we would like it. Unless we have an immediate solu-

—————— *Frame 1.1   What is a problem?* ——————

A problem is . . .

'Problem solving' is the art of finding ways to get from where you are to where you want to be (assuming you do not already know how). The 'problem', therefore, is the gap between the present situation and a more desirable one.

Vincent Nolan (1989, p. 4)

A problem can be defined as any situation in which a gap is perceived to exist between what is and what should be.

Arthur B. VanGundy Jr (1988, p. 3)

We usually refer to ourselves as having a problem if things are not as we would like them to be, and we are not quite sure what to do about it.

Colin Eden, Sue Jones and David Sims (1983, p. 12)

. . . any situation in which an expected level of performance is not being achieved and in which the cause of the unacceptable performance is unknown.

Charles Kepner and Benjamin Tregoe (1981, p. 34)

A problem . . . is a condition characterized by a sense of mis-match, which eludes precise definition, between what is perceived to be actuality and what is perceived might become actuality.

Peter Checkland (1981, p. 155)

A problem is a situation in which 'a decision-making individual or group has alternative courses of action available, . . . the choice made can have a significant effect, and . . . the decision maker has some doubt as to which alternative should be selected'.

Russell Ackoff (1981, p. 20)

tion there is a real problem, and it's ours. So, we do not have to know about a problem in order to have one. But we do need to have perceived a problem before we can be expected to do something about it.

1.3   Can I solve this problem?

If we do not know how to resolve a particular situation we may have two difficulties. We may have difficulties in defining precisely what the problem is. And we may have difficulties in finding a possible solution *when* we have decided on the best way of looking at (defining) the problem. But, directly or indirectly, we must be able to do something about a problem situation once we have resolved what this should be, or there is very little point in doing any problem solving in the first place. As a 'lone' problem solver, if *we* do not have the authority and resources to implement our solution, then implementing it will be made more difficult because we have to rely on our skills to influence somebody else who does have the power. And motivating others to do something is seldom an easy or a simple task.

Our perceptions play a key role in many aspects of problem solving, and here they are of particular interest because they determine what we think we are able to accomplish by way of a solution. It is our perception of our 'power to act' (or of our skill to influence) that is really important; this needs to be considered when starting to tackle a problem situation. Our perception will be modified by the prevailing organizational culture in which the problem solving is to take place. In organizations with an emphasis on flexible working and internal markets, where we are often actively encouraged away from narrow specialisms and responsibilities, we may have a situation where all problems are deemed to belong to the organization and thus to everyone in it. In this type of culture we are likely to feel that we have more personal power than we would have elsewhere. Our perception of our power will also vary with time, as culture changes and opportunities come and go.

There are inherent difficulties in influencing other people and persuading them to do things. Some people believe that if we do not possess the power to implement a solution *directly*, there is effectively little we can do about a particular problem. In such circumstances, we would be better off attempting to resolve a different but related problem, one for which we do have the power to do something about. I have a problem:

> I wish we could abolish all forms of chemical, biological and nuclear weapons.

As an individual there is little or nothing I can do about this problem *directly*. However, stating the problem as:

> How can I help to increase the awareness of others to the potentially devastating effect that the use of these weapons would have on the whole of our planet?

gives me a direction I can move in.

- I can join/make donations to organizations already working towards this end.
- I can write letters/articles about the subject and send them to anyone who I think might publish them.

- I can start a discussion on the subject in the bar of the 'World's End' public house.

1.4   Who owns a problem?

Tied to these notions of whether or not we recognize a problem and are able to do something about it is the whole question of problem ownership. There are differing views as to who qualifies as an owner of a particular problem situation and how much power and influence is a prerequisite for this. For instance, can someone who fails to recognize that he or she has a problem be a problem-owner? There is general agreement that the owner of a problem is any person who is 'dissatisfied' with a situation and wishes it were otherwise (which assumes recognition of the problem). However, there is less consensus over the importance of a problem-owner's ability to implement a solution. Definitions of potential problem-owners seem to be spread along a 'power to act' continuum stretching from those who have the direct power to implement a solution to those who are just the 'victims' of the situation and will be affected by any solution that is proposed, and who often have very little power or influence.

This difference of opinion is most prevalent in discussions concerning circumstances where several people share the same problem. The same problem situation can be seen in many ways by many people: which *definition* of this problem situation are we the owner of, and can we do anything about the problem when viewed in that way? If we redefine a problem in such a way that it comes within our own domain of power and influence, then our definition of the problem can be made to reflect not only our particular perception of the problem situation but also our individual power to effect a solution. When we embark on joint problem solving, we should each consider the limitations imposed (by our situational and contingent power) on our abilities to implement a solution, and define the problem accordingly. Then no matter who we are or how much power and influence we have, not only do we have a valid stake in the problem, but we should also be able to accomplish something with regard to its resolution. This view of problem ownership should remind us of the possibility that other people may have a stake in *any* problem situation that concerns us and it is likely that there are other valid and differing views as to what this problem is.

But what of situations where we are asked to help somebody else who has a problem – where initially we have no ownership of the problem? If we are called in as an outside consultant for this purpose, we cannot and should not attempt to solve that person's problem for them. Our role is solely to help *them* resolve their own problem. We should endeavour not to get involved with the **content** of the problem situation: we are there to facilitate the problem resolving **process**.

To **resolve** a problem is to select a course of action that yields an outcome that is good enough, that satisfices. . . . this approach relies heavily on past experience and current trial and error for its inputs. It is qualitatively, not quantitatively, oriented; it is rooted deeply in common sense, and it makes extensive use of subjective judgements.

To **solve** a problem is to select a course of action that is believed to yield the best possible outcome, that optimizes. . . . this approach is largely based on scientific methods, techniques and tools. It makes use of mathematical models and real or simulated experimentation; therefore, it relies heavily on observation and measurement and aspires to complete objectivity.

To **dissolve** a problem is to change the nature, and/or environment, of the entity in which it is imbedded so as to remove the problem. [This approach idealizes because its] objective is to change the system involved or its environment in such a way as to bring it closer to an ultimately desired state, one in which the problem cannot or does not arise.

Russell Ackoff (1981, pp. 20–1)

1.5   Problem solving or resolving?

I have been using the word 'resolve' above, where I might have used the word 'solve'. This is deliberate. I prefer the word 'resolve' because it describes better what we actually mean by 'real-world' problem solving. *Chambers' Twentieth Century Dictionary* (1972) offers the following meanings of 'resolve':

> to make visible the details of; to separate into components; to analyse; to determine; to transform; to free from doubt or difficulty; to dissipate; to solve.

When involved in the process of problem solving we may do some, many or all of these things.

Other authors have found the term 'problem solving' to be inadequate and many find it necessary at least to distinguish between problem identification and problem solving. In particular, Russell Ackoff (1981) has gone further in an attempt to clarify what it is we do with problems in order to improve a problem situation, and has spoken of 'resolving', 'solving' and 'dissolving' problems. Frame 1.2 contains a brief summary of the meanings he ascribes to these terms.

Ackoff suggests that only when using scientific methods where our intent is to optimize the situation through experimentation and quantitative analysis, for example management science's Operational Research (OR) techniques, should we refer to what we are doing as 'solving' problems. There is some debate as to whether such optimization is ever actually possible with the sort of problems that we will be dealing with (see Chapter 3).

This book is mostly about how we go about identifying which is the most useful way of looking at a problem situation and resolving what courses of action we should take in order to improve things. And according to Ackoff's classification system, most of the techniques mentioned (for example, Brainstorming and Synectics) appear to be primarily problem *resolving* techniques, though Soft Systems Methodology, due to its holistic approach, is the most likely one also to be considered a problem *dissolving* technique. The use of any of these strategies may subsequently indicate the desirability of employing Operational Research (OR) and other quantitative methods to optimize a chosen course of action, thus *solving* a problem. However, I shall use the term 'problem solving' because of its common and widespread usage.

We will be looking into what precisely is involved in problem solving (or rather, resolving and dissolving) shortly, but first I think that it is useful to investigate whether there are different sorts of problem, and if so, whether we should treat them differently?

1.6   Are there different types of problem?

Consider a couple of situations that might be thought of by some people as being problematical,

> We are constructing the flat triangular structure shown in Figure 1.1 according to the measurements given. Although we have sufficient information to build the structure, it would be useful if we knew the size of the other angle because this information could be used to check the accuracy of our construction when we are finished. What is the angle?

The solution to this 'problem' is 42°, which can be found by the application of simple trigonometry. This is a fairly straightforward problem and some people might dispute that it qualifies as a problem at all.

> Peripherals Unlimited, a small electronics manufacturing company, produce and sell three microcomputer peripheral products: a letter quality dot matrix printer, the CP80; a single 3.5″ floppy disc drive, the CD35; and a 14″ high resolution colour monitor, the CV14. Their production draws different demands on the resources needed to

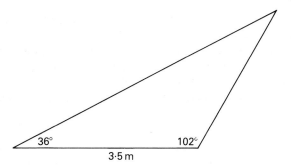

Figure 1.1 *Triangle problem.*

Table 1.1 *Peripherals Unlimited*

Product	Machine time (min)	Labour (hr)	Raw materials (£)
CP80	10	2	90
CD35	15	3	45
CV14	25	2	50

produce them, as shown in Table 1.1. The estimated contributions (to profit) from the CP80, CD35 and CV14 are £130, £95 and £105 respectively.

The machine time available for cutting, folding and drilling the case and chassis components is limited to 40 hours per week until such time as a second machine can be purchased. Likewise labour, which is mostly used for the completion of the final units from sub-assemblies, is restricted to 210 hours per week and there is no possibility of hiring any more staff in the foreseeable future. With regard to 'raw materials', since the greater part of this cost is the purchase of ready-built Taiwanese sub-assemblies, there is no externally imposed limit on the number available. However, with an eye on its cashflow, it is the company's present policy not to tie up more than £6000 per week on this.

Due to Peripherals Unlimited's relatively small production capacity they believe they can sell as many printers and monitors as they can make. The market for external disc drives, however, is still expanding and for the moment the company feels that they are unlikely to sell more than 50 units per week. Peripherals Unlimited want to ensure that they are making the best use of their available resources, and have asked us to advise them on how many of each product type should be produced per week in order to maximize their profit.

The solution to this 'problem' is that (on purely financial grounds) they should make 12 CP80s, 24 CD35s and 76 CV14s per week. But this is not a problem, it is a decision waiting to be made. There may have been a problem once, for example, 'How can Peripherals Unlimited rationalize its operations so as to be in the best possible position for 1993?' But to get to the situation described above they should have identified all the possible courses of action that could have been taken which were both feasible and desirable, and *decided* that a solution to the problem of how to get into the best possible position for 1993 was to modify their production mix solely on the basis of maximizing their profit. That is the solution, not the arithmetic calculation that follows it.

It could be said that determining the most cost-effective product mix is part of the research Peripherals Unlimited needs to do in order to decide whether altering the production schedule *is* one of the most appropriate actions to take. That still does not make it a problem. Linear Programming and other mathematical/statistical techniques, often grouped together under the heading of OR, and the computer software that assists their implementation, are correctly termed Decision Support Systems. They help us make decisions, not solve problems.

The problem solving strategies and techniques described later in this book should be thought of as a 'front end' to the traditional methods of management science. There are many good books already on OR, and so very little further mention of these methods will be found in this text.

1.7 Classifying problems

A number of problem classifications exist. These only help to distinguish *real* problems (the sort which the problem solving techniques and strategies mentioned in this book are designed to help us resolve) from situations like the two described above. However, we will briefly examine these classifications as they bring to light some problems we often have with problem solving.

1.7.1 Reducing problems to size

We can differentiate between **complex** and **simple** problems. This describes the structure of the problem situation, not the ease or difficulty with which we can write down a statement of what we think the problem is. The complexity of this structure reflects how far-reaching a problem and its implications are, and whether it involves people.

The Triangle 'problem' was simple by anyone's definition; Peripherals Unlimited's 'problem' is simple to anyone familiar with the techniques of OR.

Some people suggest that complex problems should be broken down into manageable portions. Others say this is often the worst thing to do. Breaking a problem down may mean that we fail to consider the interactions between the small part we have chosen to solve and its immediate environment. The breaking down of a problem in order to facilitate its solution is referred to as **restructuring** the problem. We should be aware of the danger of 'missing the problem' in situations where we are obliged by circumstances to do this: we may break a problem into bits, solve all these bits and fail to realize that the real problem existed in the interaction between these bits. This is what systems people call a **boundary problem**, and the Soft Systems approach described later is an attempt to overcome this dilemma. The following scenario provides a simple illustration of this.

> The marketing section of a company complains that the production section is not effective. They feel frustrated because after all their efforts seeking out new customers and obtaining more orders than ever in the past, they are being embarrassed by complaints from these customers about the failure of orders to arrive before the agreed delivery dates. The production section on the other hand claims that they are already working to maximum capacity, and that impossible demands and deadlines are being imposed on them by the unrealistic promises that the marketing section has been making to customers.

The fault may lie within a particular section; perhaps marketing *is* making unrealistic promises, perhaps production *is* understaffed in relation to the recent increase in business. But the problem may in fact be one of bad communications between the sections:

- Marketing not fully realizing the scheduling limitations that production works to.
- Marketing inadvertently/inappropriately referring to every order as high priority.
- Marketing failing to appreciate the notice production requires for a special 'one-off' run.
- Production not keeping marketing furnished with up-to-date information about finished goods in stock, work in progress and future production commitments.

If this complex problem were to be broken down on a sectional basis, it might never be solved.

At one time Operational Research (OR) was heralded as the answer to every manager's problems. It claimed to be able to deal with the problems of management in *all* their complexity. 'OR is the application of the methods of science to complex problems arising in the direction and management of large systems of men, machines, materials and money in industry, business, government and defence. The distinctive approach is to develop a scientific model of the system, incorporating measurements of factors such as chance and risk, with which to predict and compare the outcomes of alternative decisions, strategies or controls. The purpose is to help management determine its policy and actions scientifically'. Enthusiasm for the techniques of OR transferred from wartime operations to the practice of management in the 1950s, quickly turned to disillusionment during the 1970s.

In reality, most effort in adapting OR for use on management problems was concentrated on refining certain quantitative methods, and developing these for use in specific and recurring situations. The belief that certain management problems turn up repeatedly encourages managers to assume that any given problem situation is likely to be one or more of the following specific 'problem' types (Wild, 1972):

allocation problems
inventory problems
replacement problems
queueing problems
sequencing and routing problems
search problems (i.e. concerned with location)
competitive or bidding problems

Not only does this tendency tempt us to restructure problem situations and to do so in a restricted way, so that we may end up solving totally the wrong problem and missing the real one completely, but it is based on a false premise. Often the uniqueness of a situation makes it problematical and this apparent contradiction between theory and reality could explain why few managers actually use OR. An antidote to this is to recognize that the real problem often lies several stages before the point where we decide whether we need to employ OR techniques or not. OR can be useful in certain circumstances – it allows us to model certain specific situations and (so long as we do not over-simplify reality in our model) provides us with answers to questions such as 'Which is our most cost-effective product mix?' 'How many service points do we need in order to reduce customer waiting time to a couple of minutes?' But it is of little use with a large majority of real world problems. Jay Forrester (1961) contended that this was not because managers were incapable of understanding or applying the techniques of OR, but because the techniques themselves are just not capable of handling the complex decisions that managers have to make.

1.7.2   The problem of knowing what the problem is

We can also classify problems on how **well-defined** or **ill-defined** they are. Are we sure of what the problem really is? Do we feel confident that we know in which 'direction' we should look for a possible solution?

The Triangle problem was extremely well defined. We know exactly what we are dealing with, a plane triangular structure some of whose dimensions are known exactly. There is only one possible problem definition, and there can only be one solution. We know precisely what we have to find out, the third angle, and how to do this. Exactly the

Redefining the problem breakdown ———————————— *Frame 1.3*

You are travelling alone in your car to a very important meeting. Fifteen minutes from your destination (30 minutes before the meeting), your car engine loses power, cuts out and you glide to a standstill on a busy clearway in the middle of a thunderstorm.

You certainly have a problem. But what is it?

How to get the car started again.
How to effect an immediate repair to . . .
How to reach my destination as quickly as possible.
How to find alternative transport.
I wish I had wings.
I wish I could teleport to my destination.
I wish it would stop raining.
I wish I had stayed in bed today.
How to get the car off the clearway into a safe parking area.
How to communicate with the RAC/my office/my destination.
I wish I could think up a new excuse for my boss/wife/etc.
I wish I could afford a more reliable means of transport.
I wish I knew how to fix cars.
How to get myself and/or car back home.
I wish I could afford the repair.
How to get the car to a scrap yard at no cost.
How to keep warm and dry.
I wish I were a member of the AA.
I wish I had a Datsun.
I wish I had a radio telephone.

same comments can be made about Peripherals Unlimited's problem.

When a problem is ill defined and even when we think we know what the problem is, we should try to view the problem from many angles to ensure that we are actually attempting to solve the 'right' or most appropriate one. A simple example of this is illustrated in Frame 1.3. This process of looking around the stated problem is referred to as **redefining the problem**. The Synectics approach described later places great emphasis on this concept.

1.7.3   Tame and wicked problems

Yet another classification system, which again only separates real problems from the others, divides problems into **tame** and **wicked**. The

───── *Frame 1.4   'Wicked' problems* ─────

Wicked problems have the following features:

- They do not have a definitive problem description,
- There is no certain way of knowing when you have reached the best solution.
- Their possible solutions are not true or false but somewhere between good and bad,
- There is no immediate or ultimate way of testing the merit of a solution,
- They have an infinite number of possible solutions,
- The problem situation shows no precise indications as to what are/are not permissible ways of reaching a solution.
- Each problem is essentially unique,
- There are many ways of looking at (defining) the problem and each one suggests a 'different' direction in which we should perhaps look for a solution,
- Every wicked problem can be thought of as a symptom of another problem,
- There is seldom any opportunity to determine a solution by 'trial and error',
- It is usually imperative that we find a 'correct' solution, preferably at the first attempt.

Rittel and Webber (1974)

features of a wicked problem are paraphrased in Frame 1.4 to illustrate the type of situation we *are* hoping to deal with.

Simple, well-defined and tame problems are not our major concern here. Taken one at a time, they are relatively easy to deal with. However, even simple problems can be difficult to handle if they arrive together in large numbers. If they are not to overload our problem solving efforts, we will need to prioritize them and plan a schedule for their resolution. It is mainly the wicked variety with which we need help, and we will look at these *real* problems again, to see if their nature suggests the use of one problem solving strategy rather than another. Before this we are going to look at what stages might or should be involved in such a strategy.

Resolving problems

2

I am about to present another problem (a wicked problem). Before I do, it would be useful for you to plan how you would tackle it. You know nothing about the nature of the problem except that it is going to be considerably different from the Triangle problem in Chapter 1. Try to list a number of steps or stages you think that you are likely to go through in order to solve this new problem. In order to get the most out of the next few pages you should make an attempt to plan your problem solving strategy and then try to use it to tackle the problem situation in Frame 2.1.

You plan is probably reasonably workable. Did you feel there was room for improvement in your problem solving process? Ask yourself the following questions:

The Desert Island predicament ——————————— *Frame 2.1* ——

You have been shipwrecked on a small uninhabited island miles away from the nearest civilization. After a quick look around, you discover the following items washed up on the shoreline:

assorted rope
glass bottles
ripped sails
driftwood
three empty oil drums
some large sea shells
two plastic sacks

How are you going to get out of this predicament?

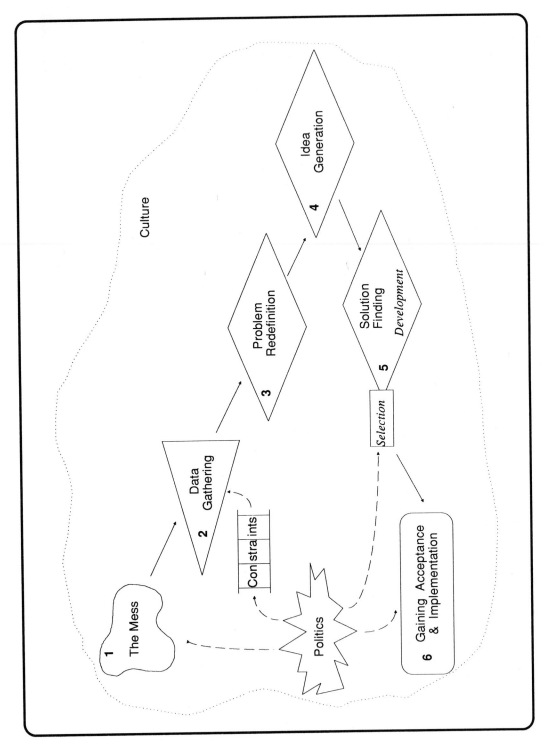

Figure 2.1 *A problem solving model.*

- Did you have more than one possible solution?
- Did you look at the problem situation from various viewpoints?
  - (a) How to make an escape from the island.
  - (b) How to build a raft.
  - (c) How to survive on the island.
  - (d) How to construct a shelter/find food.
  - (e) How to maximize the possibilities of being rescued.
  - (f) How to communicate with the outside world.
- Are you certain that you were actually solving the right problem?
- When you thought of an idea did you make a note of the idea, and then try thinking of some more, or start evaluating the merit of that one idea immediately?
- Did you feel you needed more information or someone else to help you to solve the problem and/or to 'bounce' ideas off?
- Can you honestly say that there is no way in which you could have improved the way you tackled this problem?

Although it was not the sort of real world problem that you have to deal with every day it has many of the some features, being badly defined and open-ended. How might a problem solving strategy that was adequate to solve this 'problem' need to be refined to tackle organizational problems?

The questions above are intended to make us question how our problem solving strategy might benefit from being changed. We shall be addressing each of these in more detail in the next few chapters.

2.1   A general problem solving model

There are several **models** around, usually comprising a list of steps or activities that people tend to do during the process of problem solving. It is not necessary either to know of or strictly adhere to any particular model in order to be an effective problem solver. Most of the problem solving strategies discussed later tend to have their own steps or stages. The model shown in Figure 3.1 (modified from Sidney Parnes' work) serves as a reminder of the various stages we *may* need.

2.1.1   The 'Mess'

We start with the realization that a problem exists. Since this implies that things are not as we wish them, we will probably experience feelings of uneasiness, doubt, etc., but to bring order out of this chaos we must at least be prepared to get down into the middle of it. Any real world problem situation will appear immensely complicated at first sight. We feel intimidated by its complexity, and will long for some way of simplifying it – some way of imposing order on the chaos. We feel threatened and inadequate, anxious about how we can demonstrate competence, about how we can demonstrate that we are on top of the situation. But we must resist this temptation.

At this point we should be asking ourselves questions such as:

What is the situation now?
Is there really a problem?
Is it my problem?
Why do I want to solve the problem?
Where do I want to be?

2.1.2   Data gathering

In this 'fact' finding stage it may be necessary for us to gather:

- **objective data** – the who, what, where, when, why and how of the situation;
- **subjective data** – opinions, attitudes, feelings and beliefs;
- details of any **constraints** that exist (or are thought to exist) on the system – legal, financial, time, etc.;
- anything else(?).

2.1.3   Defining the problem

This crucial stage in problem solving can be referred to as Problem *Re*definition as there may be several valid ways of viewing the problem that all need to be considered. If we do not start from the right place we will be lucky to stumble on a lasting solution. General advice is to note the problem definition as given, then take time to think of other ways of describing it – try to get different 'angles' on the problem situation.

2.1.4   Generating ideas

At this stage we should remember not to evaluate our ideas too soon. Although some selection of ideas will be necessary before we move to the next phase, no judgements or criticisms should be made whilst we are trying to generate them.

2.1.5   Solution finding

Now we gently evaluate and develop the most promising of our ideas. We should first try to open things up, be creative, try some lateral thinking, before we attempt to select items to be carried forward to the next step. This choice we eventually have to make is not simply selecting the best solutions according to some abstract, absolute or objective criteria. It involves 'political' considerations as well. It is often an involved and complex decision making process, where we decide which

---

Acceptable solutions to real problems ——————— *Frame 2.2* ——

The desert island problem, although fun to think about and useful as a starting point for discussing problem solving strategies, is really a problem in isolation. We can test our individual knowledge of survival tactics and exercise our imaginations on raft design, but there is very little in the way of an external system or environment whose possible interest in the problem situation we should attend to, and which could place restrictions on the range of our possible solutions. Not only is most organizational problem solving a group process, but often other groups have a stake in the problem solving group's operations. So what constitutes an acceptable solution is often decided by the group itself, and may also be constrained by these wider interactions. In other words, the problem solving takes place within a context.

A simple illustration of the difficulty of deciding what constitutes an acceptable solution is to consider the following solutions to the problem of 'How to combat air pollution from car exhausts', all of which are possible. Which would be appropriate in a management report to the managing director of a major car manufacturer: ban all cars, ban internal combustion power, invest £x million in research and development into alternative energy sources, redesign *all* his company's engines to run on unleaded petrol, fit catalytic converters, conduct an advertising campaign *saying* that all his company's cars are cleaner?

Presumably the first two are unacceptable, but what of the other four? Most car manufacturing companies have gone or are moving in the direction of the fourth solution, but the fifth seems eminently reasonable and would a company unable immediately to adopt either of these two consider the last? A rich and far-sighted company might even contemplate adopting the third solution.

---

solutions are 'acceptable' in the context of the problem situation (Frame 2.2).

Before we embark on the process of gaining wider acceptance of, and commitment to, our possible solutions, we need to consider their sequencing (it is unlikely that we will be able to present all our possible solutions), and the amount of 'weight' we wish to give to each solution when we offer our ideas/solutions to other people.

2.1.6 Gaining acceptance

Finally, and often a problem in its own right, we need to 'sell' the merits of our possible solutions, **gain acceptance** for them and elicit the commitment necessary to **implement** them. There are many factors that determine success in this as will be seen later. It does not matter how innovative, imaginative, spectacular, accomplished and eminently sensible our solutions might be if we lack the authority or interpersonal skills necessary to persuade others to our view. The brilliance of our solution alone is rarely sufficient to guarantee its implementation.

2.2   Following the model

You can return from any stage to any previous stage and repeat part (or all) of the process, if appropriate. You may wish to take several problem definitions through to a solution, to generate additional ideas if difficulties are encountered developing possible solutions from your initial ideas, or even go back to get additional data if needed. While it is useful to know what stages we might have needed to go through, it should never be thought that we *must*:

- go through every stage;
- do this in the order prescribed, starting at stage 1;
- never consider the possibility of 'looping back' to repeat an earlier stage or stages, if that seems to be desirable or necessary;
- assume that the stages are discrete and never overlap.

Although often we start at step 1 and go through all the steps methodically, this is not always the case. Often our problem is identifying what is causing us concern about the situation. Once we have satisfied ourselves as to how best to describe (or define) the problem, the solution or the means of arriving at it may be fairly standard or obvious and we may only complete the first three stages of the model. If we already have a couple of ideas, and our problem is determining their feasibility, we might start with a developing/evaluating stage (step 5). This will uncover doubts or concerns we may have about these ideas and require us perhaps to start at the 'top' again, stating each concern as something we need to resolve (step 3), by perhaps gathering more data (step 2) and then generating some ideas (step 4) about ways of overcoming the concerns that we have.

2.3   Problem solving strategies

Four of the five problem solving strategies we shall encounter, Brainstorming, Synectics, Kepner–Tregoe's Rational approach and Soft Systems Methodology, are reckoned to be complete problem solving processes. That is, they contain their own steps or stages, through which we progress, and which should be comparable with those in the model. Morphological Analysis is more correctly described as a technique that can be usefully employed at different stages during our problem solving. You will be able to judge how comprehensively the four strategies address the issues raised by the model as we go on.

We shall now return to our earlier discussions about classifying problems in an attempt to determine where one strategy might be more appropriate than another.

2.3.1   Choosing a problem solving strategy

When something goes wrong with a piece of machinery, be it a car or a computer, a drilling press or a packing machine, there is always a cause or combination of causes that have produced the malfunction. Careful logical analysis of the situation will determine what has gone wrong and it is usually possible to verify that we have found the cause, and hence *the* solution. Problems involving machinery can certainly be ill defined – we may not know precisely what the problem is. If we did, we wouldn't have a machine problem. We might have a replacement part problem or a work rescheduling problem but not a machine problem. And although the problem may have arisen from a combination of causes, which all need to be identified, there is only one solution – to do whatever is necessary to rectify the fault (or possibly two solutions, if we include the possibility of scrapping the machine and buying a new one).

Most problems in the real world are not quite like this. Invariably there are a number of potential and possibly interrelated causes and, what is worse, a variety of possible solutions, some of which may be better than others. How do we know that we have thought of *all* the possible solutions? Such problems always seem to involve other people.

Another method of classification, albeit somewhat simplistic, is to divide problems into those concerned with purely mechanistic systems (machine problems), and those which involve people in some way (people problems). The Kepner–Tregoe (KT) problem solving strategy, **Problem Analysis**, seems ideally suited to 'machine' type problems. However, although it is claimed that KT's Problem Analysis can deal with all forms of problem (see Chapter 10), the general opinion is that there are better ways than this for dealing with people problems, the Synectics approach in Chapter 7 for instance.

Some people will doubtless say that all problems have people involved in them somewhere, and quote situations such as the following one.

> A new machine bought recently by Fred Nurd Ltd is not performing up to specification. It will not shape the thickness of alloy used to the desired level of precision. On contacting the designer of the machine, Fred Nurd Ltd were told that their problem was due to the fact that they were expecting the new machine to do something for which it was never intended, so what did they expect!

There will inevitably be a grey area between the two poles of this classification system, and we shall have to rely on common sense when choosing a problem solving method.

Obviously Fred Nurd Ltd had a machine problem, and presumably using KT's Problem Analysis they have discovered a possible cause, which has now been verified by the designer. Whether they still have a machine problem or now have a people problem will depend on how they define their current problem situation. it is more likely to be a people problem from now on, since problem descriptions such as the following suggest themselves:

- How do we encourage the designer to work with us to modify the machine to deal with the necessary alloy thickness?
- How could we persuade our customers to accept the slight reshaping of our product which is necessary with the new machine?
- How do we redesign our product to use either the same alloy only thinner, or a 'softer' alloy of the same thickness so that the machine can cope with it?
- How do we persuade the machine's supplier to exchange it for a more powerful variant or offer us recompense for the bad advice received?

If the problem is of the machine fault diagnosis type, then KT should serve us well, otherwise look for another strategy such as Synectics or Soft Systems Methodology (SSM). A notable exception to this rule of thumb is medical diagnosis, obviously a people problem, but one for which the Rational approach is usually better suited. What we have loosely defined as people problems still encompass a diversity of real world problems. Is there no way that we could subdivide these into classes where one problem solving strategy is better than another? The answer to this is probably 'no', but there are additional guidelines that can be offered.

Do we require a particularly innovative solution to our problem situation? Such might be the case if our problem could be stated as:

- How to 'invent' a new range of products/services?
- How can we improve an existing product/service to make it more appealing to our customers?

This list is by no means exhaustive. If a problem requires a novel or **innovative** solution, then every creative skill we can exert during the problem solving process will help. Most people would argue that we do not only need creativity when looking for something new. If we have considerable difficulty resolving a problem, this is probably because we keep drifting back to some old solutions, none of which is particularly satisfactory – we are in a thinking rut. What is needed is for us to take an apparently irrational sideways leap (lateral thinking) to discover fresh ideas, as carrying on in the same direction means continually bumping into the same brick wall.

If innovation is paramount in our considerations then we must adopt creative approaches such as Brainstorming (Chapter 6) and Synectics (Chapter 7). Brainstorming is included here primarily because it was the first serious attempt to apply the 'psychology' of creativity to real world problem solving, and its underlying 'philosophy' forms the basis of all creative problem solving approaches that have followed. **Brainstorming** is still a useful technique for acquiring large numbers of conceptually simple ideas, for example product names, ideas for adding value to an existing product, etc. **Synectics**, however, is a far more sophisticated process. In the area of idea generation alone Synectics is more powerful because where Brainstorming relies on 'connection making' to happen by relatively passive random association, in Synectics it is actively encouraged, stimulated and forced to occur. You are more likely to find that novel solution with Synectics.

Moreover, sometimes the problem situation is likely to require considerable development of an idea before it becomes a possible solution. For example, 'How can we increase our revenue from tourism without spoiling the environment?' One idea might be 'attract only rich tourists'. This idea has possibilities, but most of us would have some concerns over it – it needs developing (we need to think about its merits, and whether there are any ways of overcoming our concerns) before we can judge whether it is a possible solution or not. Brainstorming has severe limitations in this area; it is not really equipped for this type of situation at all. The Synectics process is good at **idea development**. Another area where Synectics is strong is in **problem identification**, when our need is to 'open up' the problem situation, view it from many angles and give ourselves a reasonable chance of checking that we are attempting to solve the right problem.

Individually, we may find the connection-making necessary for creativity difficult, because we only have our own mind's resources to draw upon. Although with practice we should be able to improve our abilities, research shows that a group of people working together in an appropriate climate can be more productive than the sum of their efforts working individually. Fellow group members act as resources that spark off our imagination. Whilst both Brainstorming and Synectics can be used by an individual to good effect, both work best in a group problem solving environment.

Morphological analysis (Chapter 9) is often categorized as a Creative Problem Solving (CPS) technique, presumably because it is used in situations similar to the above, where innovation is important. Essentially it is a (structured) systematic search for 'opportunities', such as new product ideas, new markets, etc., and appears to be a fairly rational (logical) way of doing this. The importance of an innovative solution is thus a guide to which methodology we might use, but not a way of classifying real problems. The use of creative thinking and CPS techniques is beneficial in the resolution of *any* real problem.

As a group problem solving strategy, Synectics works best with relatively small groups of six to eight people. A key feature of the Synectics approach is that the problem-owner(s) plays a vital role within the group in the problem solving process (see Chapter 7). These features of the Synectics process have implications for its use in problem situations with **multiple ownership**, about which more than one person feels dissatisfied, and where they should all have a part in resolving it. But if problem ownership is wider than a handful of people, we may have to restructure the problem into appropriate parts and have several groups working on it, or try something else. The **Soft Systems'** holistic approach avoids the need to restructure the problem situation, and could be a better alternative in this situation (see Chapters 7, 12 and 13).

When we do have a situation in which too many people are involved for one group to be practicable *and* subdividing the problem so that various groups can tackle a part of it is unmanageable or undesirable, there is a tendency for organizations to call in 'outside' consultants to help solve their problem. Whilst these consultants will work in close collaboration with the actual problem-owners, it may ultimately be the responsibility of the consultant to 'solve the problem'. He or she will analyse the problem situation and suggest the feasible and desirable changes that might resolve it. In other words an external consultant may be expected to and inevitably does get involved with the 'content' of the problem solving process. Synectics insist that the leader of one of their groups should not do this (see Chapter 7); SSM makes allowances for this *modus operandi*.

These situations often arise because people feel that they do not have sufficient time or resources to solve their own problem, and for this reason they resort to outside assistance. Whether we consider this attitude right or wrong is immaterial; these situations exist and if *we* are the external consultant it is likely that SSM is the most viable problem solving strategy to adopt, simply because Synectics does not permit the problem owner to 'opt out' of the problem solving process in this way. The choice between SSM or Synectics is not determined by whether you find yourself in the role of an external problem solving *facilitator* or not. If it has not been determined by practical considerations due to the complexity of the problem or widespread problem ownership, it is likely to be determined by the extent to which the problem-owners are prepared to take an active part in the problem solving (including development of the solution). Every attempt should be made to encourage as much participation by the problem-owners as possible.

The reason for these repeated references to the undesirability of trying to solve another person's problem is that, if people are not involved with the derivation of the solution to a problem situation that they have a stake in, they cannot realistically be expected to be committed to it, or its implementation (see Chapters 7, 12 and 14). Even SSM used 'carefully' in these circumstances could be doomed to disaster.

The would-be problem solver may find that, whether or not a particular problem solving strategy is appropriate, the climate in which he has to work may preclude its use. For example, in many 'hi-tech' environments, relying heavily on computer systems, or in traditionally conservative organizations such as banks and insurance companies, the employment of the creative techniques mentioned here may well be met with little understanding or sympathy. Even now, many people feel that CPS techniques are at best new fangled, strange and American. New they are not! Unorthodox and American they are, but there is nothing intrinsically bad in this. Fortunately, this is not a hard and fast rule; there are organizations operating at the frontiers of science and technology and financial institutions which employ these problem solving techniques.

2.4   Creativity, problem solving and computers

Herbert Simon has suggested (1960, pp. 1–8) that we can position decisions along a continuum running from 'highly programmed' at one end to 'highly nonprogrammed' at the other. He contended (1960b) that we had (using OR and computers) the 'technical capacity' to automate many of the decisions that fall at the programmed end of this spectrum. He also predicted that it would not be long (a couple of decades) before 'heuristic programming' would permit us to automate nonprogrammed decisions by computer as well.

Thirty years on, it is true that, if a set of rules can be written down that take us systematically through, say, an appropriate machine fault diagnosis routine (similar to those found in car maintenance manuals), an analysis of our entitlement to tax allowances and our tax liabilities, or a procedure which determines what would be the best form of insurance/ investment for us or whether we are a good credit risk, etc., then an expert system (see Frame 2.3) could be constructed that apparently possesses this expertise and which could advise us accordingly. In other words, computerization of a programmed decision is a practical reality, and is becoming quite a common occurrence.

Even if a set of rules such as these were difficult or impossible to obtain, as long as we have an appropriate set of examples of the expertise that we are interested in 'capturing' on a computer (with respect to machine faults, we would need to have for a number of breakdowns, a record of the sort of things which were checked, the 'symptoms' noticed, along with the fault that was eventually deemed to be the cause of the problem), an expert system could still be devised using a process

─── *Frame 2.3   Expert systems* ───

An expert system is a computer program that attempts to encapsulate some knowledge possessed by a human expert. This expertise need not be of a highly academic nature, but simply rare knowledge possessed by only a limited number of people within an organization, or fairly mundane information that we need access frequently but do not hold permanently in our memory, for example, train timetables.

An expert system consists of a knowledge base – a collection of facts (such as, there is a train leaving Bristol at 07.15 every weekday which stops at Reading and Slough, and arrives at London Paddington at whenever) and rules (for example, if you are travelling from Salisbury to Slough you need to change trains at Basingstoke and Reading); a means by which it can question the user and thus gain the further information (such as, desired destination and arrival time, departure point, etc.) it needs in order to perform some query ('What is the last train I can catch from Salisbury that will get to Slough by 0.9.30?') and reach a conclusion; and a procedure for working through the rules in order to deduce the most appropriate advice (on available trains) to offer the user.

known as Rule Induction or with artificial neural networks. Some people consider that this process typifies machine learning, but should/ would a computer running such an expert system be considered as having problem solving skills? I can foresee that computers may perform some rudimentary problem solving for us, once of course some human has written the expert system. But I have no fears of computers replicating human ability to solve people problems, at least not until someone develops a foolproof way of predicting human behaviour by mathematical means!

What about computer creativity? They can certainly produce '3-D' representations of buildings, cars, etc. that will permit us to look at the object from all directions, including from the 'inside'. They can generate very realistic animated graphics and reproduce the sound of any instrument in an orchestra (and a few that aren't). Impressive though these things are, it is ultimately the human operator's creativity that we are marvelling at; all the computer has done is to make it easier for that person to realize his or her ideas. The nearest a computer gets to producing what can even vaguely be referred to as creativity is the generation of fractal landscapes, which are apparently constructed from randomly generated squares 'distorted' by perspective. Though visually stunning, these are not very far in essence from the concept of a computer writing a best seller by extracting an appropriate number of words at random from a dictionary.

2.5   Summary

I shall conclude this chapter with a comparative analytic summary which may be helpful in deciding the appropriateness of a given problem solving method. Please do not feel constrained by it; it is usually better to bend the methodology to suit the problem situation, than to force a problem into a certain form so as to make the methodology applicable. Some of the originators of these techniques and strategies have actually said that their methods are not to be thought of as systematic processes that must be adhered to rigidly and with which one should never tamper, but as flexible processes that can and should be modified to meet new situations. I believe that the others, given the opportunity, would concur with this philosophy. Remember that, if you always keep on doing what you have always done it is highly unlikely that you will ever discover anything new.

Machine problems	KT Problem Analysis
Potential problems	KT Potential Problem Analysis Brainstorming
Systematic opportunity search	Morphological Analysis
Problem identification	Synectics
Innovation	Synectics Brainstorming Morphological Analysis
Large and highly complex problem situations	Soft Systems Methodology
Multiple problem ownership	Soft Systems Methodology Synectics

and not because of the method but because of the environment . . .

Conservative management	KT Problem Analysis (with as much creative thinking as you can sneak in!)
Advanced technology environment	Soft Systems Methodology

CHAPTER

3

Decisions, decisions!

Among the definitions of a problem given in Frame 1.1, you may have noticed that Ackoff's definition was somewhat different. It seems to describe a decision, not a problem. Is decision making a different process from problem solving; is one part of the other, or are we really talking about two aspects of the same thing? If we describe problem solving as something like 'finding ways of getting from a situation perceived as unsatisfactory, to one that we would rather be in' and decision making as 'making a selection between various courses of action', these processes might be thought of as separate. However, as we consider the full implications of what is involved, perhaps by expanding these 'definitions' into a number of stages, the fallacy of considering them as discrete processes becomes apparent.

In Frame 3.1 we can see two lists typical of those which people come up with when asked to identify the stages in problem solving and decision making. It is clear that there is at least one decision-making stage, 'select the best solution', within problem solving, and often many more. Moreover, people tend to find it difficult to make decisions because they have a problem 'generating alternative ways of meeting the objectives', 'determining the evaluation criteria/techniques' and sometimes 'identifying the objectives of the decision'.

Looked at this way, one process is obviously part of the other and vice versa. But which is the superior process and does it matter? The answers to these questions depend mostly on the view people take of the decision-making process itself. It is worth digressing slightly to explore these viewpoints, in order to place the problem solving techniques about to be described in context.

Problem solving v. decision making ─────────── *Frame 3.1* ──

Problem solving	Decision making
Identify and try to understand the problem	Identify the objectives (goals) of the decision
Collect relevant information and reflect on it	Find alternative ways of meeting these objectives
Generate some ideas	Determine evaluation criteria/ techniques
Develop solutions	
Select the best solution	Select best course of action
Implement it	Implement it

3.1 Decision making: a choice between alternatives?

Decision making is often thought of as a relatively simple choice between several courses of action. This is an oversimplified view as such a definition can imply that the decision-making process is a single-stage affair which happens in a fairly short space of time. It is true that some decisions we make, for example, whether or not to have another cup of coffee, do appear to be like this. We make a lot of rapid, simple choices, and often are not conscious of doing any complex analysis or comparative evaluation of available alternatives. Some routine business decisions may be like this, but many are not!

We could settle for the rational view of decision making, which has been advocated as an appropriate method for dealing with decisions other than trivial ones such as the coffee example, as our description of the decision-making process. (The list of steps in Frame 3.1 provides a rudimentary summary of the rational view, but its modern-day counterpart is better exemplified by Charles Kepner and Benjamin Tregoe's Decision Analysis described in Chapter 10.) Whilst it supports to a large extent the idea that a decision is a fairly straightforward choice between alternatives, the rational model does identify a number of steps we usually need to go through, and the process is now thought of as a conscious one. However, it also assumes that the decision-making process can be, is and should be rational. It leaves no room for intuition. You may feel that this is not the way things are with many of the decisions you have to make. If this is the case we need to think of the decision making process as something rather more than just a choice between alternative courses of action, but what?

3.2 The problem with decisions

The rational model, though seemingly an eminently sensible way of approaching choice situations, is difficult to apply in practice. Herbert

Simon (1955) criticized the rational view on the basis that it assumed an exhaustive set of alternatives readily available along with a full knowledge of their consequences and that it was also possible to measure the extent to which the consequences of each of these alternatives would achieve the desired objective. And furthermore, we could then establish a *consistent* order of preference from these measurements, and would choose the alternative that came out best. He maintained that very seldom were these assumptions valid in practice.

Simon demonstrated that in reality the essential 'ingredients' of the rational model were often compromised out of sheer necessity, resulting in an oversimplification of the whole process. He further claimed that 'there is a complete lack of evidence that, in actual human choice situations of any complexity, these computations can be, or are in fact, performed'. In his **principle of bounded rationality** (1957), he even seems to suggest that the capacity of the human brain is not up to handling the magnitude of the task of making a truly rational decision with complex real world problems. Most of the time, he said (1955), managers were settling for a satisfactory solution that suffices for the time being (**'satisficing'**), rather than pursuing the optimum solution that the rational model purported to yield.

Many real world decisions are highly complex: e.g. multiple and often conflicting objectives (see Chapter 11); the difficulties encountered devising alternatives and deciding or reaching a consensus about what the evaluation criteria should be; the personality and prejudice (mental set – see Chapter 4) of the decision maker(s); the politics of the situation (see Chapter 12); difficulties in getting reliable and relevant information. Even if we ignore the issue that many of the factors we might want to consider are unmeasurable, things would have to be drastically simplified to make them fit the rational model. Finding an optimal solution under these circumstances is virtually impossible anyway. Furthermore, as Cyert *et al.* found (1956), there are many decisions we have to make, involving just a single alternative, usually made by comparing this one possible course of action with 'some kind of explicit or implicit "level of aspiration"'. We are not searching for the best alternative, but deciding whether the one we have is good enough: Ackoff (1983) also notes that what seems rational to one person is not necessarily rational to someone else. If objective, rational decisions exist, they must depend heavily on consensus for their validity (see Chapters 10 and 11).

If the rational model of decision making is often not viable, what can we use instead? Charles Lindblom (1959) says that what managers actually do in practice is to make 'successive limited comparisons', restricting themselves to one (or a few) objectives at a time, often initially disregarding social issues. They compare the few alternatives that come easily to mind, more on the basis of past experience than anything else. This choice involves selecting alternatives and evaluation criteria simultaneously, because the appropriateness of the latter varies between alternatives. Since this process can only result in a partial solution, it is repeated endlessly as conditions and aspirations change and as the accuracy of predictions improve. Decision making was thus perceived as a cyclical, **incremental learning process**. Though still in widespread use, the successive limited comparisons style of decision making cannot, as Lindblom points out, guarantee we will not overlook potentially excellent options in our limited search for alternative courses of action, nor can it ensure that we will consider all relevant criteria in our comparative evaluation of alternatives. Complex decisions are evidently more than a simple choice between alternatives: they start to look like problems! The decision making process appears to be heuristic (guided trial and error, based on past experience) and stochastic rather than rational.

Simon (1960a) argues that the decision-making process consists of three phases, intelligence, design and choice, which he describes as follows:

- 'searching the environment for conditions calling for a decision';
- 'inventing, developing and analysing possible courses of action';
- 'selecting a particular course of action from those available'.

Clearly, this view indicates more than a choice between alternatives, implying the existence of two stages (phases) before we get to any 'choice' situation. Simon believes that executives spend far more time on the first two phases (particularly the second) than the third phase, although he concedes that this varies between individuals and the organizational levels at which they operate.

An alternative view from Sir Geoffrey Vickers (1961) describes judgement as 'the power of reaching the "right" decisions when the apparent criteria are so complex, inadequate, doubtful or conflicting as to defeat the ordinary man'. He distinguishes three broad types of judgement:

- **reality** judgements – 'about the state of affairs "out there"';
- **action** judgements – deciding 'what to do about it' and committing yourself to action on this basis; and
- **value** judgements – about 'what result was most to be desired'.

He maintained that 'the higher the level of judgement involved; the less possible it is to find an objective test by which to prove that the judgement is good'. Both action and reality judgements involve the mental processes of analysis and synthesis (fundamental components of problem solving), and an ability he calls ingenuity. Latent in these value judgements is a creative process. These last two viewpoints seem to suggest that making decisions is often the same process as problem solving, and that we should attempt to classify decisions in some way before we look any further at how we should be making them.

Frame 3.2   Types of business decision (Ansoff, 1968)

Strategic

These are long-term decisions that resolve the organization's relation to its environment. Questions such as what are its objectives and goals, whether to diversify and how best to develop and exploit its present position, which products or services it should be offering, and where these should be marketed.

Operating (Tactical)

The bulk of the decisions an organization has to make. These are short term and concerned with maximizing the efficiency of resource allocation, including such things as production scheduling, quality management, inventory control, pricing, choosing a marketing strategy, budgeting, etc.

Administrative

These decisions ensure harmonious and effective collaboration over the implementation of strategic and operational decisions, and are concerned with organizational structure (chain of command, areas of responsibility, work flows, communication channels, location of facilities and distribution networks) and the acquisition and development of resources (personnel, finance, raw materials, facilities and equipment).

3.3   Types of decision

The nature and types of decision that members of a typical business organization may have to take can vary considerably. At one extreme we have the vital, often complex, 'one-off' decisions that may determine the future of the organization, and at the other, the still significant but relatively simple routine (and often repetitive) 'day to day' running decisions. H. Igor Ansoff (1968) has classified business decisions as Strategic, Operating and Administrative (see Frame 3.2). While distinct, these categories of decisions are interdependent and complementary.

Using this classification, strategic decisions tend to be less well structured in that objectives are less clear, often conflicting, more open-ended in the number of possibilities and issues we should consider, and hence problematic and less amenable to the rational approach. Operational decisions tend to be less complex, more routine and the techniques of Operational Research (OR) are available to assist decision making here. However, it is doubtful whether such optimizing techniques are really capable of handling even this type of problem (see Chapters 2 and 11). Forrester (1961) maintained that managers seldom use quantitative techniques such as OR because these methods cannot handle the complexity of many of the decisions that they had to make, not because managers are unable to understand or apply them. Apart from illustrating the diversity of decisions, this classification does not help in deciding how we should attempt to deal with them, because some operational decisions can be exceedingly problematic and at the other extreme, the appropriateness of certain policy decisions may be obvious to all. Administrative decisions can be both routine and complex, involving as they do the actual organizing of people.

Paul Diesing (1958) has classified a manager's decision making into two parts depending on the type of decision being made. Some decisions, termed economic, could be dealt with in a rational (and quantifiable) way as above, by identifying objectives and alternative courses of action and evaluating them according to how well they could achieve these objectives. But managers also have to make social decisions, which 'attempt to change personalities and social relations in the direction of greater fundamental harmony and stability'. Decisions of this type involve intangible and unquantifiable factors such as stress, morale and self-confidence and although necessary, were not made on a rational basis.

Around the same time, Simon (1960a) suggested it was possible to position all decisions along a continuum running from 'highly programmed' at one end to 'highly nonprogrammed' at the other. 'Decisions are programmed to the extent that they are repetitive and routine, to the extent that a definite procedure has been worked out for handling them', and '. . . are nonprogrammed to the extent that they are novel, unstructured and consequential. There is no cut-and-dried method for handling the problem because it hasn't arisen before, or because its precise nature and structure are elusive or complex, or because it is so important that it deserves a custom-tailored treatment.' The implication seems to be that some decisions *may* be amenable to a rational approach. But there are other decisions which deserve a different kind of treatment altogether.

3.4   Problem solving, decision making and management

Though Simon (1960a) has suggested that the whole process of decision making can be thought of as synonymous with managing, most management texts define the process of management as something like planning, organizing, motivating, coordinating and controlling. Although decision making must play a central part in planning and organizing, what about the rest? Ansoff (1968, p. 15), claims, 'a major part of a manager's time is occupied in a daily process of making numerous and diverse decisions'. Conventional wisdom maintains that 'managers make decisions', perhaps not all the time, but certainly a lot of it. Handy (1985, pp. 360–5) however, believes this to be an inaccurate stereotype and maintains that a manager 'does not just, or mainly, "take

---

Frame 3.3   A manager's job (Mintzberg, 1975) ─────────

Arising directly from his or her formal authority we have

Interpersonal roles: Figurehead
                           Leader
                           Liaison

which give rise to

Information roles: Monitor
                         Disseminator
                         Spokesman

and these two sets of roles enable the manager to play

Decisional roles: Entrepreneur
                        Disturbance handler
                        Resource allocator
                        Negotiator

---

decisions'''. He goes on to summarize Mintzberg's ten roles (Mintzberg, 1975) (see Frame 3.3) into leading, administrating and fixing. The balance of these roles varies, he says, with the level of the job, the size of the organization and the organizational culture (see Chapter 14), but underlying all these is that 'the manager, like the GP, is the first recipient of problems', the implication being that a manager spends a lot of time *identifying* problems and finding out what can be done about them. Isn't this what Simon meant? Look again at page 28.

Any apparent difference here is mainly semantic. A certain activity is occupying a lot of a manager's time, and this activity is an important part of managing. It is simply that we call it by two different names, one of which, 'decision making', is ambiguous!

I have tried to show that if we dismiss the trivial type of decision, we are left with two basic types, the relatively straightforward choice-making situations – the programmed or economic decisions – and the rest – the ones likely to cause difficulties and require some problem solving, many planning decisions will be of this latter type. Whether we lump together these 'awkward' decisions with our 'wicked' problems and call the process for dealing with them problem solving, or carry on calling this process by two names is immaterial, so long as we realize that the way of dealing with them is essentially the same. I shall continue, in the main, to speak of this process as problem solving, because that is what we are doing most of the time.

An attempt is made to summarize what has been said here in Figure 3.1. We spend a lot of our time making decisions where the mental

Decision making involves . . .

Figure 3.1 *Problem solving and decision making.*

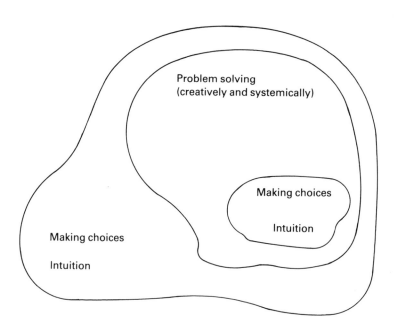

processes we use are those usually referred to as problem solving (including Ackoff's problem resolving and problem dissolving – Chapter 2). At other times we will face relatively straightforward choices (of which some may benefit from rational analysis whereas others will be just intuitive selections), in particular within the problem solving process itself. Chapter 10 presents a choice-making method, Decision Analysis, for making relatively straightforward decisions, for example, after our problem solving has ascertained what alternative courses of action are available to us and we have thrashed out how we should compare them. The rest of the book is about problem solving, or how to deal with 'awkward' decisions and 'wicked' problems!

If we have an important and complex decision to make, and we feel that the rational method or successive limited comparisons are inadequate or inappropriate, then we must: add some CPS techniques on to the 'front end' of our choice situation to help sort out our objectives; generate a comprehensive set of alternatives and gain agreement over suitable selection criteria; or adopt a systemic (holistic) approach to the whole thing.

CHAPTER

4

Where has all our creativity gone?

4.1 What is creativity?

Creativity is apparent in many fields of human endeavour, though common usage of the word often erroneously limits it to the fields of art and invention. However, if we consider only these two very 'visible' environments, our conception of creativity will tend to look at the products of someone else's creative process merely in terms of their 'value' to us as marketable or functional commodities, when attempting to assess the degree of creativity employed.

Our main interest here is though the applications of creativity within a business environment, for example, in developing new products and services and looking for opportunities for economic growth, and in managerial terms, surmounting barriers to desired goals and objectives. Such a commodified view may not be totally inappropriate, here, but to encourage this narrow view of creativity would be wasteful of many of the ideas and techniques discussed in the later chapters. These can help us be more creative in dealing with many aspects of our lives, and will not always result in a tangible product, let alone one that somebody else thinks is creative.

Carl Rogers (1954) maintained that 'there must be something observable, some product of creation' in order for us to talk usefully of a creative process having taken place. He further insists that the product must be a 'novel construction' and have 'the stamp of the individual' who created it evident upon it. But he also suggests that one of the 'inner conditions' for creativity is the realization that determining the value of these products should reside with the individual who created them and *not someone else* (see Frame 4.1).

Debates on the nature of creativity continue. We will also consider situations where the resolution of a problem is not novel or unusual, but

---

Conditions for constructive creativity ———————————— *Frame 4.1*

Carl Rogers (1954, pp. 67–8) suggested the following 'inner conditions' are closely associated with our creative potential:

Openness to experience
'a lack of rigidity . . . permeability of boundaries in concepts, beliefs, perceptions, and hypotheses . . . a tolerance for ambiguity where ambiguity exists . . . the ability to receive much conflicting information without forcing closure upon the situation'.

An internal locus of evaluation
A belief that the value of our creative products is established not by the praise and criticism of others but by ourselves.

The ability to toy with elements and concepts
'the ability to play spontaneously with ideas, colors, shapes, relationships – to juggle elements into impossible juxtapositions, to shape wild hypotheses, to make the given problematic, to express the ridiculous, to translate from one form to another, to transform into improbable equivalents'.

---

the process by which it has been attained is nevertheless ingenious, demonstrating both flair and imagination. Here the process is creative. Simply 'making out' in our everyday lives can be a creative process; is being an entrepreneur, an inventor or a Van Gogh any more creative than bringing up four children as a single parent drawing state benefits?

Wherever and however true creativity is manifested, it is commonly believed that the same mental process has been used to produce it. According to Rogers, 'there is no fundamental difference in the creative process as it is evidenced in painting a picture, composing a symphony, devising new instruments of killing, developing a scientific theory, discovering new procedures in human relationships . . .'. Much research into creativity has been directed at attempting to discover what is actually involved in these mental processes. The best known of these are the 'factor analysis' studies of J. P. Guilford (1962). Factor analysis is a sophisticated statistical method that attempts to uncover the underlying factors or variables that give rise to a set of observed measurements. For example, if we have a group of tests that purport to measure some aspect of creativity and we apply these to a number of people, then factor analysis will help us to identify what factors constitute creativity. In Frame 4.2 we can see a summary of the results of J. P. Guilford's research (1962).

Since we are concerned with problem solving, we will take these

Frame 4.2 What is creativity?

The psychologist J. P. Guilford initially hypothesized (1964) that there were at least seven distinct creative thinking abilities:

- sensitivity (alertness) to problems;
- fluency of thinking;
- flexibility of thinking;
- originality of thinking;
- ability to analyse and (in particular) synthesize information;
- ability to 'redefine' things ('to transform the meaning or use or function of an object so as to give it a new role').

Guilford was able to validate all but the abilities to analyse and synthesize. He concluded that these abilities must exist but because they are not uniform processes they did not 'show up' in his tests. He did establish four types of 'fluency' – Word, Ideational, Associational and Expressional – and two types of 'flexibility', Spontaneous and Adaptive.

Along with Cognition, Memory and Evaluation, Guilford identified two types of 'productive' thinking which 'generate new information from known and remembered information': Divergent – thinking 'in different directions, sometimes searching, sometimes seeking variety'; and Convergent – thinking which leads 'to one right answer or to a recognized best or conventional answer'. Most creative abilities Guilford found came into the category of divergent thinking, but Sensitivity and Redefinition are classified within evaluation and convergent thinking respectively. For creative thinking to exist we must have cognition – 'Without having information there is no intellectual performance of any kind' and we must have a good memory in order to retain learned information.

mental processes as our main concern and not worry about whether any 'end product' is also creative. From now on this is what I shall refer to as creativity.

In a complementary definition of creativity, Sidney Parnes (1972), refers to the three Ss of creativity – Sensitivity, Serendipity and Synergy.

- **Sensitivity** can mean both, an increased awareness of those little peculiarities of life – those inconsistencies, discontinuities and disparities associated with people, things and ideas – which are a fundamental part of the world we live in, and also an increased awareness of the processes involved in the personal and social interactions between ourselves and others.

- **Serendipity** is usually defined as the faculty of making happy chance finds.
- **Synergy** is the name given to the phenomenon associated with systems of people, things, or ideas, whereby they are more effective, more useful, more significant and/or exhibit some behaviour or property, in combination, that could not have been predicted by an examination of their individual attributes, behaviours or properties.

Sensitivity implies being more observant and more knowledgeable about 'the way things are', thus increasing the likelihood of our producing fortuitous ideas, relationships, etc. But to be truly creative we must also appreciate the relevance of these random 'finds' to the task in hand. The essence of creativity is the ability to make connections between seemingly irrelevant and unrelated objects, ideas, information and events.

This definition is less orientated towards the 'end product' than some and it provides us with a starting point for our search to find ways of facilitating the mental processes of creativity. It suggests that we should strive to be more aware of what is happening around us, be more open-minded, and that there might be a 'connection making' skill we can develop. The practical techniques in use appear to validate this view of creativity.

This view of creativity could tend to reinforce the idea that creative thinking is an 'exceptional' occurrence, that most of us do not experience or do so only to a small degree and then infrequently. I do not believe that creativity is an 'exceptional' product. Most of us can be, and probably are, more creative than we perceive ourselves to be; though in some of us this ability may be inhibited; our creative thinking skills can be enhanced with practice like any other skill.

4.2   The creative downturn

As young children we produce uninhibited drawings and appropriate but technically or grammatically incorrect descriptions of the world we find ourselves in, and invent imaginative adventures in which to act out roles. Because everything is new, there are many opportunities to demonstrate our creativity as we explore the world.

As we grow into adulthood we develop 'levels of competence' in order to deal adequately with the problems of life. For most of us, our artistic endeavours become a secondary (leisure) activity. We strive for precision in our communications so as to be better understood, and we stop making up dream worlds. Dealing with perceived reality is paramount. Our activities might require a degree of creativity, but others are less likely to see them as interesting or creative and our chances of appearing to be creative diminish accordingly. Whether we are actually less creative than we were as children; whether we have less opportunities to display our creativity, or do display it but in different ways; or whether we just perceive ourselves as less creative, our creativity appears to diminish.

There are two major explanations of this hypothesized 'creative downturn'. The first argues that we have 'lost control' of certain thinking operations that are fundamental to creativity. To regain full command of these processes we need to accept that certain 'child-like' thinking operations *do* have a place in adult problem solving. In the second explanation the existence of various psychological 'blocks', some of which are innate while others form as we mature, hinder our ability to 'get' ideas.

The common theme in both of these views is that at least part of the problem stems from our upbringing. Our society, our culture and our educational system, equip us adequately for most aspects of our lives, but at the expense of our ability to think creatively. All the 'material' necessary for producing creative ideas *is* 'available' at a sub- or non-conscious level in our minds; what we require is the means of making them conscious.

George Prince (1976) devised his 'Mindspring' theory in an attempt to show the relationship between our learning and creative problem solving skills and to suggest why they are often perceived to have diminished by the time we reach maturity. He suggested that six thinking operations are involved in learning and problem solving:

- wishing
- retrieving
- imaging
- comparing
- transforming
- storing

The following example demonstrates how we might use these six thinking operations in a typical learning/problem solving situation. Sitting at a personal computer trying to use a new piece of software, the machine responds with an incomprehensible error message and refuses to do what we want it to. We start to do some **wishing**:

I wish I had saved all the work I have done.
I wish that I could back-track from this impasse.
I wish I knew what I have done wrong and how to get out of this mess.

In other words, we make an attempt to determine what really is our problem. We then start **retrieving** any past experiences we have of using other computers and other pieces of software, that have ended in a similar situation. We **form mental images** of these situations, replaying in our minds how they occurred and what we did in an attempt to recover from them. We **compare** these past experiences with the present situation and **transform** or adapt them in line with our most recent

George Prince's Mindspring theory ———————————— Frame 4.3 —

- There are six discrete thinking operations: Wishing, Retrieving, Imaging, Comparing, Transforming and Storing.
- All thinking operations are purposeful and their products will fall somewhere on the spectrum: irrelevant – approximately relevant – precisely relevant.
- Learning involves the same thinking operations as problem solving.
- Certain of these thinking operations (Wishing, Transforming and Imaging) tend to be repressed as we grow older and this decreases our learning and problem solving efficiency. (Our culture 'inadvertently' causes us to associate these operations with wrongness.) This situation is worsened by the natural decline of our mental abilities with age.
- These repressed operations can be restored to awareness, increasing learning and problem solving efficiency. This is not a difficult task, though the use of them tends to bring on anxiety.

perceptions. It is these modified mental images that will (we hope) help us to understand and thus resolve the present problem. At the end of all this we **store** away this new experience for future reference.

When we were young virtually all our experiences were new, and we spent most of our time trying to make sense of them. To do this we had to make considerable use of *all* six of these thinking operations. But the novelty of the circumstances ensured that we used the thinking operations of wishing, imaging and transforming in particular.

As children we did a lot of wishing. We wished that we had the toy that we saw someone else playing with. We wished that we were someone else, or could be somewhere else. We wished that we knew how to deal with all these new situations. When things seemed to be 'unobtainable' our usual way of dealing with this was to imagine what they would be like, but we had to do this on the basis of limited past experience. When wishing for the impossible and when trying to make sense of the actual, we had to rely heavily on our ability to transform our mental images, as most retrieved experiences were only approximately like the new situation. It was also essential that the images we formed from retrieved memories were vivid and detailed enough so that we *could* adapt them and play with them in our attempt to understand the world.

What George Prince noticed was that as we grow older we *appear* to use the operations of wishing, imaging and transformation less and less. We do not actually stop using them, we just cease to be aware of using them. Yet they may be the basis of all creative thought. According to Prince (1976, p. 291)

Wishing is an efficient form of goal setting, a technique for problem identification, 'the natural first step in affecting change', and a powerful motivator.

Transforming is at the very heart of learning. We learn by refining the precision of our stereotyped memories. Without transforming there can be no change, no learning.

Imaging not only facilitates the comparison and manipulation of ideas, but is also an essential part of our memory processes.

Prince suggests that as adults these operations have become 'internalized' and are usually carried out at a non-conscious level. He accounts for this phenomenon by suggesting that as we grow up we associate these operations with 'wrongness'. And we soon learn that being 'wrong' can be painful. Essential though these thinking operations are, we find it difficult to perform them consciously and repress them to an unconscious level. We learn that we cannot have everything that we wish for. Our parents, teachers and peers *tell* us that it is 'wrong' to wish for certain things. We find it difficult to differentiate which things it is all right to wish for and which are not, so we curtail our wishing perhaps more than we need to.

We are able to manipulate mental images much faster than another person can talk, and so we tend to 'think ahead' of the speaker. We try to imagine what the other person is going to say. Inevitably we find out that many of these images are wrong. Unfortunately we come to believe that it is the process itself which is 'wrong'.

We have already noted that transformation is a very important part of learning. However, when we were children and described an aeroplane as a 'bus with wings', we may once again have been told that we were 'wrong', and others may have laughed at us for making such 'mistakes'. Being very resourceful at that age we soon learned to *ask* what the mystery object was, rather than to risk another 'incorrect' transformation.

Frame 4.4 lists those things which Prince believed were characteristics of routine and creative thinking (Prince, 1976, p. 292).

An alternative view of our apparent lack of creative talents is to picture our mind as containing all the necessary raw material (memories and experiences) for creativity from which we should be able to make connections with the problem situation that will eventually lead to the production of novel ideas and possible solutions. Unfortunately, these ideas and innovative solutions are prevented from emerging from our subconcious minds by various mental 'blocks'. In this respect, our mind is a bit like a dormant but not extinct volcano: the creative fire is being held back by the crusty cap that has formed over many years. Only very rarely (and with difficulty) does our volcano erupt with an idea. These mental blocks affect each of us in different ways. Some of them could be the mechanism for Prince's 'self-censor'; this severely evaluates our

---

Routine and creative thinking (Prince, 1976) ———— *Frame 4.4*

Routine thinking is characterized by:

- Wishes that are reasonably attainable;
- retrievals that fit the situation perfectly, and which
- require little transformation;
- comparisons that result in precise fits;
- it is logical and precise;
- we feel comfortable and certain;
- little or no learning takes place;
- it involves a high degree of rightness;
- there is little worth storing (nothing new!).

Creative thinking is characterized by:

- wishes that may not be achievable;
- retrievals that are at best approximate, but may not fit at all;
- necessarily high level of transformation;
- comparisons that lead to more wishes, transformations, retrievals, etc.;
- it is non-logical and approximate;
- we feel confused, uncertain, anxious, excited, afraid;
- there is a high propensity for learning;
- it involves a feeling of wrongness;
- there are things worth storing.

---

ideas and only lets us voice the 'carefully thought out' ones. Other blocks may work at a deeper level than this, inhibiting the thinking processes themselves.

James L. Adams (1974) has compiled a list of more than 25 of these conceptual 'blocks' that make it difficult for us to think creatively, classifying them as perceptual, emotional, cultural, environmental, intellectual or expressive blocks.

4.3   Perceptual blocks

It is well known that our senses can easily be misled when the mind receives *confused* data from the sense organs. However, perceptual blocks result from the way the mind tries to manage all of the data it receives from our senses. Whilst this process may be optimized for most of our everyday living it has inappropriate side effects when it comes to problem solving. Because our senses are so critical in perceiving the world these blocks are probably the most significant factors undermining our creativity.

4.3.1   Stereotyping

It would be impossible to remember every detail of every experience and so our mind only stores in its long-term memory 'important' information. It appears to do this by looking for patterns in the data it receives that will permit it to 'pigeon hole' new information along with similar experiences. When we recall this information we get an imprecise image of the original experience with the irrelevant details removed. Consequently we often see only what we expect to see based on the pattern of our previous experience. Perhaps the most common manifestation is the tendency, on meeting people for the first time, to form instant and lasting judgements about them based on obvious features such as clothes, hair or accent.

Unfortunately our attitudes, opinions and beliefs affect our perception as well. The tendency we have to notice certain things (of particular interest to us) more than others (mental set) only serves to reinforce these preconceived notions (halo effect), and can also lead to what is called a self-fulfilling prophecy.

If we take our stereotyped memories too literally we may overlook a significant feature of a new problem situation because we do not remember it (as being important) on some previous occasion, or incorrectly assume something exists or is significant simply because that is the way we remember things were the last time.

4.3.2   Difficulty in isolating the problem

It is often true that 'you can't see the wood for the trees'. We can experience difficulty in isolating the problem from the masses of irrelevant data surrounding it. If we allow ourselves to become enmeshed in these superficial details our solutions may be inadequate, or worse, we may fail to recognize the real problem altogether.

4.3.3   Tunnel vision

All too often when we start to solve a problem we make assumptions about it: we impose inappropriate boundaries or constraints on the problem situation, and hence limitations on what we can do about it. These boundaries and constraints may exist in reality – or they may not. Although this block may seem the opposite of the one above, it is possible to suffer from both.

4.3.4   Inability to perceive the problem situation from various viewpoints

This block has two dimensions. Firstly, we may have difficulty in seeing a shared problem from someone else's viewpoint. Secondly, we may be

The desire to be creative — Frame 4.5

To Calvin W. Taylor (1962, p. 181) motivation may be a strong component of creativity. Here are some 'motivational characteristics' that have been suggested:

- a curiosity or inquiringness of mind;
- an intellectual persistence;
- a need for recognition for achievement;
- a need for variety;
- a need for autonomy;
- a preference for complex order;
- a tolerance of ambiguity;
- a need for mastery of a problem;
- an insatiability for intellectual ordering.

unable to see our own problem in a number of different ways which, amongst other things, can lead us to confuse cause with effect. Whether we are working alone or with others it is important for us to get different perspectives on the problem situation to ensure we are actually trying to solve the right one.

4.3.5 Saturation

Extremely familiar inputs from our senses are often disregarded by our conscious mind to prevent 'overloading' it. Think of something you see every day, your television set perhaps, and try to draw it. Did you get every detail correct? Tape record an evening at home with the family: do you remember that clock ticking on the wall and the aircraft or bus passing by outside?

We may overlook these everyday phenomena when one of them is, or could give us a clue to, the actual cause of a problem.

4.3.6 Failure to use all our senses effectively

Blindfold yourself and hold your nose. Then try to tell the difference between the taste of a raw potato and a piece of apple. Without your senses of smell and sight, your sense of taste may be inadequate. Our senses frequently work in an interconnected manner. Failing to use all of them efficiently may cause us to miss an important part of the problem.

4.4 Emotional blocks

Our emotions and desires can interfere with both our ability to form thoughts and mental images, and the freedom with which we can then transform and manipulate these. They can also inhibit us from voicing our ideas. These emotional blocks seem to be linked to motivation, that 'something' which drives us to expend effort, enthusiasm, emotion, etc., in doing certain things. (Frames 4.5 and 5.2)

4.4.1   Obsessive desire for security and order

A desire for security and order is a common trait. We develop habits to make our lives easier, more predictable, more secure and free from anxiety. An extreme desire for this state can result in an intolerance of ambiguity which inhibits creativity. We must be able to tolerate chaos, to immerse ourselves in the 'mess' of the problem situation, in order to resolve it.

4.4.2   Fear of making a mistake

No one likes appearing naive or foolish and being laughed at as a consequence. Our self image is important to us and can depend heavily on what we feel other people think of us. Making mistakes is a natural part of learning but we are often afraid of making mistakes because we believe that others will think less of us. The only thing about making mistakes that we should be criticized for is not learning something from them.

4.4.3   Unwillingness to take a risk

Although there is some debate over what precisely motivates us, a common factor seems to be a desire for self-fulfilment. Unfortunately, attaining this invariably involves taking a risk. It may be relatively harmless or could involve something as drastic as our professional credibility financial ruin of life itself. We are wisely taught to err on the side of safety and not to take any unnecessary risks but are seldom told how to assess them. So we tend not to take *any* risks. Because most people fear to take risks, it is important to be gentle and constructive when evaluating and criticizing other people's ideas.

4.4.4   Lack of motivation

Since problem solving is a risky business, we need to be highly motivated to get involved. For some it is the expectancy of the exciting mental challenge of the problem, for others the chance to pursue a personal interest. Sometimes the possibility of monetary reward can be the stimulus. But without sufficient motivation of some kind we may well fail at our problem solving.

4.4.5   Inability to reflect on ideas

The solution to a difficult problem can often come after a daydream or on waking up after a sleep. Certainly being able to relax, to mull over ideas calmly, away from a crisis atmosphere, and to reflect on the various possibilities help the problem solving process. Conversely, pressure and anxiety due to as perceived lack of time on feelings of insecurity can only hinder our problem solving.

4.4.6   Trying to solve problems too quickly

Some people are always rushing around frantically trying to get things done quickly, trying to get things back to normal as soon as possible. This may be due to emotional insecurity or perhaps a desire to hide incompetence. The danger is that by rushing at things we start with the first or most obvious problem definition, rather than the most appropriate one. We may also allocate insufficient time to reflect on our ideas or rush our evaluation thus risking the premature rejection of unusual ideas. We are likely to end up with an inadequate solution. We may even 'solve' the wrong problem.

4.4.7   A preference for judgement

We have a need to explain and justify why things related to ourselves are the way we perceive them to be. This process of 'attribution' is important because it enables us to determine our level of personal achievement. Because of this we are ceaselessly evaluating situations and thus get into the habit of judging and criticizing everything. This is undesirable in problem solving which should be approached with an open mind. Also, our fear of making mistakes 'encourages' us to criticize rather than to offer ideas also. Remember that if we judge and criticize other people's ideas they are more likely to judge and criticize us. We also need to know why others are thinking feeling and behaving in the way they are. The process of attribution may lead us to misjudge their *intentions* as well.

4.4.8   Lack of imagination or imaginative control

Some people find it hard to use their imagination fully. They have difficulty thinking, let alone saying, apparently illogical, impractical or irrelevant things. Mental imagery and fantasy are important in CPS. However, we must always be aware of the difference between fantasy and reality as ultimately we must interpret our fantastic speculations in the real world of our problem situation.

4.5   Cultural blocks

Our society places limitations on what is acceptable for us to say or do. Our upbringing helps to ensure that these limitations are so ingrained that they affect our thinking as well as our actions. The organizations to which we belong also have cultures that produce similar effects. Often the bases of these cultural limitations are highly dubious. Recently in Britain, a senior policewoman was criticized in some newspapers for going swimming (at a private party) in her underwear. Would she have been criticized had she worn a bikini swimsuit which consists of essentially the same garments? Of the many shared beliefs and values that go to make up our culture most that affect our creativity are based on false premises.

4.5.1   Problem solving is a serious business

We have a tendency to believe that problem solving should require considerable mental effort. If we are not actually experiencing 'discomfort' we are obviously not working hard enough. Problem solving is usually something we have to do rather than choose to do. Yet being comfortable and relaxed may well be the best way to approach solving a problem. Being too serious can lead to stress which will in turn decrease productivity and effectiveness and will also make us susceptible to the next two blocks.

4.5.2   Daydreaming and reflection are a waste of time

The importance of having the time and the inclination to mull over problem situations and to reflect on ideas and possible solutions cannot be overstated.

4.5.3   Fun and playfulness are only for children!

Laughter at a business meeting is often taken to indicate that group members are not taking things seriously enough. For adults, work and leisure are normally disjoint activities, yet CPS can and should be fun. Indeed 'child-like' mental playfulness can considerably enhance creativity. J. G. March (1976) wrote: 'Playfulness is the deliberate, temporary relaxation of rules in order to explore the possibilities of alternative rules'. Playfulness allows experimentation which is very important in CPS. This seldom gets out of hand since experienced practitioners of CPS seem to develop a natural awareness of when their enjoyment of the situation could be becoming detrimental to a group's productivity.

4.5.4   Logic is better than intuition!

A popular myth in Western cultures is that something that can be proved by scientific method has more merit than something felt intuitively to be correct. We have a tendency to overvalue logic, objectivity, quantitative data and practicality and undervalue intuition and subjective quality judgements. Effective problem solvers need a good balance between the two types of thinking.

4.5.5   Tradition is better than changes!

Some cultures put much time and effort into preserving traditional ways of life. To attempt change in such a culture means that the benefits of the change must be sold effectively. There is nothing wrong with keeping traditions, provided that they are good traditions. However, if we are going to challenge a tradition it is important to show that we are not doing so *just* because it is old. And an over-protectionist attitude to tradition, which gives rise to a dislike, distrust or fear of change, inhibits creativity and progress. Without new ideas we stagnate.

4.5.6   Taboos

Some things are not just unacceptable to say or do, they are unthinkable, or at least difficult to think of without feelings of guilt. However, these taboos often block off from our conscious minds areas of thought that might provide ideas for a solution to our problem. Thinking of taboo subjects offends no-one.

4.5.7   Organizational taboos

Typical of organizational taboos are certain ideas, policies or processes that were tried once before and which resulted in disaster. Everyone takes delight in putting right the innocent newcomer who dares propose such a discredited solution, but what if this solution (perhaps in a modified form) is now feasible and we refuse to reconsider it. Who is being foolish? Contravening organizational norms (see Chapter 15) is another common form of taboo.

4.5.8   Management and leadership style

The intuitive judgements, fantasies and the often wild and unconsidered ideas which are so essential for creativity seldom occur except in an atmosphere of mutual trust within a group where normal cultural and emotional blocks have been lifted. Whether or not an organization encourages participative management generally, a problem solving group must be democratically run. In an autocratically governed work group we will not be encouraged to run against organizational norms and we are thus unlikely to be creative.

4.5.9   Lack of group support

To produce an environment that supports creative thinking the group dynamics must be appropriate. We need the emotional support, co-operation and approval of our fellow group members. All need to be committed to the group's objectives and must be willing to sacrifice their own position or opinions for the common good.

4.5.10   Reluctance to implement ideas

Any unwillingness by an organization to implement new ideas will be frustrating and dampen the creative effort. Expectations again; if little or nothing ever actually gets done about the situations we are trying to improve, we will be less likely to try so hard next time around. This problem is further compounded because successful CPS groups may come up with too many ideas to implement or with ideas at the wrong time. The first of these we will just have to live with, to overcome feelings of guilt about not pursuing *all* our ideas. The second requires further consideration. We will want to tell someone of our ideas but the offering of an unsolicited idea may be treated as an unwelcome distraction or it may cause offence because it is seen as an implied criticism. The solution to this may be to have an organizational policy similar to that suggested by Synetics Limited whereby the originators of ideas may freely publish them on the understanding that the recipient is under no obligation to process, or even acknowledge, the idea.

4.6   Environmental blocks

4.6.1   Distractions

Some organizations will take employees away from the office when problem solving has to be done. This is to combat the common environmental block of physical distractions such as phone-calls and interruptions. Obviously distractions can only hinder problem solving, but one person's distraction (for example loud music) may be an essential element of another's ideal working environment.

The next three blocks were suggested by Stevens (1989, pp. 51–2).

4.6.2   Monotony

When dealing with monotonous tasks we often switch our brain to 'auto-pilot'. In consequence we may fail to notice a problem when it arises. We may also be more susceptible to distractions, especially other matters that require our consideration. A good way to combat this specific distraction is regularly to take a few seconds' break, write down our thoughts concerning this other matter, and then return to the task in hand.

4.6.3   Physical and mental discomfort

Poor lighting, uncomfortable seating and inadequate heating/air conditioning can be a cause of distraction. They can also make us tired and irritable and contribute to feelings of lethargy or stress. Pressure of work, whether due to unrealistic deadlines or previous procrastination, also causes stress. Stress and anxiety are not normally conducive to problem solving.

4.6.4   Lack of communication

Getting access to the data we need to solve a problem usually involves us in talking to other people. We may also feel that they too should be involved in our problem solving and that we should get together for this purpose. Inability to achieve these things hinders problem solving as well as leading to frustration and yet more stress. An organization's structure will have implications with regard to the structure and efficiency of its communication channels and the ease with which we can gather information and meet with others.

4.7   Intellectual and expressive blocks

4.7.1   Incorrect choice of problem solving language

There are variety of problem solving languages at our disposal, for example, visualization (using mental images), verbalization and mathematics. A given problem is often easier to solve using one rather than another. And so we should experiment with different problem solving languages.

4.7.2   Inflexible or inadequate use of problem solving skills and strategies

Using a particular problem solving skill too exclusively or at the wrong time can hinder problem solving. Often, it is appropriate to use creative thinking to open a problem up when first starting to solve that particular problem. Later, logical or analytical skills may be an appropriate way of refining the solution. Using analytical skills too early in the process of resolution can be a mistake. When using a particular problem solving strategy (such as those described later) be prepared to use them flexibly.

4.7.3   Lack of correct information

It is usually important to have all the possible relevant data and to sift through it looking for directions, implications, limitations and connections, before embarking on problem solving.

4.7.4   Incorrect or inadequate means of expression

Accurate communication with another human being is always difficult. Many factors increase this difficulty such as the use of jargon, giving quantitative information in written rather than tabular or graphical form, describing something in words when a small sketch would illustrate the object being described more simply and quickly, using a complex photograph instead of a simple diagram emphasizing important features. Always make sure you are using the most effective method of communication. Paraphrasing back to someone what they have said to you is an effective way of ensuring that you have understood their idea or possible solution.

4.8   Creativity revived

Now that we have seen how and why our creative talents may have become inhibited, what can we do to improve matters? The advice offered in the 'rules' below, which are all based on the findings of people working in this field, offers a good start.

4.8.1   Ground rules for creative thinking

- Welcome every idea, no matter how wild it is it has some merit. If nothing else it will fire our or someone else's imagination.
- Hold back on criticizing an idea – remember that it is difficult enough to get an idea past *our* 'self-censor', so don't be too quick to criticize somebody else's idea. And make sure you understand another person's idea before you evaluate it.
- Remember that we always have some knowledge or experience which can help us solve a given problem.
- Don't be afraid to indulge in some 'childlike' behaviour – as in wishing, imagination, mental playfulness, etc.
- Never forget that other people perceive problem situations in ways different from you – treat this as an advantage, a way of helping you get different viewpoints, to help you establish which is the most appropriate one to work with.
- Always think of a mistake or failure as an opportunity to learn, not as a thing we did 'wrong'. If we just forget about it, we could do it again!

These 'ground rules' are largely interdependent, and we should try to incorporate *all* of them within our everyday problem solving strategies *at once*. More realistically, we could use them as a sort of checklist to indicate how creative our current behaviour is, and for identifying and initiating corrective actions.

4.8.2   The 'beginning' idea

First of all we should learn to value the 'beginning' idea, that is, one that has not been carefully thought out. We have seen that cultural disapproval of being 'wrong', making mistakes and appearing foolish, can lead us to voice only carefully thought out ideas. Rarely do we 'publish' beginning ideas and then only in climates where we are sure not to be ridiculed or taken advantage of. Ideally, we need to promote a climate in which we can all safely 'let our hair down' and feel able to disregard the inhibitions that normally limit our creative thinking. The problem is that we cannot always guarantee that we will be called upon to problem solve in such a 'friendly' climate.

Given that ours is a less than perfect problem solving environment, we should begin by supporting others brave enough to voice beginning ideas. The least we can do is not reject their beginning ideas because they are naive, unusual or incomplete, and refrain from gaining emotional capital out of their unwillingness to offer them. We should indicate unambiguously that we are pleased to receive their beginning ideas, and where appropriate, credit people for having inspired one of our ideas. Also, since someone has to make the first move, we should try to be less reserved about offering our beginning ideas. In a potentially 'hostile' climate, I find that prefacing a beginning idea with an appropriate 'apology' 'This is just a wild idea, I don't know if we can do anything with it . . .' or 'A thought has just occurred to me, but I haven't had the chance to think it through as yet . . .' makes me feel less anxious about voicing it. Even so someone is almost certain to say 'Yes it certainly *was* a wild idea!' or 'We can tell that you haven't thought *that* one through!', but such criticism will probably be seen by others as the deliberate 'put down' it was intended to be, unhelpful, and of less worth than our beginning idea.

If we do feel unable to voice beginning ideas, and only offer 'carefully thought out' ideas, others will not see how these ideas have evolved, or be able to contribute to their development. All that is left for them to do is to accept or reject our idea. By not offering ideas early, we do not get the benefit of other people's thoughts, ideas and opinions. Our idea may be the poorer for that. We need to overcome our (natural?) inhibitions and be more prepared to 'publish' imperfect ideas.

Next time you do some problem solving: 'Do some wishing, and, even though it makes you anxious, allow yourself to be confused and un-

---
Frame 4.7   *Most useless ideas for an acetate sheet*

Nuclear fall-out shelter	Paper weight
Spare wheel	Contraceptive
Spectacles	Nose warmer/ear muffs
Parachute	Cooking utensil
Headware	Incinerator
Missile launcher	Fire extinguisher
Aqualung	Piggy Bank
Furniture: chair, table, stool	Toilet
Footwear	Handkerchief/toilet paper
Channel Tunnel excavator	Pea shooter
Transportation: boat, car, plane	Car park
Clothing: trousers, dress	Glass cutter
Oven-proof dish	Windows
Food	Crash helmet
Tower block foundations/support	Golf clubs
Jet engine	Key
Knife, razor blade, etc.	
---

certain and do some mistaken thinking. It won't hurt you; you don't have to act on it (Prince, 1980).

4.8.3   Most Useless Ideas Competition

As a means of freeing the mind, this exercise should be equally effective carried out individually or in a group. The idea is to find the most useless, ridiculous, totally impractical application for a common, every-day item.

I often find that a useful article for these exercises is a clear acetate overhead projector transparency. A typical set of responses is shown in Frame 4.7 (they have only been slightly censored!).

Some even more creative ideas often appear by taking each of the ideas in turn and trying to find five good points about the suggestion. For example, 'If we did make our Nuclear Fallout Shelter out of a sheet of acetate, what would be the advantages of this "building" material?'

- You could see the bombs coming.
- You can see when its safe to come out again.
- Waterproof; the fallout would be washed off by the rain.
- It would be portable; fold it up, put it in your back pocket and carry it around with you just in case.

┌─ *Forced Relationships* ────────────────────── *Frame 4.8* ─┐

The concept of Forced Relationships is attributed to Charles S. Whiting and is described as ways in which we can induce original ideas from two normally unrelated ideas by 'forcing' ourselves to think of some connection between them. One variation on this theme is picking words (usually only nouns and verbs) at random from a dictionary to help with the development of an idea.

For instance, supposing we were looking for new ideas for a table lamp – the word from the dictionary might be 'fluke': a flounder, the barb on an anchor, an accidental success. Forcing a connection would lead us to think of such ideas as:

- A lamp with a large flat base (perhaps the whole 'work surface') that will not fall over.
- A lamp with a hook, magnet or suction pad that could be attached in any convenient position.
- A lamp with a 'flatter' reflector to provide a greater area of illumination.

There is nothing particularly revolutionary about these ideas, but 'fluke' was only the *first* word picked from the dictionary.

└───┘

- It's cheaper than conventional methods, and about as effective as the advice offered in the Government pamphlet 'Protect and Survive'.

There is a 'moral' to this exercise which is worth stating: 'No matter how stupid an idea may seem to be it has *some* value'. Do not underestimate the value of those 'wild' ideas. They are the source material that what we need to spark off our imagination.

If you are desperately trying for new ideas to help resolve a particular problem, but without success, then try this technique on something directly related to the problem. Imagine the wildest, most impractical or stupid ways in which you could solve the problem. Then list the good points of your 'useless' ideas: it is possible that you will make realistic connections with the problem. At the very least you will begin to clarify some of the qualities you need in your solutions.

4.8.4   Forced relationships

If you are still having difficulties, then try deliberately forcing some connections (see Frame 4.8), but do not even think about evaluating them at this time. Only when you have lots of ideas (useful, interesting, speculative, whatever), is it time to think about their merits – and even then it may be too soon (see Chapter 6).

_____ Frame 4.9   *Value Analysis* _____

> Value Analysis is a technique which examines the components that go to make up a particular item, and compares the cost of producing them to the value of the function that they perform. If the cost of producing a component is disproportionately high compared with its utility, better ways are looked for to provide its function.

4.8.5   Checklists

Another useful device to stimulate new ideas is to use a checklist, similar to the one given in Chapter 6. These contain many questions, such as those shown below in bold type, intended to stimulate the imagination by acting as prompts to looking at the problem situation from different aspects.

Engine oil for cars is often sold in 5 litre tins. You may also know that when these tins are full, it is notoriously difficult to top up the oil level in an engine without pouring oil all over it. Looking for ways of improving this 'delivery system', this checklist might have suggested that we add something to it (**Magnify – What can I add?**), such as the plastic tube with a 'lip' at both ends commonly inserted into the screw cap and 'pulled out' to form a primitive spout on these tins. Another word from the checklist (**Substitute – What other ingredients, materials . . . ?**) might suggest that we make the 'tin' out of another material – some form of plastic in which we could mould a better spout. (I suspect, however that the move to plastic containers was more the result of Value Analysis, see Frame 4.9.) Some of you may have already noticed the 'ultimate' solution. One oil company now sells an oil in a 'highly modified' plastic container that comes with a proper spout and can subsequently be used as a petrol can (**Magnify – Multi-purpose?**). Further explanation of the use of checklists, more useful questions, and another example of their use can be found in Chapter 6.

Do not expect your ideas to emerge fully evolved and perfected. That idea you may have had about selling oil in polythene sachets, or large cardboard 'milk' cartons where, if you are careful, you can tear them so as to be able to refold the top of the carton into a spout, may not be as silly as it first seemed. You can get wine and tomato ketchup in bags; and all manner of milk products, fruit juices and pasata (sieved tomatos) in cardboard cartons at the moment. Do not be too critical too soon!

4.8.6   Approximate thinking

I have an approximate experience that's approximately relevant to anything – doesn't matter what it is! Getting myself to realize that it's not mistaken to use that, enables me to dip into a huge amount of my potential. (Prince, 1980).

Each of us has a vast, diverse and essentially unique collection of thoughts, images and experiences stored away in our memories. Probability alone suggests we must have something relevant to dealing with a new situation or resolving a particular problem, but we often fail to realize this. Research in Creative Problem Solving indicates that we all have some recollections that are approximately relevant to any given problem that we have to tackle.

4.8.7   Analogies

William J. J. Gordon (1961, p. 54), suggests that the essence of creativity is the mental act of 'making the familiar strange' a 'conscious attempt to achieve a new look at the same old world, people, ideas, feelings, and things'. He describes how we might use techniques variously referred to as analogies or metaphors to facilitate the making of these unlikely connections. He identifies (1961, pp. 36–56) four types of analogy: Personal, Direct, Symbolic and Fantasy Analogies.

Personal Analogy

Here, we imagine what it must be like to 'be' the object of our interest or concern, and use this 'experience' to help resolve a problem. Suppose we were looking for ways of improving a propelling pencil. In your role as a propelling pencil, you think 'Every time my lead breaks somebody twists my extremities with both hands (painful!) and this interrupts my writing. It's not my fault. It's that idiot holding me who was pushing too hard! I was doing OK and deserve a pat on the head and not a punishment. Anyway, why don't they give me unbreakable lead or at least protect the normal stuff somehow: it doesn't break when it's inside me.' It may be that such a personal analogy was responsible for the new pencils that extrude more lead when pressed on top like a retractable ballpoint pen, and which have a protuding metal tube protecting the lead.

Direct Analogy

Here we make a fairly straightforward comparison between the object or situation under consideration and something similar but from a totally different environment.

Returning to the propelling pencil and the problems we have refilling it, having to take it apart to transfer lead from the store at the top of the pencil. An image that came immediately to mind was of some friends of mine hand-milking their goats. Could we use a squeezing and pulling motion (fed by gravity) to draw in a new lead for our pencil, whilst the old one is being used up. Biology is a useful field to examine when looking for parallel situations such as this. One of my refillable pencils actually does have such a gravity-fed 'autofeed' mechanism that funnels a 'new' lead towards the tip of the pencil, where it is grabbed by a 'ring clamp' device. I noticed this *after* I had my 'goat' idea and confess to being both pleased and disappointed to find someone had already perfected 'my' idea.

This example illustrates two very important points. Firstly, it is totally immaterial that I do not really understand how a goat's mammary glands operate, my 'approximate knowledge' of the way a goat's teats are manipulated was sufficient to start me thinking about a possible solution to my problem.

Secondly, direct analogies work best when living entities are used as an analogue for an inanimate object, as in the example above. They also work well the other way round. Take for example the problem of dealing with redundant employees with whom there is nothing wrong except that their services are no longer required. We might think of them as empty wine bottles. Rather than just throw these people on the scrap heap of life, we could ponder the merits of 'bottle banks'. Because of current altruistic feelings about ecology and the conservation of resources, people are prepared to sort bottles by colour (clear, green, brown, etc.) and transport them to a bottle bank, thus reducing 'collection' costs to glass manufacturers, and making recycling an economic proposition. Could we identify transferable skills that our redundant employees might possess and classify them accordingly? Are they really 'redundant' (it may be that they can be retrained more cheaply than training a new person from scratch). If they are redundant, do they qualify for subsidized retraining schemes, which will increase the likelihood of their finding alternative employment?

Symbolic Analogy

For this type of analogy we need to be able to sum up the essence of our problem situation, in some symbolic and highly evocative way.

In the early days of Synectics, 'book titles' were often used for this purpose. Prince (1970, pp. 95–6) suggests that first we should try to write down the indispensable characteristics of the object, action or idea that we are investigating, providing us with a list of words. Then we ask what is paradoxical or contrary about one or more of these words in connection with idea, action or object. We then try to form from these thoughts word-pairs ('book titles') that are 'aesthetically pleasing, surprising, even poetic'. Examples of the sort of thing Prince means are:

- a familiar surprise
- a disciplined freedom

- a dependable intermittency
- an ephemeral solidity

If we return to the redundancy problem discussed above, the essential characteristic of these employees is that they are

redundant – excessive, inessential, obsolescent, old-fashioned, superfluous, surplus, unnecessary, unwanted, useless

Now we think of words connected with these employees that are contradictory to any of these. Although these employees are redundant, they still possess certain **skills** and experience, they are not without some **potential** or utility . . .

potential – capability, capacity, possibility, promise, utility, value – future, hidden, latent, unrealized

skill   – ability, accomplishment, aptitude, competence, experience, expertise, facility, ingenuity, practicality

After this we combine these words into pairs (the 'book titles'), for example

- a redundant potential
- a surplus value
- an old-fashioned future
- a superfluous utility
- a hidden obsolescence
- a promising uselessness

Having generated a few 'book titles', one or more of these word-pairs would be used as the 'quality' required in what we will refer to in Chapter 8 as an Example Excursion. Briefly explained we would try to think of examples of say 'superfluous utility' from the worlds of Warfare, Biology and Transportation. This might yield 'nuclear weapons', 'pairs of organs in the human species' and 'spare sets of wheels on lorries', respectively. Then we try to make connections between these ideas and our original problem, that of redundant employees. Here are just a few 'beginning' ideas that these comparisons suggested to me.

Nuclear weapons: The super-powers have far more nuclear weapons than they realistically need to win a war, let alone to act as a deterrent. However, it could be argued that this surfeit has been useful in preventing a *war*, because of the fear of Nuclear Armageddon. It would now seem that the sheer number of these weapons, and the *expense* of maintaining them, has obliged these nations to bargain for arms reductions, and that this process could lead to the development of an atmosphere of cooperation, trust, perhaps even friendship, between these nations. Can you relate this to the problems found in an overstaffed company?

As regards pairs of organs in humans, in nature we can find many examples of 'build-in' redundancy, many of our organs, for example our lungs and kidneys, are duplicated, though we do not actually need two of them. Here nature is providing a 'back-up' provision in case one of them should go wrong. The 'spare organs' idea made me wonder whether companies may feel that it was cost-effective to keep a 'spare crew' available 'on-call' in case of illness or other emergencies. Or, if this is not viable for an individual company, then that industry as a whole might consider organizing and financing a system of 'back-up' employees. A less ambitious alternative might be to set up a register of employee skills and experience (like the existing system for 'supply' teachers) which could be made available to others who might have a need for these people.

What about the notion of spare sets of wheels on lorries? These days, with increasingly heavier loads being carried by road, we often see spare sets of wheels on the larger lorries which are used when the vehicle is heavily laden, but are jacked up off the road when the lorry is unladen. This idea suggested the notion that it may be cost-effective to keep some redundant employees on a 'retainer' basis, in case we may need them again. Some income and a partial connection with the company may be seen by them as better than nothing.

The 'book title' concept was eventually dropped (wrongly I believe) in favour of a type of symbolic analogy which is not easy to describe or to generate. William Gordon (1961, pp. 45–8) cites one example of its use, namely, that of using the 'Indian rope trick' as an analogy for a jack, but would we have thought of doing that? The criterion for selecting this type of symbolic analogy is that it should 'use objective and impersonal images'.

We are bombarded continuously with visual (and often intentionally symbolic) images in the form of films, television and advertisements. These images can be extremely productive when it comes to generating ideas. Extract a character or situation from a film you have seen as a symbolic analogy, and use this to suggest ideas about the problem. One word of warning, do not take a character or situation that too closely parallels the object of your current problem solving.

To demonstrate how we might use this idea, let us consider the problem situation described in Frame 4.10. I found it impossible not to compare Harry Pearson with the two main characters in M.A.S.H. The film and TV series focus on two doctors working in a US Mobile Army Surgical Hospital during the Korean War. They are portrayed as having a total disregard for the authority and morality of their (often incompetent) senior officers. They also deliberately flaunt their disrespect for unjustifiable regulations, and are able (or perhaps 'allowed') to get away with not wearing regulation uniforms, having a still in their quarters and a blatant indifference to rank. They get away with this

---

NAF Electronic Systems ———————————————— *Frame 4.10* ——

The management of NAF are concerned about the attitude and behaviour of one of their service engineers, Harry Pearson. Harry is a highly experienced service engineer and has been with the company many years without a blemish on his work record. Six months ago he was 'reassigned' from his usual work because his expertise was desperately needed to sort out the many problems that were occurring with a new product range of televisions.

In recent months, despite many warnings, Harry has been repeatedly breaking company 'rules' by 'extending' guarantees, supplying replacement parts at cost, replacing faulty equipment by new and often different models of television when he 'should' have repaired the fault and by advising customers to purchase TVs produced by NAF's competitors. Harry has always maintained a good rapport with those of NAF's customers with whom he has dealt, and recently there has been a barrage of complimentary letters to the company about the promptness, courtesy and professionalism with which he has done his job. There has even been a letter from a satisfied customer mentioning him by name published in a national magazine.

Why is Harry recklessly going against company policy? What can be done about him?

---

because they *are* good surgeons, desperately needed by the war effort. I asked, 'Why are the two main characters in M.A.S.H. acting the way they are?' and then tried to transpose the answers I obtained into the NAF problem situation. The results of this are given in Frame 4.11; the 'transposed' answers are shown in parentheses.

If familiar with M.A.S.H. your likely perception of the moral theme will be similar to one or more of the viewpoints listed in Frame 4.11, but probably not all of them. I have tried to put my feelings to one side and to consider what *could* be an 'objective' explanation of such behaviour. I am attempting to use this highly visual recollection to provide a number of initial ideas about what the problem could be and that should serve as the basis of discussions with Harry about the true causes of his present attitude and behaviour. Rather than having no idea as to what Harry is about, we now at least have some possibilities, and by asking pertinent questions we can determine whether we are on the right track, and if so, discuss with Harry what would constitute a mutually acceptable solution.

Career Excursion

Straddling the divide between Personal and Symbolic Analogies lies what Synectics (see Chapter 7) terms a Career Excursion. In brief, when

---

Frame 4.11   Symbolic Analogy: transposition from the characters in M.A.S.H. to Harry Pearson of NAF

Why are they the way they are? Because of . . .

- an over-riding altruistic interest in the welfare of . . . their patients (his customers) . . . who have been . . . conscripted (conned) . . . into . . . a pointless, and not of their own choosing, war (buying a worthless product).
- a reaction to . . . the horror of their environment (the totally alien philosophy of the new management), . . . and the incredible wastage of . . . human life, something they value highly (his time, expertise and resources, not to mention the destruction of the quality image that the company's products used to have).
- a rebellious attitude against being . . . forced to do something they dislike, don't believe in, cannot see the point of (reassigned to service a new, cheaper, lower quality/prestige product range).
- a psychological need to . . . 'let off steam', by behaving irresponsibly whenever the pressure is off (to avert the many 'unpleasantnesses' that *he* is now receiving from dissatisfied customers) . . . , in order to preserve . . . their sanity (his self-esteem).
- a hope that such actions might lead to . . . a dishonourable discharge and being sent home (him being returned to the job that he was happy doing).

---

faced with a problem situation or problematic object, a Career Excursion involves asking questions such as:

If I were a Sports Personality, School Teacher, Judge, Monk, Fireman

What would I think of this situation?
What would I (want to) do with this object?
How would I want things to be different?

We try to imagine what it would be like if we were looking at the situation or object in a role totally different from its normal one. We might, for example, look for ways of 'adding value' to a clipboard. These were once used mainly by 'time and motion' experts and the like, but are now available cheaply in a number of different colours and styles. How can we add that 'extra something' to the basic design in order to encourage people to buy another before their existing one wears out? Let us assume that our starting point is a rigid moulded plastic clipboard.

Our **Sports Personality** might say

Well, what I need is a clipboard with a stop-watch built in, I know you can get pens, rulers and, as far as I know, possibly clipboards with simple digital watches in them, but that's not much good to me. A full-function stop-watch is another matter altogether. At the moment I have to fix my stopwatch to my clipboard with elastic bands. I often take groups of kids orienteering at the weekends, and we have a similar problem, only this time we could do with a built-in compass.

Our **School Teacher** complains

We lend our pupils clipboards when we take them out on educational visits, so they can record their answers to questions we ask them. The trouble is, too many of them get 'lost'. We can't afford to keep replacing them. I've thought that indelibly marking them with the school's name and address might alleviate this. I've also thought of advertising the local fish and chip shop, record shop or something on the clipboard, to try to gain sponsorship from local retailers.

Both examples illustrate now putting yourself in another role can produce useful ideas.

Fantasy Analogy

This type of analogy takes a number of different forms. A less fantastic form involves mentally disobeying or ignoring scientific, organizational or cultural laws or rules to see the benefits of not being restricted by them. If this helps us to find some quality or thing in this fantasy world that we like or we think would resolve our problem, then we try to find ways of achieving this within the laws we have temporarily dismissed. In a similar way we can mentally realize our wishes pertaining to the problem – do some 'wishful thinking' or 'wish fulfilment'. We then analyse what it is about these wishes that appeals to us, and try to incorporate this into a more practical solution. These forms are useful to the lone problem solver. There are other forms such as the use of mental imagery (see Chapter 7), or the telling of fantastic stories, which work best with a group because they rely on the interaction of people's imaginations to add to and/or send the storyline in unexpected directions.

5 Working in groups

It has been claimed that many strategies and techniques designed to encourage creative thinking work best in a group setting. Comments and ideas made by other people fire our imaginations, and in the right circumstances we have a tendency to build on other people's ideas. However, the conclusions of research conducted into group productivity are mixed; for example, Arnold Meadow and Sidney Parnes in the 1950s seemed to verify that a Brainstorming group was more productive than an equal number of individuals working alone, but not using Brainstorming principles (see Chapter 6). Others have indicated that a Brainstorming group is not as productive as that same number of individuals working alone, but who are also using Brainstorming.

Subsequent research on enhancing group productivity has tended to concentrate on factors such as group cohesiveness. According to David Buchanan and Andrzej Huczynski (1985, p. 203), the level of cohesiveness of a group can be estimated from such things as 'whether members arrive on time, the degree of trust and support between them and the amount of satisfaction they gain from their group membership'. Irving Janis (1982) suggested that in some cohesive groups, an overriding desire for consensus and unanimity can lead to poor decision making due to the suppression of internal dissent and the consequent failure adequately to evaluate alternatives. Generally it is felt that group cohesiveness is an important positive factor determining productivity. As far as creative thinking is concerned, trust and support (see Chapter 4) are vital elements of an environment that enhances creativity.

Jay Hall (1971) concluded that what made a group more effective than individuals was when they *actively searched for areas of disagreement* early on in their discussions, and then resolved the subsequent conflicts into a consensus decision. Ineffective groups tended to 'opt out' of such conflicts and reached a common view by averaging their diverse opinions.

This led him to devise a set of rules for reaching a consensus (these can be found paraphrased at the end of the 'Lost at Sea' exercise at the end of this chapter. A 'well formed' group *can* come up with more and 'better' ideas for solutions and can make better decisions than individual members of the group working on their own.

Before we look at some strategies that enhance creative thinking, we should look at how best the 'dynamics' of the situation should be arranged so as to encourage the group members to think more creatively. This involves discussion of two main issues, first leadership, and secondly, being a good team member. Together, the interpersonal skills required of these roles can ensure that an appropriate 'climate' for creativity is both established and maintained.

5.1   Leadership

Most people believe that groups must have leaders, though some observers feel that 'creative' groups do not seem to have one permanent and easily recognizable leader. They seldom do have a 'traditional' style leader, but in virtually all cases such a group needs and has a leader of some kind, though it is not always self-evident who this leader is because different leadership styles are involved and because with an 'experienced' creative group the person assuming the role of leader may vary as the group's objectives change. People find themselves in a leadership role for a variety of reasons and possibly could obtain that position solely by virtue of personal charisma, tradition (for example, by birth or seniority), situation (being in the right place at the right time) or by appointment.

If our group requires a leader, it is essential that he or she is a Functional Leader (see Frame 5.1), who holds the position because of the way they adjust their behaviour to meet both the task-related and the personal and interpersonal needs of the group. Primarily, this leadership style needs to be fundamentally democratic rather than authoritarian. We want the members of the group to contribute all they can to the group's task and an authoritarian, task-orientated approach is not conducive to this, especially if what we want are 'beginning' or half-formed ideas! However, effectiveness with a democratic, people-orientated style of leadership requires rather more from the leader's behaviour. Robert Bales (1956) suggests that it is untenable to have a leadership style concerned both with the needs of the task and those of the people within the group, and that groups perform best when the roles of task leader and human relations 'manager' are occupied by different people. Bales identified the task specialists by asking group members questions such as, 'Who contributed the best ideas for solving the problem?' and 'Who did the most to guide the discussion and keep it moving effectively?' The human relations specialists were likewise

Frame 5.1   Action-centred leadership

The concept of Functional Leadership was pioneered by John Adair. His model of leadership maintains that leadership effectiveness comes from what the leader does to meet the needs of the task, the group *and* the individuals within it. It encourages a flexible style of leadership which may be predominantly concerned with the task, the group, or an individual, depending on the priorities and the circumstances.

Examples of the functions the leader needs to fulfil are:

- Task: defining tasks and setting objectives, planning the tasks, allocating work responsibilities and resources, setting, monitoring and controlling the quality of performance, time-keeping.
- Group: establishing behavioural norms by example, building team spirit, encouraging and providing a sense of purpose, maintaining discipline, ensuring good communications, acting as spokesperson for the group.
- Individual: attending to personal problems, providing motivation, recognizing and using individual abilities and contributions, providing positive feedback, training and developing skills.

identified with the question 'Who do you like?' A third group role emerged from this analysis, that of the 'scapegoat'.

Joe Kelly (1969, p. 217) describes the interplay between these two leadership roles as follows:

> it is possible to think of the task specialist as working at the task which structures the behaviour and attitudes of the group members, and which frequently makes people anxious and disturbs the equilibrium of the group. The anxiety generated by this kind of initiative may well be siphoned off and directed towards the scapegoat. The human relations specialist, who is usually a very warm and receptive personality, now comes to the fore and takes care of the casualties, bandages up the victim, and sponges down the task specialist, without diverting the group too much from its primary purpose of achieving the task.

Fiedler concluded that the suitability of a task as opposed to a people-orientated approach is connected with the relative favourableness of the task or problem situation. The task-orientated leaders seemed to him to be more effective in the extreme situations (very favourable and very unfavourable conditions), whereas the people-orientated leaders were more effective at other times. The favourableness of the conditions depended on whether the task was highly structured or unstructured, whether the leader's positional power was high or low (see Chapter 14), and whether the followers felt that their relationships with the leader were good, moderate or poor. These three variables are difficult to measure, a leader having to rely heavily on intuition when selecting a leadership style on this basis alone. Also this view of leadership ignores the needs of the followers and that sometimes a leader's technical competence is more important than his or her personality. All the same, it does demonstrate the importance of the context.

5.1.1   Process leadership

Generally, most CPS groups benefit from having what we call a process leader who is neither the problem-owner nor task specialist. Process leaders take little or on part in the problem content, but monitor group dynamics so that they can 'guide' the problem solving process through the most appropriate techniques and strategies after first having established and then whilst maintaining a suitably conducive group 'climate'. They do not offer any ideas, develop any solutions or perform any evaluation during the problem solving session. The precise nature of their input to the content of the problem depends on the methodology being employed. In Brainstorming (see Chapter 6), for instance, the leader, though generally contributing no ideas during the actual session, does offer direction for the group's ideas, and may do some 'sifting' of them afterwards. To this extent he is not a true process leader. The leader of a Synectics style group (see Chapter 7), should not take any part in the problem content whatsoever, because the group always contains a problem-owner (or client) who performs these functions when invited to do so by the leader.

This division between content and process seems to correspond with that of task and people at first sight. The problem-owner is the task specialist, whilst the process leader looks after the well-being of the group, but there is a major difference. The process leader of a Synectics style group *does* take care of the psychological needs of the individual and of the group. She is encouraging and supportive whilst ensuring that the climactic 'rules' are adhered to, but at the same time she guides the group through the problem solving process. This separates the task specialist from the process leading, and eliminates many potential conflicts, without taking the ultimate task control away from the problem-owner.

This experience with CPS groups suggests that the traditional style of meeting and chairmanship is not ideal for problem solving, as the 'traditional' leader or meeting chairperson tends to choose the direction of discussion, make instant judgements on relevance and usefulness, stick rigidly to the agenda and allocate assignments and tasks. While these are all important activities when used appropriately, George Prince (1970, pp. 3–4) believes that traditional style meetings are invariably less productive than they could be because:

- It is not always clear to group members precisely what is required of them – does the chairperson want to give information, gather ideas, seek reactions or genuinely solve problems?
- When meetings are used to solve problems or help make decisions 'creativity is a vital component because it develops alternatives, enriches possibilities and imagines consequences'. The chairperson can discourage the conditions necessary for creativity.
- The chairperson is invariably the person with the most senior 'rank' and 'it is accepted practice for him to use this power and for other members to play to it'.
- Our tendency to criticize ideas prematurely (see Chapter 4, 6) results in many useful ideas being abandoned.

It is generally considered to be poor leadership not to make it clear as to what the leader is doing, and what your expectations of the group members are. The other failings are all ultimately functions of the task specialist, being the leader of the process. Prince believes (1970, pp. 5–8) that people at meetings exhibit a behaviour that is a combination of sensitivity and aggressiveness, which ostensibly seem to be in conflict, but which are precisely the qualities we need for inspired problem solving. 'Aggressiveness presses us to adventure beyond the rules, to speculate outrageously. . . . Sensitivity alerts us to both opportunities and shortcomings.'

The chairman must ensure that these are used constructively. However, traditional meetings are very often perceived as competitions. If, as inevitably happens, we experience some disparagement, we then devote our attention and skills to repairing and refurbishing our self-image, preferably at the expense of our rivals. Having an impartial process leader helps us get away from these old attitudes. Prince concludes that a good leader is one who:

- defends each group member's image, because he or she 'knows that each member cherishes his own individuality above any problem to be solved';
- directs all aggression against the problem; and
- demonstrates that a meeting can be a winning situation for everyone concerned.

The ability to do these things is certainly something we would expect from a process leader; referring back to what a functional leader does (in Frame 5.1), a process leader performs many of these functions as well. In fact, a process leader should be fulfilling *all* the 'group' and 'individual' maintenance functions, and *most* of the 'task' functions as well. The exceptions here will be some overall planning of the problem solving activity which will usually be done by *both* the process leader and problem-owner together; in 'defining tasks (problems) and setting objectives' this activity can be left solely to the problem-owner.

In current thinking on leadership, Diane-Marie Hosking and Ian Morley (1988, pp. 90–1) suggest that 'the only sure means of identifying leaders is through the analysis of leadership processes'. They maintain that by studying the leadership process, the leader–follower relationship, certain 'acts' emerge was contributing to a 'social order' that protects and promotes the values and interests of the groups to which we belong. Leaders are those who 'consistently make effective contributions to social order, and are both expected and perceived to do so by fellow participants'. These 'leadership acts' are performed with a degree of skill, and Hosking and Morley say the skills of leadership are similar to those of 'negotiating'. Klaus Bartolke, however, commenting on their ideas in the same text (pp. 153–5), questions whether the concept of equating leadership skills with those of negotiating is universally applicable and, although calling it a 'useful theoretical construction', suggests that in some situations the skills of joint problem solving may be more appropriate.

5.1.2   Leadership and group development

The four stages we are believed to go through as we come together to form a group are described in most management texts, so a brief description should suffice here. Initially, we will be tentatively trying to determine the group's purpose, its composition, who should lead it, and our place within it (**forming**). This is followed by a conflict stage where these matters are thrashed out (**storming**). If we survive this process, we can then settle down to establishing the way we intend to fulfil the group's function and what behaviours and degrees of openness, trust, etc. are appropriate for achieving this end (**norming**). Only then can our group start **performing** productively. As far as problem solving groups are concerned, the establishment of the composition, purpose and norms of the group is usually in the domain of the process leader. Our only concern then is how to get to the performing stage as soon as possible. If we assume that our leader can skilfully perform the necessary 'leadership acts' and can quickly gain the group's trust and commitment and communicate and demonstrate the appropriate behaviours required of the group, then the warm-up exercises recommended elsewhere in this book will serve to reinforce these desired group norms.

5.1.3   Whatever happened to competition?

Prince's third aspect of good leadership, that of bringing about 'a winning situation for everyone' by eliminating the competitive attitude often found in meetings, raises the question of whether competition should be at the very heart of business. Obviously our product or service needs to be 'competitive' in that it has to have at least as much to offer as any comparable product or service available or else our business will not survive. But do we need to compete against other organizations in the sense of winning more sales at their expense? It would seem that the answer to this question is, not necessarily.

In recent years a 'new' management strategy has been evolving that could have a considerable impact on the commercial outlook of many organizations and companies in the near future. It reappraises the notion of 'competition' and addresses the possibilities of the concept of 'building markets'. John Sculley introduces us (1988, p. 137) to the idea of a 'Third Wave' company as follows:

> I've poured myself mentally and physically into the world of industrial competition (at Pepsi, one of the best second-wave companies). I've also discovered a new world (at Apple) where business has less to do with competition and more to do with building markets, where success is measured not by share points but by enlarging the playing field for everyone, thereby making the industry stronger – not just for us and at another player's expense.

In some instances the 'Third Wave' philosophy of 'winning situations for everyone' is not appropriate, for instance, when several television companies are competing for a single franchise. The 'market' cannot be easily expanded because of the limited number of frequencies available within the internationally agreed television broadcast bands. But most of the time, organizations can work 'together' in this way for the benefit of all. The 'Third Wave' philosophy can and does work.

As individuals we each possess different needs, abilities, aspirations and goals, but because we *are* individuals, we have an even greater need to cooperate with others in order to fulfil these things. Organizations are after all 'groups of people united by a common goal', though as Gareth Morgan remarks (1989, p. 30), such a phrase masks 'almost all the interesting features of organizations in practice . . . they are rarely so rational and so united as the definition suggests'. If it is possible for the notion of building together so as to create a 'winning situation for everyone' to work *between* groups of people (or organizations) with different and perhaps conflicting goals, it ought to be equally applicable *within* groups, at any level from the whole organization down to that of a small group of individuals. This whole idea seems to be linked with that of motivation, which is clearly important to our discussion of leader–follower relationships.

5.1.4   Autonomy, teamwork and motivation

Creative Problem Solving and teamwork are inextricably linked. The 'climate' of openness, trust and general emotional support required for creative thinking, once established and maintained for a while, has a tendency to spill over into the relationships between group members outside of the problem solving sessions. Almost inevitably, the overall team spirit of a group that works regularly together in this way will improve. Synectics recognized this phenomenon in their experiences with managers as facilitators/trainers in CPS and innovation. This led to the development of the concept of 'Autonomous Teamwork' (also referred to as Innovative Teamwork by Synectics Inc. and 'selfish co-operation' in Nolan, 1981), which evolved via this idea of 'winning situations for everyone'. Synectics have been putting this concept into practice for many years, both in connection with teambuilding and, like Apple Computer, by extending their philosophy to include their business competitors as well. But our interest here is in regard to team-building. Vincent Nolan (1989, pp. 238–9) describes autonomous team-work as follows:

> People work with maximum commitment and energy when they are doing what they have chosen to do, and are doing it in the way they believe is best for them. If they have no emotional ownership of the task, if they are doing it only because they have been told to, or because it is merely a means of earning a living, they cannot bring their full energy and enthusiasm to it. . . . As well as valuing their personal autonomy, people also like to work with others; they like to be helpful, to be supported and to identify with a whole (prefer-ably successful) that is larger than themselves. It is natural, there-fore, for people to work in a team, especially if it operates in a way that values and encourages individual autonomy.

This suggests that to secure the highest level of motivation (see Frame 5.2) and commitment from a group of people, we should do our best to preserve their individual autonomy over the way they make their con-tributions to the group's general aims. Some system has to be in place for this to work, one that provides, frequent opportunities for us to exchange openly with each other our needs, wishes and frustrations and to discuss, contribute to and make a special effort to reach con-sensus over the team's objectives, strategies and values, and the means to resolve (but not compromise on) the 'conflict of interests' which will inevitably arise. It also requires a certain amount of positive effort on the part of the individuals concerned, and relies on them taking re-sponsibility for their own actions.

When we 'join' a group we enter into an implicit psychological con-tract. We agree to help with the group's objectives in anticipation that

---

Frame 5.2   Motivation —————————————————

Abraham H. Maslow (1943) suggested that there were five groups of needs that drove us onwards:

Physiological needs	food, sex, sleep, sheer activity, etc.
Safety needs	a safe, orderly, threat-free, predictable, organized environment.
Love needs	love, affection and belonging (feeling part of a group).
Esteem needs	self-respect and self-esteem (strength, achievement, adequacy, confidence, independence, freedom) and the esteem of others (reputation or prestige: recognition, attention, importance or appreciation).
Need for Self Actualization	self fulfilment.

Somewhere within these groups lies a desire to know and to understand.

Clayton Alderfer has recently proposed that these needs can be classified into just three groups, spread along a *horizontal* continuum:

Existence needs	Material desires (physiological needs, security, money, etc.)
Relatedness needs	People relationships (social and esteem needs)
Growth needs	Self-actualization (creative desires)

However, these 'Intrinsic' theories of motivation though appealing are now thought to be inadequate. Charles Handy (1985, pp. 34–42) offers the following as our best current thinking on motivation. His model (based on Expectancy Theory) assumes that we are self-activating beings and can to some degree control our own destiny and our own responses to the pressures that others bring to bear on us, we can select our goals and choose the paths we take in an attempt to attain them. Each of us has a set of needs (such as those suggested by Maslow and Aldefer) and a set of desired results, and so we perform a calculation to determine how much 'E' (which stands for effort, energy, excitement, enthusiasm, emotion, expenditure of time, expenditure of money, expenditure of passion, etc.) to invest in a particular course of action. This decision, although often unconscious or instinctive, can at other times be conscious and deliberate.

The way we do this calculation is different for each of us and is based on three elements:

● the strength (salience) of the need,
● the likelihood that the amount of 'E' we intend to expend will lead to a particular result,

- the effectiveness (instrumentality) of this result in regard to reducing the need.

These are related to our self concept, the roles we occupy, the extent to which the terms of our psychological contract are met and, of course, our perception of all these things. If any of these elements are zero, then we do nothing!

(See also Georgopoulos *et al.* (1957), Vroom (1964) and Lawler (1969).

membership of that group will satisfy our needs for security, friendship, belonging, support, empowerment, a sense of achievement, etc. As long as we perceive this contract as being 'honoured' we are motivated to contribute to the group's activities, and prepared to take these responsibilities. Synectics are quite specific that we should feel responsible for it is those things we actually *do* to further the team aims, and refer to this as our 'action responsibility'. This, along with 'open-minded communication' and creative problem solving skills (see Chapter 7), form the basis of autonomous teamwork.

Within this area of action responsibility, Nolan states, 'team members are left to carry out their own job in their own way, without advice, help, ideas, criticism or opinions from their own colleagues, unless they ask for such, except when what they are doing or proposing to do impacts on another team member's area of responsibility' (1989, p. 243). The team is there to offer help only when asked for, thus respecting the individual's autonomy, and will assume that the individual is able to ask for this help when it is needed. It is an essential part of this kind of teamwork that requiring help is viewed as a willingness to learn, and not as an inadequacy, which is more usual in our culture. Unsolicited offers of help are not unheard of in such a team, however there is an obligation on the giver to ensure that the offer is not seen as a criticism.

The team must also provide the day-to-day emotional support and encouragement we need, to achieve our own objectives and those of the team and to enhance our self-confidence and self-esteem. The keystone of all of this is mutual trust, or the assumption that everyone is working to their best in order to achieve both their own and the team's objectives. While an atmosphere of mutual trust takes a long time to build it can very easily be destroyed. The advice Nolan offers is always to 'assume constructive intent on the part of colleagues, particularly when things go wrong'. Finally, at least one member of the team should be skilled in CPS, so that when conflicts of interest do occur, as they will do, the team is able to generate alternative ways of meeting the same given objective. This should enable us to find an alternative which will satisfy all those concerned and hence resolve the conflict.

────── *Frame 5.3* '*Best fit' leadership* ──────

Charles B. Handy (1985, pp. 103–11) has argued a good case for what he calls a 'best fit' approach to leadership, which assumes that 'there is no such thing as the "right" style of leadership, but that leadership will be most effective when the requirements of the leader, the subordinates and the task fit together.' To achieve this fit, each of these 'factors' need to be given a rough placing on a scale running from 'tight' to 'flexible'.

Leader – Here we are concerned with the leader's preferred style of operating and his or her personal characteristics. The scoring of this factor comes from whether the style is autocratic or democratic (Charles Handy prefers the terms 'structuring', 'supportive'), and thus depends on the leader's:

- value system (on how he/she should be a leader);
- confidence in his/her subordinates;
- habitual (usual) style;
- assessment of the importance of his/her personal contribution;
- perceived need for predictability of the outcome (and hence control).

Subordinates – It is their preferred style of leadership in the light of the circumstances that interests us here, so the scoring of this factor depend on their:

- estimate of their own intelligence and competence;
- their psychological contract with that group and that leader;
- interest in the problem and their view of its importance;
- tolerance for ambiguity or their need for structure;

and

- the past experience of the group;
- cultural factors.

Task – The job, its objectives and its technology, will also suggest whether things should be structured or open-ended. The scoring here will depend on the:

- kind of task;
- time-scale;
- complexity;
- whether 'mistakes' matter;
- importance of the task.

If, after each of these has been given an 'objective' score on the tight/flexible scale (usually by the leader), they do not fit (have approximately the same score), attempts are made to adjust the factors until a fit is obtained. The 'freedom' with which this adjustment can take place is thought to depend on a fourth factor.

Environment – The organizational setting of the leader, his group and the importance of the task. The key aspects of this are the:

- power position of the leader in the total organization;
- relationship of the leader to his group;
- organizational norms;
- structure and technology of the organization;
- variety of tasks;
- variety of subordinates.

All other things being equal, it is easiest (for us as leader) to change our leadership style, hence the flexibility requirement in earlier 'style' theories of leadership, but sometimes it may be more appropriate to develop a new way of working for the group or to redefine the problem.

In all this it must not be forgotten that the group leader is also its 'ambassador' and its role 'model'.

5.2 Leadership revisited

Summarized below is some general advice on leading this new 'breed' of team, provided by Nolan (1989, pp. 266–7):

> . . . the more the environment a team works in requires innovation, and the greater the extent of external change, the more team members need a style of leadership that is open, honest and constructive.

- Be yourself. Your personal integrity is your most valuable asset.
- Know yourself; exploit your strengths and get help where you need it.
- Define your role as leader. People need to know where they stand; to know that, they need to know where you stand.
- Provide a model of behaviour that you want practised in the team.
- Always disclose what you are thinking and planning to do.
- Give constructive feedback.
- Give honours judiciously.
- Be consistent.

This approach is complementary to Handy's (1985, p. 115) 'best fit' approach to leadership (see Frame 5.3), which he says implies that the characteristics of a good leader should be:

- a high tolerance for ambiguity and an ability to handle open-ended problems;
- an aptitude for differentiating between the needs of people and the needs of the situation;
- a clear self-concept, and hence a tendency to possess self-confidence;
- a high reservoir of ('E' factors) excitement, enthusiasm, emotion, etc., in particular, energy;

- a preparedness to set moderately high standards for him/herself and his/her co-workers, and to give and receive feedback on performance.

This 'best fit' approach is essentially an extension of the contingency theories we started out with (page 64). Is this the end of the story? Hunt *et al.* (1988, p. 1) comment on the diversity, and controversial nature, of recent leadership research; that we still appear to be some way away from achieving consensus on what constitutes effective leadership, or on precisely what 'leadership' is. The recent views of Hosking and Morley have been briefly introduced, but alongside this we find that certain aspects of the earlier trait and style theories seem to be re-emerging and acquiring a new upsurge of interest. For example, the concept of **charismatic leadership** is currently being reappraised from the perspective that it is not 'solely a function of the leader's personality' but is more to do with the perceptions of followers which may or may not be situationally contingent. Charismatic leadership is often defined these days as something like . . . a new or different view of things portrayed by the leader which is perceived by his/her followers as being 'cognitively, emotionally, behaviorally and consequentially "real" for them' (Boal and Bryson, 1988, p. 12).

Closely related to charismatic leadership is the concept of **transformational leadership** (Frame 5.4). Where the latter differs is that it actively encourages followers to think for themselves and to develop their own 'visions' to further the group's objectives. Bruce Avolio and Bernard Bass say that apart from charisma, 'transformational leaders also need the ability to recognize the needs, aspirations, and values of their followers and the skill to conceive and articulate strategies and goals that will predispose the followers to exert their best efforts' (1988, pp. 36–8). Transformational leaders must also be able to 'read' situational factors, such as the prevailing organizational culture in order to determine what is possible and when the time is right to attempt changes in the outlook of individuals and/or organizations. These leaders do not just 'react to environmental circumstances – they create them'. Is this another way of describing a process leader?

Commenting on Avolio and Bass' ideas, Jill Graham is optimistic about transformational leadership, because not only does it encourage follower autonomy but it has the means to sustain it. 'Individualized consideration and intellectual stimulation are the pump primers used by transformational leaders to make followers more self-confident, self-reliant, and critical people, all of which reduces the likelihood that followers will fall into habituated subordination' (1988, pp. 73–9). In fact, she sees intellectual stimulation as 'facilitating radical thinking, even to the extent of inviting followers to challenge the positions of the leader'.

┌─*Transformational leadership and beyond* ─────── *Frame 5.4* ──────

Bruce Avolio and Bernard Bass (1988) advocate (pp. 30–5) a model of leadership developed by Bernard Bass (1985) which incorporates both previous thoughts on transformational leadership (James MacGregor Burns, 1978) and some earlier ideas concerning transactional leadership. This model attempts to explain how through 'heightened motivation', followers are encouraged to 'perform beyond expectations'. Although the main emphasis is on the 'transformational' aspects of leadership, they maintain that in order to be an effective transformational leader, we must have the skills of a transactional leader as well.

Bernard Bass claims to have identified five factors within what Avolio and Bass see as effective leadership. Two are those of **transactional leadership** (a form of leadership essentially rooted in path–goal theory):

- '**Contingent reward.** The leader is seen as frequently telling subordinates what to do to achieve a desired reward for their efforts.
- **Management-by-exception.** The leader avoids giving directions if the old ways are working . . . [and] . . . intervenes only if standards are not met.'

The different interpretation now being placed on these factors is that it is by encouraging them 'to work for transcendental goals instead of immediate self-interests and for achievement and self-actualization instead of safety and security', that followers are motivated to perform beyond expectations.

The other three of Bass's five factors are **transformational leadership** factors:

- '**Charisma.** The leader instils pride, faith, and respect, has a gift for seeing what is really important, and has a sense of mission (or vision) which is effectively articulated.
- **Individualized consideration.** The leader delegates projects to stimulate and create learning experiences, pays personal attention to followers' needs – especially those who seem neglected – and treats each follower with respect and as an individual.
- **Intellectual stimulation.** The leader provides ideas that result in a rethinking of old ways, and enables followers to look at problems from many angles and resolve problems that were at a standstill.'

There has been a trend for many years now to distinguish 'supervision' and possibly also 'management', from 'leadership'. The diagrammatical representation of the functions of management in Figure 5.1, showing the 'usual' five functions (see Chapter 3), plus a sixth

Figure 5.1 *Leadership, supervision and management.*

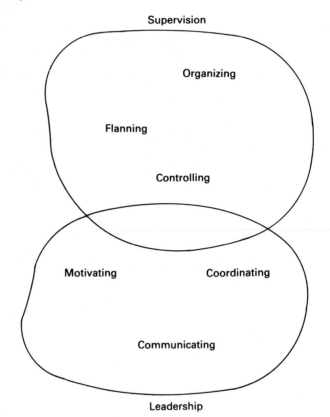

Management is . . .

Supervision

Organizing

Flanning

Controlling

Motivating   Coordinating

Communicating

Leadership

one 'communicating', illustrates this split. Although undoubtedly an oversimplification, Figure 5.1 does make the distinctions that, first, supervision and leadership have little or nothing in common and that, secondly, as a consequence of this, our traditional view of managing can no longer be seen as the same thing as leadership (see Chapter 14). Graham (1988, pp. 74–8) notes that **supervision** is usually associated with a leader–subordinate relationship implicit in which is a certain 'coerced compliance' brought about by 'the fear of punishments, the promise of rewards, or the desire to fulfil contractual obligations', and which is maintained by the use of positional power (reward, coercion and legitimacy). In connection with leadership, we speak of a leader–follower relationship where followers are psychologically linked to the organization because of identification (involvement based on pride of affiliation) and/or internalization (involvement based on a congruence between individual and organizational values), along with which comes the idea that 'followers freely choose to be influenced by those who lead them', and which relies on the use of personal power (expert and referent).

Appealing though this description of transformational leadership may be in that it appears to support the concept of 'autonomous teamwork', Graham warns us that when measuring the impact of transformational leadership on the basis of effective follower performance there is a distinct risk of attributing inappropriate characteristics to the leader (including many popular myths). And this is assuming that the charisma that a leader is perceived to have *is* partly the cause of effective follower performance. Enhanced follower performance could well be due to something that possibly has nothing to do with the leadership, for example, being intrinsically motivated by the task itself.

Finally, two quotes that summarize leadership rather nicely:

> A leader can only be a leader if followers are willing to follow. (Buchanan and Huczynski, 1985, p. 389)

> Leadership is the lifting of a man's [or woman's] vision to higher sights, the raising of a man's performance to a higher standard, the building of a man's personality beyond its normal limitations. (Drucker, 1955, p. 195)

5.3   Group membership

5.3.1   What goes on during a group activity?

Effective communication is an integral part of successful problem solving. Without it, we are unable adequately to ascertain other people's cognitions, beliefs, attitudes, opinions, expectations and values concerning the problem situation, or subsequently to relay back to the owners of the problem our ideas and possible solutions. In a group problem solving situation, not only do we have the above interchanges of information taking place, but this is being done face-to-face amidst all of the usual interpersonal interactions occurring within the group. We may also be asking people to do or say some 'strange' things, which makes it paramount that every participant must understand what is expected of them, and what the 'ground rules' are. So let us now look at the communication process within a group.

Robert Bales in the late 1940s/1950s identified 12 types of communication between members of a problem solving group. These are summarized in Frame 5.5. Groups B and C are associated with the task being performed by the group, whereas A and D relate to the human relations within the group. Together these acts determine the type and quality of the process employed by the group to reach its objectives. These different acts of communication were observed from overt behaviour and checked by questioning group members afterwards.

─── *Frame 5.5*   *Communication within groups* ───

Classification of Acts of Communication (Bales, 1956, p. 267)

A. Positive reactions
- Shows solidarity, raises others' status, jokes, gives help, reward
- Shows tension release, shows satisfaction, laughs
- Agrees, shows passive acceptance, understands, concurs, complies

B. Problem Solving Attempts
- Gives suggestion, direction, implying autonomy for other
- Gives opinion, evaluation, analysis, expresses feeling, wish
- Gives orientation, information, repeats, clarifies, confirms

C. Questions
- Asks for orientation, information, repetition, confirmation
- Asks for opinion, evaluation, analysis, expression of feeling
- Asks for suggestion, direction, possible ways of action

D. Negative reactions
- Disagrees, shows passive rejection, formality, withholds help
- Shows tension increase, asks for help, withdraws 'out of field'
- Shows antagonism, deflates others' status, defends or asserts self

Given that it is commonly felt that these acts of communication constitute an exhaustive list of behaviours, which do we wish to encourage for creative thinking and problem solving, and which should we try to eliminate? At first sight it would appear that those in group D are of little or no value and are thus best discouraged. However, Bales himself identified group C as being generally negative with respect to accomplishing the task, and others have since tended to agree with him.

Synectics similarly believe that there are four main interactions that take place when people work in groups, which affect the group's productivity. These can be described as:

- offering ideas, suggestions and information to the group;
- supporting someone else's contribution;
- evaluating or rejecting someone else's contribution;
- asking questions.

While these activities are a very natural and necessary part of working in a group, Synectics warn that these four interactions are just as likely to have a detrimental effect on a group's productivity. For example, questions can be used as a 'put down': You're not really suggesting that we do that are you?' Other examples of the negative effects of these interactions are:

- Ideas can be used as the ammunition in one-upmanship games.
- Someone may present an idea so forcefully that it inadvertently overshadows or excludes equally worthy contributions from less forceful group members.
- Praising the merits of an idea ingenuously, or just more than it is worth, is a fairly effective way of killing an idea.
- Too much support too soon may also encourage a group to settle on a solution before it has been adequately thought through.
- Being prematurely critical of an idea may at best cause a basically good idea to be rejected, and at worst may inhibit further *positive* participation from the contributor.

We should also remember that the effect of these interactions can be contrary to their intentions, no matter how positive they may have been.

Synectics place particular emphasis on the use of questions. We often need to ask questions to clarify our understanding of what someone else has said, and to gather information. But questions asked at the wrong time, for instance, when it is not desirable or really necessary to understand what has just been said (see In–Out Listening in section 7.7), inevitably slow down the flow of ideas. Synectics also believe that often what is actually happening when people ask questions is that they are checking out the 'goodness' of their idea prior to voicing it – the old 'self-censor' again (Chapter 4). What they are really saying is 'Who, what, when, why or how is . . . , because if such and such is the case, perhaps we could . . . (idea).' One very simple thing each of us can do, which in the long term can considerably improve our communications, is to (honestly) give the reason for wanting to know the answer to a question, as we ask it.

As we have been looking at aspects of leadership and the typical interpersonal interactions that take place within a group we have been dealing with some of the behaviours required of the members of a creative work group. Chapter 4 contains other indications of our expectations of their contributions and now would seem to be a good time to summarize all of these qualities.

5.3.2   Group membership skills

Almost all of us are quite expert on many matters of group process, but, curiously, we seldom use what we know to improve the operation of groups. We are expert in the sense that we can go home after a meeting and describe the group's psychology and social structure in considerable detail over dinner, and we know which particular behaviours were dysfunctional to the group. (Leavitt, 1978, p. 198).

My experience concurs with this opinion and I believe that our first responsibility as members of any group is to be open about our feelings, and to attempt to deal with any perceived 'injustices'. This may exacerbate any interpersonal conflict present in the group, but as Harold Leavitt goes on to say (p. 211), 'the preferred course would seem to be to promote rather than limit communication, that is, to accept and deal with information about personal feelings and personal needs as well as with information about pertinent facts'. The variety of perceptions, opinions and personalities amongst group members is one of its most valuable resources.

In a CPS group, everyone is expected to give freely of their ideas, both obviously useful or interesting ideas and wildly speculative ones. Thus we have an obligation to suppress as best we can any conceptual blocks that we possess, and also our natural tendency to criticize others immediately they make a suggestion. The personal and interpersonal skills required by a group or team member (when they are not leading) are nicely summed up by Colin Hastings *et al.* (1986, pp. 97–8) who speak of the need for team members to be 'active followers' and say about these people that

> They know when to be in on the action and when to pull out. They know when to give help and when to ask for help. At times they will provide push and direction but equally they are able to allow themselves to be pulled by others. Their willingness to follow does not come from the passive obedience to the leader or others, but from their active loyalty, respect and personal commitment to all the members of the team. They are willing to be led by any of the team members provided that they can be persuaded that it is in the best interests of the team as a whole. But above all they assume responsibility. They take it upon themselves for instance to ensure that they understand how their role affects other people's roles. They are driven by a desire not to let other people down, and when, as can always happen, this looks likely they take active steps to help their colleagues avoid or minimise the consequent problems.

> When they don't understand they ask. Members of Superteams have no fear of looking foolish if they don't know because they recognise that they will need to learn from and value each other if the team is to benefit from its diversity of talent.

Particularly note the references concerning asking for help; this, as we have seen, is a fundamental aspect of 'autonomous teamwork'. If we are given this autonomy, and have taken responsibility for our own actions, we will be left alone to get on with it without interference from others. This means that if we need help we are *expected* to ask for it.

5.4 Selecting groups/teams

Many people have tried to 'convert' Bales's classification into a list of group roles, patterns of behaviour that a person may adopt when participating in group working. His original four roles (task specialist, human relations specialist, scapegoat and the rest of the group) have been expanded to as many as 15. Some researchers have 'divided' their roles between task/problem related and people/process related sub-groups, others not. This dilemma indicates the existence of 'grey' roles that defy this type of sub-classification. For instance, the 'gate-keeper' was a role popular a few years ago – someone who knows a lot of things or where to find them out. This is a useful person, with access to a wealth of information and contacts, but is this role assisting the problem directly, or the process of problem solving?

There is a method for ensuring the balance of teams based on the use of Kolb's Learning Style Inventory (1976), which highlights the connection between how we learn and our problem solving skills (see Mind-spring theory, section 4.2 above). This Inventory furnishes four scores which indicate the extent to which we prefer to use active experimentation, reflective observation, concrete experience and abstract conceptualization as methods of learning. It is suggested that teams should have all-round performance, with at least one team member who is predominant in a particular quadrant for all four quadrants in Figure 5.2. This figure also shows how certain group roles and the left/right brain concept have been associated with this grid in the past.

Listed in Frame 5.5 are the group roles identified by Belbin (1981) (see also Handy, 1985, pp. 166–7) as being needed for a 'fully effective group', with other roles I came across at the Manchester Business School in the early 1980s, and the six management styles of 'Action Profiling', another technique used for selecting and ensuring the balance of a group.

I have equated the descriptions of the two sets of roles with each other and with these management styles, by comparing Belbin's description of his eight roles, Carol-Lynne Moore's summary of the six styles 'measured' by Action Profiling (1982, p. 16) and my recollection of the 'MBS' roles. There appears be some consensus between these three views of group/team roles, though there were two instances where this 'match' proved a little troublesome. First, the Company Worker, the 'practical organizer' whose forte is 'schedules, charts and

Figure 5.2 *Learning style.*

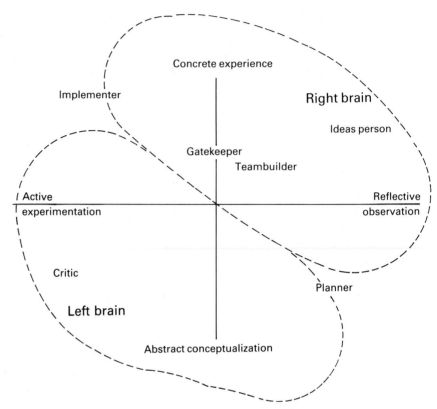

The 'Coordinator' is usually positioned in the centre but that does not reflect his/her all-round capability

Frame 5.6 *Group roles*

R. M. Belbin	*Source unknown* (MBS)	*Action Profiling*
Chairman	Coordinator	
Team worker	Teambuilder	
Shaper		Determined
Resource-investigator	Gatekeeper	
Plant	Ideas-person	Exploratory
Monitor-evaluator	Critic	{ Investigative, Evaluative }
Company worker	{ Implementer, Planner }	Anticipatory
Finisher		Timing

plans', is certainly an Implementer, but sounds like a Planner as well, two diametrically opposed types on the Learning Style grid. Whilst it is by no means impossible to find someone with that propensity, I suspect it would require two people to fulfil that role. Secondly, I had a little trouble assigning the Anticipatory and Timing styles of Action Profiling, since both the Company Worker and the Finisher, the person who 'checks the details' and 'chases' us about keeping to schedule, seem to have aspects of both these styles. The 'Shaper', about whom little is revealed here, is described by Belbin as 'highly-strung, outgoing and dominant', full of drive and passion, predominantly a task-orientated person, who perceives him or herself (usually wrongly) as ideal material for chairperson. Although it is not a 'perfect fit' by any means, I would expect to see many of these qualities in the average task specialist.

Very seldom do we have the luxury of choosing our team and so it is perhaps a little unrealistic to put forward these roles solely as a tool for group selection. However, they can be used as a sort of 'checklist' to determine how 'balanced' our group is and could possibly offer assistance in selecting additional or replacement members for the team. A word of warning for anyone intending to check the 'balance' of a group; we need to guard against such an exercise throwing up a 'halo' effect (see Chapter 4) around the perceived shortcomings of the present group membership.

If we assume that our group has a process leader with coordinating and team-building skills, a determined task specialist/problem-owner (shaper), and preferably a gatekeeper already, five additional personality traits can be identified that would be useful to us. We would like to have: someone who is imaginative and prepared to speculate openly and explore ideas (ideas-person); someone who tends to be analytic and logical (investigative) and has a natural tendency to evaluate possibilities (critic, 'analyst' is a slightly less pejorative term); a practically minded person who quickly sees how something can be done or organized and can/will carry this through (implementer); somebody whom I would describe as a person who pays minute attention to details and has a good sense of timing (finisher); and finally someone who is a good planner, perceptive to the necessary stages of development and who can anticipate the consequences of these (planner). It should always be remembered that real people will possess several of these qualities and will do so in varying proportions. The advice is to select a group of people who together provide a complete set of the qualities mentioned above.

5.5   Action Profiles

Our 'Action Profile' describes the 'style' with which we approach problems (apply 'attention' to the problem situation), make decisions (establish our 'intention' to choose between the alternatives generated by the problem solving) and go about the implementation of the chosen course of action (exhibit our 'commitment' to that decision). These three aspects of problem solving and decision making contribute six basic management styles (investigative, determined, timing, and exploratory, evaluative, anticipatory), depending on whether we are a more 'assertive' or 'perspective' person. No one style is 'right', we are a mixture of various proportions of all six. The aim is once again to ensure that the team is strong in all areas. Knowing a person's Action Profile tells us how that person likes to work, and takes away much of the frustration caused by them 'unexpectedly' not doing things in quite the way that we would have done!

Action Profiles also show our propensity to share our problem solving and decision making processes with others, or to work on our own, as well as ratings on several other more general decision making skills, such as adaptability. It does not attempt to measure our aptitude at problem solving and decision making. Synectics Ltd use Action Profiling not only to attempt to ensure an overall balance in their team, but also to highlight and forewarn team members where potential clashes might occur between individuals because of their differing styles of working, so that these individuals can compensate for this in advance when dealing with each other, and, since the consultants often work in pairs, to match them up in a complementary way.

5.6   Summary

The key points to be derived from this chapter are, first, that for CPS and many other groups as well, what we require is a different type of leader from the conventional stereotypes, a process leader who can create the atmosphere of openness and trust required for creativity. Secondly, though our process leader is an important factor in ensuring a successful outcome from our group's endeavours, he or she cannot do this alone. Along with our process leader must come a willing band of highly motivated and committed, *active* followers, prepared to share the responsibility for any success, and provide emotional support in times of difficulty. Lastly, high degrees of autonomy and emotional involvement in the group's activities (elicited from feeling that their individuality is valued) would appear to be factors in ensuring the high level of motivation required.

5.7   Group consensus exercise

[Lost at Sea]
You are adrift on a private yacht in the South Pacific. A fire of unknown origin has destroyed much of the yacht and its contents. The yacht is

now slowly sinking. Your location is unclear because of the destruction of the main navigational equipment, and because you and the crew were distracted trying to bring the fire under control. Your best estimate is that you are approximately one thousand nautical miles south-west of the nearest known landfall.

Below is a list of 15 items salvaged intact and undamaged after the fire. In addition to these articles, you have a serviceable rubber life raft complete with oars, which is large enough to carry yourself, the crew and *some* of the items listed below. The total contents of all of the survivors' pockets are a packet of cigarettes, several books of matches and five one dollar bills.

You (individually) must rank the 15 items below in terms of their importance to your survival, so that a choice can be made of which to take with you in the life raft. Give the rank of 1 to the most important item and 15 to the least important.

sextant
shaving mirror
5-gallon can of water
mosquito netting
one case of US Army C rations
map of the Pacific Ocean
seat cushion (a Coast Guard approved buoyancy aid)
small transistor radio
shark repellent
20 square feet of opaque plastic sheeting
one quart of 160° proof Puerto Rican rum
15 feet of nylon rope
two boxes of chocolate bars
fishing kit
2-gallon can of petrol/oil mixture

Now repeat this task as a group decision-making exercise. Your group should ensure that the rank for each of the 15 survival items *must* be agreed upon by each group member, before it becomes part of the group decision. Consensus like this is difficult to reach, therefore not every ranking will meet with everyone's complete approval. As a group, try to make each ranking one with which *all* group members can at least *partially* agree. Appendix 1 has some hints for a possible solution.

In attaining consensus, the following guidelines should be observed:

- Avoid arguing for your own individual judgements. Approach the task on the basis of logic, and consider carefully the comments of others.
- This is not a competition; if a stalemate is reached over something, search for a mutually acceptable alternative.

- Do not alter your opinions just so as to avoid conflict and reach agreement. Support only those suggestions which are basically similar or complementary to your own, and change your mind only when something has been objectively and logically argued. Always be suspicious of a quick agreement.
- Avoid 'conflict reducing' techniques such as a majority vote, averaging or the 'trading' of points of agreement when reaching your consensus.
- View differences of opinions as a help rather than a hindrance in decision making. They are natural and should be expected. A wide range of information and opinions can lead to better solutions.

Brainstorming

When a group of people get together to produce ideas, solve problems, etc., often the first thing that happens to the ideas or possible solutions put forward is that they are criticized, torn apart or dismissed from further discussion. Sometimes an idea may deserve this fate, but often they are useful, interesting or appealing ideas that have a few minor 'faults' which could be remedied if we were to try. In this situation the best that is likely to happen is that an idea from which we might have developed a solution is lost, one hopes only temporarily. Unfortunately this may deter the idea-giver from contributing fully to the group; the group may then lose a potentially valuable resource. At worst the idea-giver turns against the group, or against the member responsible for the criticism. We then have what Synectics call a 'Revenge Cycle'. The idea-giver retreats into his 'shell' thinking mainly about 'crucifying' his opponents the next time they speak (see Chapter 4).

The main differences between Brainstorming and previous methods of problem solving is its insistence that absolutely no criticism whatso-ever (whether spoken or implied by visual expressions, body language or grunts) is allowed during the generation of ideas. This does not mean that there is no evaluation of ideas, just that it is postponed until later, usually in a separate session.

It is not easy to create an atmosphere in which criticism is postponed, even temporarily. As we saw in Chapter 4, people come to meetings with differing viewpoints and desires, and a self-concept to enhance or protect. These things, coupled with the usual differentials of status and power that exist within groups, tend to lead to an atmosphere of com-petition, especially when group members are trying to impress others with their contributions. But neither is creating such an atmosphere impossible.

─── *Frame 6.1   Outline of the Brainstorming process* ───

- Pre-meeting with the problem-owner to define the problem, determine its suitability, and to discuss what constitutes an acceptable solution.
- Warm-up session – which may include problem redefinition in its later stages.
- Brainstorming session – incorporating additional techniques: Wildest Idea, Checklists and Attribute Listing as appropriate.
- Subsequent acquisition of ideas.
- Selection of most promising ideas.
- Development of selected ideas.
- Verification and presentation of selected ideas.

A key property of a Brainstorming session is the much larger quantity of ideas produced compared with individual problem solving or the more usual group problem solving techniques. Not all the ideas produced will be brilliant, but there are usually a lot of useful ones. This productivity of Brainstorming groups has been attributed to several factors. The power of association of the human mind is well known (though perhaps not really understood), and when a group of individuals are assembled and encouraged to produce ideas by association the effect is a dramatic increase in the number of ideas produced, what Alex Osborn refers to as 'Social Facilitation'. When judgement is suspended, one person's idea quickly triggers ideas in the minds of others, causing a 'snowball' effect. Groups also usually come up with more ideas than the same number of individuals working alone. It has also been demonstrated that the more wild or speculative these ideas are, the more dramatic this effect. A certain amount of constructive rivalry – the challenge to produce more, better or wilder ideas – also acts as a stimulant.

6.1   What is Brainstorming?

Brainstorming was conceived originally as a 'complete' problem solving process, intended to provide the means for dealing with several of the stages we tend to go through when tackling a problem. When compared with the stages in the problem solving 'model' presented in Chapter 3, the Brainstorming process involves redefining the problem, generating ideas and finding possible solutions, developing feasible solutions and evaluating solutions. An outline of the whole process is given in Frame 6.1.

The pre-meeting normally involves just the leader and client. One reason for this is to make the leader aware of the constraints on the range of acceptable solutions in any real world situation, owing to financial, social, political and legal considerations or just client pre-

┌─*Rules of Brainstorming* ──────────────────── *Frame 6.2* ──┐
- No criticism is allowed – evaluation of ideas must be withheld until later.
- 'Free-wheeling' is encouraged – 'the wilder the idea, the better'.
- Quantity is wanted – the greater the number of ideas, the more likely is the chance of having useful, interesting or appealing ones.
- Combination and improvement – try to 'build' on other people's ideas.

ferences so that the leader can guide the group's efforts. However, because it is difficult for someone to be conscious of these constraints and still remain uncritical, it is probably best if the Brainstorming group itself remains unaware of them.

Brainstorming is essentially a group problem solving process as it relies on the interactions between the ideas and imaginations of group members for its success and productivity. This does not mean that when faced with solving a problem alone we should not utilize Brainstorming, but, because we only have our own mind from which to draw inspiration, we will probably need some assistance from additional techniques such as a Checklist like the one in section 6.5.2, and Forced Relationships (see Frame 4.7, p. 52). Even within group problem solving sessions advantages can be gained by 'breaking off' from the normal proceedings and individually writing down some Brainstormed ideas (in what are called 'trigger' sessions). The creative 'climate' within the group is developed and maintained by the group leader's 'gentle enforcement' of strict adherence to the four rules of Brainstorming; these are summarized in Frame 6.2. The leader in this context is not a typical meeting chairman, but a process leader as defined in Chapter 5.

There are a number of reasons for this insistence on the observance of these rules. Apart from the earlier comments about 'losing' ideas and 'upsetting' fellow group members, permitting criticism at the idea generation stage affects the productivity of our imaginations and the 'flow' of ideas. We tend to use our imaginative resources to construct defences for our ideas rather than for thinking up new ones. This reduces the quantity of ideas that we are likely to get, let alone the quantity we will express and record.

A conscious effort to produce 'wilder', more speculative ideas is almost as important as the postponement of criticism. Not only do these ideas tend to set and maintain the 'atmosphere', reducing tension, relaxing the participants and providing the 'fun' element of problem solving, they also fire the imaginations of other group members. This ultimately leads to the acquisition of a larger number of innovative ideas. Although this is the main purpose of the wild ideas, a surprisingly large

---

Frame 6.3   Building on other people's ideas

Finding names for a new Uni-sex perfume:

'The Master and Mistress'
'How about something French sounding?'
'Messieurs et Mesdemoiselles'
'Maestro'
'Deux Chevaux'
'Lovebirds'

'Deux Chevaux' is a simple 'build' on the idea of trying something French and the car name 'Maestro'. It has a certain 'ring' to it, though people would probably not want to think that they were wandering around smelling of 'two horses'! Having said that, there is a successful ladies' perfume called 'Tramp'.

---

proportion of them do lead to a problem solution. Who would have thought that such a 'stupid' idea as repeatedly striking overhead telephone lines with the wing tip of a light aircraft as it flies over them would lead to a solution of the problem of a 3-inch build-up of frost along 700 miles of these lines disrupting long distance communications! A simple modification of this idea worked; replace the aircraft by a helicopter and use the downdraught of the rotors to dislodge the frost.

Finally, experience has shown that the best ideas often come from a combination and/or development of several other ideas, and so we are encouraged to 'build' on other people's ideas whenever possible (see Frame 6.3, and Chapter 7). We will also see later that Osborn recommends that further 'builds' should be attempted, when we subsequently begin to evaluate the ideas we have generated.

6.2   When to use Brainstorming

It used to be thought that virtually all problems could benefit from a Brainstorming approach, though some might need breaking down into parts to ensure that problem was not too general. Brainstorming is not now considered suitable for complex problems and even in the 1950s Osborn advised that 'the guiding principle is that a problem should be simple rather than complex. Failure to narrow the problem to a single target can seriously mar the success of any brainstorm session' (1957, p. 238).

The problem 'How can we improve the profitability of our "household products" division?' is far too diverse a problem situation for

---
Typical applications of Brainstorming —————— *Frame 6.4* —

- Finding a name for a new product/service.
- Finding alternative uses/new markets for existing products.
- What improvements can we make to this product/service/process?
- Where can we find more time/space/resources so that we can . . . ?
- Potential problem analysis.
- Obtaining a cross-section of views on a specific topic.

Brainstorming to tackle in one go (if at all). If we were to attack this problem from a number of specific 'viewpoints' – such as: How can we reduce production costs of our leading household product? What other markets are there for our plastic containers? What additional products could we 'easily' add to our existing range? How can we improve the marketing of our kitchen-ware? – we would stand a greater chance of success. Although addressing *one* of these problem definitions is feasible with Brainstorming, tackling all of them may not be. There will be a limit to the number of Brainstorming sessions that time permits, even if we ignore any additional difficulties likely to be caused by the perceived interconnectedness of some of these specific problem definitions.

Brainstorming is not normally used with complex problems these days owing to a change in opinion over the desirability of restructuring such problems. Not only is it difficult to separate a complex problem situation into a number of discrete and independent parts, but this process may result in the actual problem area being 'missed' completely. Other methods seek to avoid the dangers of restructuring a problem, for example, the Soft Systems Methodology described in Chapter 12. Osborn paraphrases his own advice with 'orientation of aim is often half the battle'. This particular observation is realized by the inclusion of an entire stage 'Goal Wishing' (see Chapter 7) in the early part of the Synectics process. Brainstorming is best used only on quite specific problem areas (see Frame 6.4); these other problem solving strategies are better on more complex problems.

Tudor Rickards (1974) has listed a number of specific problem areas for which Brainstorming may be unsuitable. Among these are problems requiring a high level of technical expertise, problems involving the manipulation and motivation of people, and those problems where written material needs to be created and/or considered.

One feature that may indicate a problem is suitable for Brainstorming is if the merit of the ideas or possible solutions once acquired is fairly self-evident, and/or they do not require much further development before they become feasible, for example finding a name for a new product.

6.3   Conducting a Brainstorming session

6.3.1   The size and composition of the group

Group sizes from half a dozen or so up to a couple of hundred have been tried in the past, though experience suggests that approximately a dozen people is the ideal. A compromise has to be made between enough people to get a steady flow of ideas easily and a small enough group to be manageable. In too large a group ideas may be forgotten or lost, leading to frustration, and time may be 'available' for us to evaluate and perhaps censor our own ideas. If a group contains a couple of people who are 'good' at, and willing to come up with, wild ideas, the group size can be smaller and still be as productive.

Osborn originally suggested that these groups should consist of a leader, an associate leader, five 'regulars' (experienced Brainstormers) and five 'guests' with a 'knowledge' of or experience related (perhaps tenuously) to the problem area (for example with a marketing problem these might include a 'typical consumer'). There are no hard and fast rules on composition, although it is generally thought that the inclusion of experienced Brainstormers is very desirable, as is a group with a wide spread of backgrounds. A group made up of only 'experts' in the problem area is very undesirable, and some would say that having more than one expert can cause problems (see Chapters 5, 7). The more diverse (due to experience, expertise or ideology) the participants, the more difficult it is for the leader to ensure that those opinions are voiced in a positive way; if the leader succeeds in this, the more creative will be the ideas. Osborn believes that a positive attitude towards the task in hand and the processes used is more important than proven creativity.

Life is made easier if all the participants are of equal 'rank' within the organization. This is true for all Creative Problem Solving because group members are expected to say things that in other circumstances might be thought silly. However, a group of equal rank is neither always possible nor desirable. If our problem was 'How can we improve communications within the organization?' an input from people at various levels in the organization should obviously be sought. This makes it important to ensure that the correct 'climate' has been established (see Chapters 4 and 5) and that everyone knows the rules and what is expected from them, so that *within* the group they are effectively equal. There may also be problems in getting everyone wanted for a particularly group together at the right time in the right place and keeping them there. This will require considerable planning.

6.3.2   Preparing for a Brainstorming session

If, as suggested, the Brainstorming group contains some 'novices', then these 'new' guests need to be given some idea of what to expect. Preferably, they should at least have taken part in a training session, and are thus not totally inexperienced, but if they have never participated in any form of Brainstorming before, they should be sent a description of the Brainstorming process which includes an explanation of its purpose and its rules.

All participants should be sent a 'background' memo, informing them of (1) the time and place of the meeting, and (2) giving them an indication of the problem to be brainstormed, along with some 'typical' ideas.

Finally the group leader needs to note down their own ideas in order to gain some impression as to the 'directions' they consider it worth guiding the group along on the day. A checklist may be useful for this (see section 6.5.2).

6.3.3   When is the best time to hold a Brainstorming session?

Timing depends largely on the group's motivation. Osborn favours morning sessions, suggesting that starting a little while before a light 'working' lunch is also successful as it improves the informality of the occasion. This should not be confused with traditional meetings and conferences which span a coffee break, lunch break, etc. where, perhaps because of inherent faults in the traditional process (see Chapter 5), these informal breaks are often deemed to be the most useful part of the process!

6.3.4   Where is the best place to hold a Brainstorming session?

Individual Brainstorming can be accomplished anywhere we can cut ourselves off sufficiently from our environment (although we may want to use our environment to fire our imagination). For group CPS sessions we generally need an informal and relaxed atmosphere; the venue should be cut off from external distractions and interruptions such as telephone calls, the seating should be comfortable and arranged in such a way as to inhibit breaking up into a number of sub-meetings, and there should be flipcharts and wallspace so that all ideas can be put up for all to see. The traditional image of a board room (with its long rectangular table and upright chairs) is not usually considered to be an ideal arrangement. A round table would improve matters, but the general consensus seems to favour 'easy' chairs surrounding low 'coffee' tables.

6.3.5   The tasks of the secretary and leader during the meeting

A member of the group should take on the role of secretary and should normally be positioned near the leader. The secretary should write up all the ideas offered and may paraphrase them, though if possible this should be avoided. No form of censorship or bias should be invoked. Osborn advises that the ideas should be numbered as they are written up, because knowing how many ideas have been produced acts as an encouragement. He also states that reading from pre-prepared lists should not be allowed.

The Brainstorming process begins with the leader explaining the problem that the group is to work on and reminding the group of the 'ground rules'. The leader should then use a warm-up exercise, to set up a 'climate' which ensures that no 'external' criticism comes from the other group members when we start putting forward ideas. The leader should also encourage the participants not to allow their own built-in 'self-censor' (see Chapter 4) to stop them from putting ideas forward, especially since often our critical faculties are so in-grained that we are not always aware of the self-censor's operation. Techniques such as Synectics' Excursions (see Chapter 7) help to overcome this.

During the course of the Brainstorming session proper, the leader has a number of other tasks to accomplish, such as enforcing the rules and counteracting the tendency of the group to break up into several smaller meetings. Since combinations of ideas are what is most wanted, the leader must also give 'builds' priority when ideas are flowing fast. Originally participants were asked to raise their hands when they had an idea to contribute, and Osborn recommended snapping one's fingers to indicate a 'build', although this may not be 'appropriate' in all cultures.

Lastly, the leader should remind the group that if ideas are coming too fast for the leader and secretary to 'manage', then the group members should note down their ideas on paper until they get a chance to suggest them.

6.4   An application of Brainstorming: naming a product

One of the most frequent applications of Brainstorming is naming a new product or service. To illustrate the Brainstorming process we will now work through such a problem. A brief outline of the story surrounding our product is given in Frame 6.5.

On the day of the Brainstorming session, the first thing we need to do after the introductions is to 'get into the mood' of the occasion.

6.4.1   The warm-up session

It is difficult to Brainstorm from a cold start. My favourite device for a warm-up exercise is the 'Most Useless Ideas Competition' (see Chapter 4). However, this can take up too much time if one works through the whole competition, so here is an alternative warm-up exercise, 'pet hates'.

The members of the group are invited to divulge those relatively

An illustrative example: Drug Stores Ltd ——————— Frame 6.5 ——

Drug Stores Ltd is a nationwide chain store, with 130 branches throughout the country. They sell a wide range of proprietary brands of cosmetics and toiletries, 'over the counter' pills and medicines, and a limited number of 'health' foods and drinks, plus a number of miscellaneous items. Drug Stores are about to launch their 'own brand' of cosmetics and are trying to think up a suitable name for this new range of products. They are hoping that these products will appeal primarily to the 'younger' woman, and provide them with a strong foothold in this market.

Pet hates ——————————————————————— Frame 6.6 ——

My next-door neighbours' dog (and its habit of fouling my lawn).
Bind weed and couch grass.
People who drop litter.
Drivers who deliberately use the wrong lane at roundabouts.
People who drive at 65 in the fast lane on motorways.
The individual who 'restyled' the front wing of my car last week and did not stop to apologise.*
The speed at which some solicitors and insurance companies operate.*
Picking up my children's clothes/toys/sweet-papers.
My family's inability to turn any lights off.
The ease and speed with which my children get their clothes dirty.
People who leave the tops off toothpaste or squeeze the tube in the middle.

trivial things which cause them to spend an inordinate amount of time being anxious, concerned or angered about them. All suggestions are written up on white boards, flipcharts, etc. without any comments except encouraging ones – the sillier a person thinks these ideas are, the better for our purpose. 'I don't like being told I am losing my temper, when I am!' 'My wife apparently doesn't appreciate the helpful advice I always see fit to give her, before she drives my car!' We should never dismiss 'wild' or unorthodox ideas as silly or irrelevant. At the very least they may cause some laughter, help the group to relax and add some fun to the proceedings, and they will probably spark off somebody else's imagination as well (see Chapter 4). A typical list of this sort of thing is given in Frame 6.6. Incidentally, James Adams points out (1979, p. 113) that when addressed specifically at aspects of products and services that annoy us, this can be a useful means of 'searching' for new products and services or improvements to existing ones.

Frame 6.7   Drug Stores Ltd: a name for a new range of cosmetics

New Faces	Fantasy	Lady of the Night
Complexions	Wishing Well	Bondage
Bright Eyes	Images	S & M
Camouflage	Reflections	Stallion
Deception	War Paint	Pagan
Metamorphosis	Creations	Neanderthal
Naturelle	Ecstasy	Inuendo
Illusions	Bitch	Aura
Images	Street Corner Look	Peaches & Cream
Collage	Red Light	English Roses
Dreams		

The little things which regularly irritate one person are usually amusing to others and the laughter which inevitably occurs 'breaks the ice'. Often people share similar 'pet hates' and saying so helps to forge sympathetic and supportive bonding between group members. This exercise may also permit the airing of something that has been preying on someone's mind prior to the session, thus clearing the air of things that would have prevented them from making a full contribution to the group's efforts. (The items marked with an asterisk in Frame 6.6 are possible examples of this.) This exercise is carried on for several minutes, by which time the group members should be beginning to relax. The leader should encourage everyone in the group to contribute but not by identifying noncontributors. An alternative warm-up exercise is to encourage group members to describe the most stupid or embarrassing thing they have done this week/month. If it succeeds, these revelations of our 'weaknesses' or failures break down the 'walls' that people build around themselves, but it does require a group leader who inspires trust, friendliness and confidence to solicit these rather more 'soul baring' responses and to carry off this type of exercise.

The next stage in the process is the Brainstorming session 'proper'. The list shown in Frame 6.7 was obtained by a group of students during a training session, and took approximately 15 minutes to achieve (a few ideas have had to be censored before publication!). Some of these suggestions are probably not going to go much further in the process ('S & M' and 'Bondage' for example), but as catalysts for our imaginations they have already served their purpose. However, there are many quite reasonable suggestions in this list, which I am sure you will agree are at least as marketable as existing product names (such as 'Evette', 'No. 7', 'No. 17', 'Classic', 'Italian', 'Rascale', 'Over the Rainbow' and 'Maxi').

6.4.2   The 'slump' and the 'wildest idea'

Eventually in all Brainstorming sessions the number of ideas emerging from the group starts to tail off. This 'slump' is particularly noticeable after the initial ideas are exhausted, if there has been little or no 'building'. Adams (1979) stresses the importance of 'pushing' ourselves through this period, since it is usually in these later stages where the best ideas appear; failure to do this means that the session 'will not live up to its potential'. One technique for 'rejuvenating' a session, particularly if it is languishing due to a lack of speculative ideas, is a 'Wildest Idea Competition' whereby the group are asked to suggest the most fanciful ways they can think of for solving the problem. As leader we would also use this technique if no-one was trying to build on the more speculative ideas – we would use the speculative idea as the starting point for some 'wishful thinking'.

6.4.3   The processing (and evaluation) of ideas

After the Brainstorming session is completed, the ideas generated have to be evaluated. Osborn said that despite some disagreement about this, most people believe that evaluation should be done by a panel of people different from those who took part in the original session, thus preventing any 'my baby' problems coming into the evaluation. However, the original group will experience frustration if no feedback is available concerning the fate of their ideas. Osborn suggests that the 'most promising' ideas should now be selected (usually by the original group leader) and passed to an evaluating panel for further consideration, but he does not indicate how rigorous this screening procedure should be. There is a danger here: this selection of the 'good' ideas from the 'bad' can be a retrogressive step. Nolan (1989, p. 60) believes that there is a distinct possibility that 'new' ideas may not be considered to be 'good' ideas because they have no track record (see Chapter 7). Allowing the original idea-generating group to make the selection and to take part in the evaluation may ensure the retention of more of the 'new' speculative or unusual ideas, but the real solution is probably to have a more sophisticated and 'idea friendly' evaluation process such as that incorporated into the Synectics approach (see Itemized Response in Chapter 7).

Osborn breaks down the processing of the ideas into several stages:

(1)   Subsequent acquisition of ideas

On the basis that the participants frequently come up with more ideas after the Brainstorming session, when they have had a chance to 'sleep on it', participants should be canvassed for additional ideas after the event. One way to do this is to send to each participant a list of the ideas produced in the session along with a request for any further thoughts that group members may have had no reflection. If this can be accomplished by personal contact a greater number of returns will probably be achieved.

(2)   Selection of ideas

Usually the group leader 'screens' the ideas, removing those not likely to benefit from further consideration, leaving those that seem 'most promising'. Osborn would probably define 'most promising' more tightly than I do and because of this I need to incorporate an additional selection process after Osborn's stage (3). I would not eliminate all the speculative ideas as there is some merit in retaining these at least until the next stage. However, in most Brainstorming sessions suggestions are made which serve process purposes (relaxing the group, sparking off the imagination of others, etc.) but which would seem questionable if repeated outside the Brainstorming session. These 'ideas' and perhaps also the more impractical ones would be eliminated; for example, we would abandon those names produced which are too similar to an existing product or have an 'unfortunate' translation in another language.

(3)   Development of the selected ideas

The best ideas, it is claimed, 'are usually combinations of other ideas' and participants have already been encouraged to 'build' on the ideas of others. However, Osborn suggests that further 'building' by the evaluation panel with the screened list of ideas can have particularly beneficial effects.

(4)   Verification

The merit of the ideas selected above should now be ascertained by the most appropriate means; the potential success of our new product, its name or the chosen marketing campaign can be 'checked out' by market research.

(5)   Presentation of the 'best' ideas

Osborn suggests (p. 254) that good advice to start with when considering the presentation of the results of a Brainstorming session is: 'The way to sell an idea to another is to state your case moderately and accurately' (Benjamin Franklin) and, 'The time to discuss an idea with others is after you have thought it through' (Dr William J. Reilly).

┌─ *Reverse Brainstorming* ──────────────────────── *Frame 6.8* ─┐

There is some uncertainty as to what constitutes Reverse Brainstorming; my use of the term means taking each idea (product name) and thinking of everything that is wrong, missing or 'bad' about the idea. We unleash the critical faculties that we have been holding back on for so long now, and become as destructive and negative as we can. The ideas for product names that end up with the least 'wrong' with them (in terms of quantity and seriousness) should be our best ones. There is, however, nothing inherent in the Reverse Brainstorming process which distinguishes the more serious faults from the minor ones.

Before embarking on a Reverse Brainstorming session we should have some idea of what sort of faults we might be looking for. (Attribute Listing could help with the selection of these 'damning criteria'.) Rickards (1974) suggests using Reverse Brainstorming after obtaining a possible solution as part of the planning stage prior to implementation. The purpose is to list all the possible (unlikely, perhaps impossible) things that could go wrong, and otherwise mar, hold up or prevent successful implementation. This is essentially an application of *normal* Brainstorming in a trouble-shooting context, a creative process where we list all the things (likely or otherwise) that might go wrong, *without criticism* and without worrying initially about estimating the validity or seriousness of these potential problems (see Chapter 11).

We must now go through these stages with the ideas we have for a name for Drug Stores' new product range. Let us assume we have supplemented our list of names by a few more thought of after the Brainstorming session (1). How can we now reduce this to our short-list which will ultimately be subjected to the verification process? I prefer to let the original group play a major part in this. We first need to make an initial selection (2) to eliminate the 'non-starters'. We want to retain most of the more novel or unusual ideas at this stage. After removing these 'non-starters' we would hold another meeting (3) whose primary task is to see if any further ideas can be found by a combination and/or development of the ideas we have so far. We now need to perform the additional selection process mentioned earlier, before going on to Osborn's verification stage (4). For this type of problem I tend to use 'Reverse Brainstorming' (described in Frame 6.8) to evaluate the list of ideas as this coarse method of selection is often all that is required. However, although Reverse Brainstorming may 'suggest' suitable assessment criteria for our ideas, before starting any final selection we should be fairly clear as to what these ought to be. We should not rely on the Reverse Brainstorming process to provide them. Frame 6.9

Frame 6.9   Drug Stores Ltd: What makes a product name successful?

Possible **selection criteria** (desirable qualities) might be:

- Memorable
- Unique
- Ease of incorporation into a jingle/slogan
- Mass appeal
- Descriptive
- Projects the right image, degree of quality, etc.

On this basis we might reject names from our list if:

- the name is too long to incorporate into a 'snappy' slogan;
- it does not have mass appeal or will not (we think) appeal to the type of customer we wish to attract;
- the name has 'unfortunate', strange or inappropriate connotations.

This would rule out names such as 'New Faces', 'War Paint' and 'Bitch'. Not having any one of the 'desirable qualities' listed above may have been thought of as a 'fault' in our Reverse Brainstorming session.

suggests some possible criteria for our problem and indicates which of our ideas may now have been eliminated from further consideration.

If we have more ideas left after this than our current need requires, we can change the gradation of our filter from coarse to fine by involving more of the criteria in Frame 6.9, but even now we should think very carefully before totally rejecting an idea. For example, 'Bright Eyes' might well be a usable name for eye make-up (if the rabbit connotation is not a problem), although not particularly suitable for an entire range of cosmetics. There is a case for retaining many of our ideas for a future occasion. Our short-list might be:

- Illusions
- Images
- Naturelle
- Reflections
- Red light

If we need a more sophisticated evaluation of the short-list to reduce these ideas down to one or two, then we can adopt the 'grid' method mentioned later in this chapter and in section 10.4, Decision Analysis.

6.5   A second application: new markets for an existing product

Another common use of Brainstorming is the search for new ways of using an existing product. This search is usually instigated by a per-

---
Another illustrative example: Dispensable Plastics Ltd —   Frame 6.10

We have been asked to participate in a Brainstorming session for Dispensable Plastics Ltd, one of the major manufacturers of plastic cups for automatic drink-dispensing machines. This company is concerned that they have virtually only this one market for their products, apart from a small proportion of retail sales which they make through chain stores for private catering, e.g. for children's parties. They would like to find a new 'outlet' for their products, just in case anything should ever 'go wrong' with the drink-dispenser business. The problem we are going to Brainstorm is 'What other things can we use a plastic cup for apart from serving hot and cold drinks in it?'

---

ceived need to find alternative markets for the product, thus permitting diversification without too many operational changes. Some reasons why a company might want to do this are:

- Someone has asked the question, 'Are there any opportunities being missed?
- If the demand for the product is beginning to tail off, because it is coming to the end of its natural life cycle, and its manufacturers may be trying to 'stall' the coming demise of their product whilst they build up other aspects of their business to compensate.
- Perhaps a catastrophic change in the market has occurred.
- Perhaps the longevity of the product's life has surpassed all reasonable expectations and, although the product is still selling well, this must come to an end soon and the company wishes to investigate contingency plans for what else they can do with their product.

A 'favourite' product for demonstrating this application of Brainstorming is the common red house brick. However, for the purposes of illustrating the process here I will relegate the red brick to a reader's exercise and have chosen another well-known item to investigate instead (see Frame 6.10). We will assume that we have already had our warm-up session, and are ready to Brainstorm some new uses for this product.

6.5.1   Attribute listing

A 'cut-down' version of a technique called Attribute Listing (accredited to Robert P. Crawford and usually linked with Value Analysis, see Chapter 10) is particularly useful when applied before searching for alternative uses. Essentially this involves Brainstorming the assets, features or properties that the item has. The 'full' version continues to consider systematically how each of these attributes could be improved,

---- *Frame 6.11   Attributes of a plastic cup* ----

Round	Cylindrical
Brittle	Can be cut
Cheap	Hole at one end
Washable	Holds hot liquids
White/coloured/patterned	Stackable
Indentations on bottom	Reinforcing ring/lip at top
Some have insulating properties	

---- *Frame 6.12   Ideas Checklist* ----

PUT TO OTHER USES
New ways to use it as it is?
Other uses if modified?

ADAPT
What else could be adapted?
What else is like this?
What can I make this look like?
What other ideas does this suggest?
Does the past offer a parallel?
What idea can I incorporate?
What other process could be adapted for this task?
What could I copy?
Whose style can I emulate?
How can we make this better and cheaper?

MODIFY
New angle?
Change meaning?
Change colour, motion, sound, odour, taste, form, shape?
Other changes?
What other 'packaging'?

MAGNIFY
What can I add?
Extra feature, ingredient?
Stronger? Larger? Higher? Longer? Thicker? Extra value? More
    time? Greater frequency?
Duplicate?
Multi-purpose?
Multiply? More in a package?
Exaggerate? Over-state?

MINIFY
What can I subtract?

Omit? Eliminate?
Smaller? Condensed? Miniature? Lower? Shorter? Lighter? Streamline?
Split up? Separate parts?
Under-state?

SUBSTITUTE
What can I substitute?
What other ingredients, materials, process, power can I use? Another
    place and time?
Another approach?
Other senses, emotions, attitudes?
Who else instead (could do this better)?
What else instead (could do this better)?

REARRANGE
Interchange components?
Another pattern, combination?
Another layout, position?
Other sequences?
Change pace, timimg? Slower? Faster? Earlier? Later?
Change schedule?
Transpose cause and effect?

REVERSE
Transpose positive and negative?
How about opposites?
Turn it back to front, upside down, inside out?
Reverse roles, e.g. with client, competitor?
Turn 'the tables', 'the other cheek'?

COMBINE
What materials, processes can I combine?
What could be merged with this?
How about a blend, an alloy, an assortment, an ensemble?
Combine units (into a single entity)?
Multi-purpose?
Combine appeals?
Combine ideas?

(Compiled from Osborn, 1957, Chapters 21–24.)

──── *Frame 6.13   Dispensable Plastics Ltd: uses of a plastic cup* ────

Flower pot
Strawberry protector
Disposable egg cup
Emergency toilet
Ink well/eye wash/birdbath
Paint pot/mixing jar
Dice shaker
Waste bins (if bigger)
Decorations – bells, flowers (if cut)
Party crackers
Column: stacked, glued rim-to-rim and base-to-base
Fire lighter
Ear trumpet/megaphone
Decorative combs (if cut)
Party hats (with elastic)
Practice golf
Protective surround (cut in random shapes or whole)
Spacers
Pencil/Sellotape/string/wool holder
Warning device (breaks with a 'crack')
Children's moon-buggy wheels
Telescope/microscope/pin-hole camera (with lenses)
Lamp reflector/shade
Pastry cutters
Bottle labels (cut to slip over neck)
Temporary lens hood for camera
Paper-weight (with heavy filling)

but for our purposes the simple listing of these attributes should make finding alternative 'uses' easier. Some of the attributes of our plastic cup are given in Frame 6.11.

Having listed as many features of the humble plastic cup as we can, we would move on to have our main Brainstorming session to find some alternative uses.

6.5.2   Checklists

Osborn discusses at length the questions we can ask ourselves to encourage our imagination. This checklist, shown in Frame 6.12, is intended to be useful for many problem situations, but should be particularly useful for our current problem. Situations where this type of checklist has been found to be particularly useful are finding applications for

┌─ *Dispensable Plastics Ltd: selection criteria for* ───── *Frame 6.14* ─┐

commercial viability of alternative uses

Great care must be taken when it comes to choosing suitable criteria, as the ones which spring easily to mind in connection with commercial viability tend to 'overlap'. For example, the amount we can spend on research and development, and in additional production costs 'modifying' the existing product, depend on what price we believe we might then be able to sell the product for, the quantity we believe we can sell and all of this affects the profitability of the project.

Possible selection criteria are:

- Likely demand
- Lifetime of product
- Profitability
- Marketability: how easily can we sell it?

└───┘

new synthetic materials, e.g. neoprene, cellophane, nylon, glass fibre; deciding what to do with waste products, scrap, etc.; and a specific example, finding new uses for telephones – time, weather, etc.

Checklists like this are invaluable for individual Brainstorming. If leading a group we could use this list prior to the session to produce a number of 'directions' in which we plan to take the members. This list can also be used as a 'regenerative' device when a group finds it difficult to 'get off the ground' or are in a rut because they believe they are unable to come up with any more than fairly obvious and mundane uses. Frame 6.13 gives some typical responses that we might expect from our Brainstorming session.

Having Brainstormed a list of ideas concerning alternative uses for plastic cups, we will need to run it through a selection procedure similar to the one used in the previous example. First of all we eliminate the 'non-starters' such as emergency toilets, then possibly hold an additional idea development session to generate some 'builds' on the ideas we have, and select suitable criteria for applying a more exacting sifting process. We are particularly concerned here with the commercial viability of our alternative uses, and some possible criteria are suggested in Frame 6.14.

When we have reduced our list to the most promising new uses, we will want to conduct a rather more sophisticated evaluation process than that offered by Reverse Brainstorming. Frame 6.15 shows a 'grid' on to which we can write these ideas in such a way that we can 'score' them against each of the criteria we have decided should be used to determine commercial viability. Simply scoring each idea on a five-point scale will be sufficient for most purposes; the system used in Frame 6.15

Frame 6.15   *The grid evaluation method*

Idea	Criteria Profit	Demand	Market		TOTAL
Flower pot	2	3	3		8
Paint palette	1	1	1		3
Lens hood	3	0	1		4
Egg cup	2	1	2		5
. . .					.
. . .					.

4 = very good; 0 = very poor

---

is 4 = very good, 3 = good, 2 = average, 1 = poor and 0 = very poor. If we feel that one or more of these criteria are more important than the others, then the 'scores' on that criterion can be weighted as appropriate. For example, if 'likely demand' is deemed twice as important as the other criteria we would multiply the score our ideas obtained on this criterion by two. From the total score we decide which of these ideas should be considered for implementation.

6.6   Conclusion

Brainstorming, perhaps starting with Adams's variation on 'pet hates' and possibly incorporating Attribute Listing and Checklists, is an effective way of tackling the problem of finding ways of improving products and services. There has not been room to give a full illustration of this here, nor indeed all other possible applications of Brainstorming. However, the issue of 'improvement' has been addressed when illustrating Forced Relationships in Chapter 4, and Morphological Forced Relationships in Chapter 9.

Regular participation in Brainstorming, and any other form of Creative Problem Solving, is claimed to bestow improvements in self-confidence, initiative and other qualities of leadership, a reduction in frustration (becaused our ideas are wanted and heard) and an attenuation of our fixations or mental set (see Chapter 4). There is no denying that Brainstorming was a considerable step forward in our attempts to deal with complex real world problems. Its underlying philosophy of not evaluating ideas too early is an extremely important concept and is now incorporated into many other more universally applicable problem solving strategies. In its more or less pure form it will be used again in Potential Problem Analysis (Chapter 10) and finding Relevant Systems (in Chapter 12). Contingency planning, for example – coping with advances in technology, long range forecasting of product markets, estimating the impact of legal and social changes on the business environment – is a common use of Brainstorming. However, Brainstorming does have its limitations with more complex problems and so in the next chapter we will examine another CPS process, Synectics. Of all the techniques and strategies grouped under the heading of Creative Problem Solving, Synectics is probably the most highly refined and most universally applicable.

7 Synectics

> Ultimate solutions to problems are rational; the process of finding them is not.
>
> William J. J. Gordon, *Synectics*, p. 11

Synectics is the name given to a body of knowledge, a collection of behavioural skills and a set of problem solving techniques. It is also the international group of companies that have developed this from 30 years of study and work with innovative groups. But it is also far more than this. The greater a person's exposure to Synectics, the more it pervades the way that person thinks to the extent that it virtually becomes a way of life (Frame 7.1).

In the words of John Alexander (1979, p. 9), a director of Synectics Ltd, the skills and procedures that comprise Synectics are designed to achieve:

- creative high quality courses of action;
- high levels of commitment and energy to agreed courses of action;
- effective cooperation between individuals and departments;
- fast progress towards objectives through innovation and conflict resolution;
- high levels of satisfaction.

Synectics achieve these benefits by enabling people to:

- develop both innovative and interpersonal skills;
- improve communication and ensure a high level of shared understanding;
- create a working climate which permits individuals to use their abilities more completely;

Synectics has been used to good effect frequently in the area of Research & Development, on such disparate items as the 'Hovis' biscuit and circular saw blades that do not cut flesh. It has also produced novel solutions to such vexing problems as persuading bears not to 'vandalize' electricity sub-stations and how an oil company can extract core samples from thousands of feet down in the earth without them losing any of their chemical qualities through changes in pressure and water dilution.

The effects of Synectics can also be found elsewhere. A major brewing company has attributed to Synectics improvements made by making their meetings shorter, more effective and more focused, whilst at the same time producing more creative options. And it has enabled members of an international pharmaceutical company to change their organizational climate not only towards openness to and acceptance of new ideas, but also to fostering teamwork by encouraging mutual appreciation and commitment.

- reduce friction between themselves and other individuals and groups;
- increase learning abilities.

One way of viewing the Synectics body of knowledge is as though it were an iceberg that consists of techniques, skills and strategies held together by a philosophy that recognizes the uniqueness and personal autonomy of individuals. Like any iceberg, the deeper you go the bigger it seems to become.

The Synectics process was originally designed to encourage the sort of innovation and creativity that we might find in a Research & Development department of an organization. But it is equally applicable to any real world problem that we are likely to encounter, due to an underlying philosophy which values our individual differences.

7.1   Outline of the Synectics process

By describing the Synectics problem solving process in the way that it is usually presented on training courses my intention is to provide a sufficient view of what Synectics can offer to enable us to start using some of its methods and principles. It is from the experience of using this simplified version of the process that the understanding and skills will develop. Synectics is more flexible and comprises more ideas, techniques and variations than can be shown here. This account is only a part of the story.

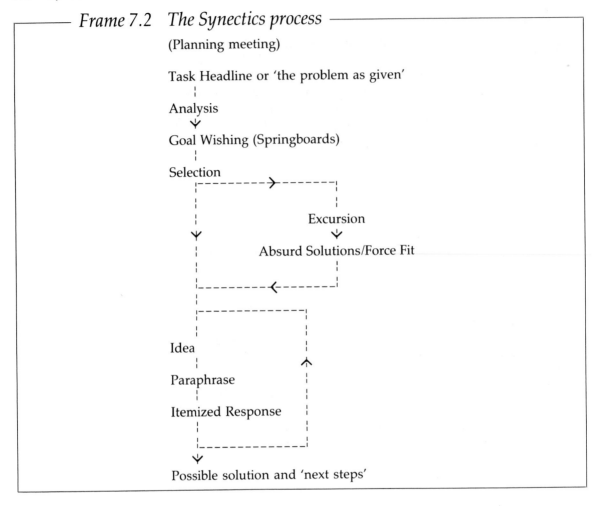

Frame 7.2   The Synectics process

(Planning meeting)

Task Headline or 'the problem as given'

Analysis

Goal Wishing (Springboards)

Selection

Excursion

Absurd Solutions/Force Fit

Idea

Paraphrase

Itemized Response

Possible solution and 'next steps'

Synectics uses the Brainstorming principles outlined in the previous chapter, but in a highly modified and more sophisticated way. The problem solving process contains a number of steps such as those shown in the Frame 7.2, but it should be stressed that these are only provided for guidance. Like other problem solving processes described in this book, we do not need to start from stage 1, nor complete all the stages in sequence, and of course iteration is permitted at any stage.

If we go through the whole process as illustrated then we would encounter three Brainstorming-like stages where speculation is welcomed and evaluation is suspended. First, in the 'Goal Wishing' stage, where the problem is opened up to try to ensure we are solving the right problem. Secondly, in gathering ideas from which we hope to obtain possible solutions and where the diagram branches into what has been called an Excursion. And finally during the evaluation/idea (solution) development stage, Itemized Response, to find ways of overcoming concerns we may have with our ideas before they can become possible solutions.

A crucial aspect of the Synectics process is that when used in a group problem solving setting, it is essential that the problem-owners (or clients) are members of the group, for it is they who will be using their selection of the ideas generated at these stages to give the group a direction in which to explore next.

7.2   When to use Synectics and its limitations

Synectics is an ideal strategy to adopt if innovation is sought, or a particularly novel solution is desired, but this should not be seen as a limiting factor. It may well be that on occasion a totally new product or way of doing something *is* required, but the reference to novelty includes a 'newness' to the problem-owner as well.

Often our real problem with resolving a particular situation is that we have been involved with the matter for so long and in such depth that we are bogged down in a rut. The more we battle to get out, the more we get stuck in the same mess, and the more the conceptual blocks of Chapter 4 will tend to make us blind to ways of escape. We desperately need a new perspective on the problem; to stand back and reflect and get right away from our problem and the previous failures to resolve the problem. The Synectics process, and in particular the Excursions, are extremely powerful tools for digging yourself out of such situations.

The only real limitation on the application of Synectics is due to practical considerations concerning group size. If the problem situation has more than a handful of problem-owners, we will be unable to resolve it with them as one group (however desirable this is). The solution is to restructure the problem situation into several parts and have several groups of people working on them, or to organize several 'parallel' groups working on the same problem. The dangers inherent in restructuring a problem have already been mentioned in Chapter 1 and there are difficulties in the latter alternative of combining the results of 'parallel' Synectics sessions (see Chapter 13).

7.3   Size and composition of a Synectics group

Although Synectics can be used as an individual problem solving technique (see Chapter 4 — analogies), it benefits from group participation. The typical Synectics group is somewhat smaller than that recommended for Brainstorming. A group of six to eight people (excluding the leader) seems to be ideal.

As with all CPS, we need a room with comfortable chairs, low tables, several flipcharts, plus sufficient wall space so that flipchart sheets can be pinned up around the room for all to see. Although the leader would normally stand in front of the seated group in order to write on the flip-charts and to convey their leadership role, it is an informal setting and people should feel free to move around. In fact it will help the leader, and add to the atmosphere of friendly cooperation, if a member of the group assists with placing flipchart sheets on the wall.

William J. J. Gordon laid down quite specific criteria for group membership and composition, suggesting that group members should be frequent users of analogies and metaphors (see Chapter 4); have an attitude of assistance, well-coordinated bodily movements and the capacity to generalize. They should possess personality traits such as emotional maturity, 'constructive childishness' and 'risk-taking' and be non-status orientated. They need to show commitment to the group and its purpose and be between 25 and 40 years of age. Though possession of many of these 'attributes' may well help proceedings, Gordon's views on group composition are now out of date in the sense that, by using the appropriate process 'tools', Synectics believe that all these qualities (except perhaps age) can be 'uncovered' in everybody.

Current practice on group selection is similar to that of a Brainstorming group. Group members should have as wide a spread of knowledge and experience as possible.

The group should not have too many 'experts'. The problem-owner will invariably be the problem content expert. If there are other content experts from the same organization, we may have a shared problem and this type of situation needs to be tackled in a slightly different way, as we shall see later. It can be useful to have a second 'technical expert' with similar technical expertise to the problem-owner, but who works in a totally different field. In one group session I was involved in, the problem-owner worked for a confectionery manufacturer and was concerned about the difficulty in getting consistent thickness of chocolate coatings on his company's products. Another group member worked for a regional Gas Board. His expertise in the behaviour of flowing 'liquids', coupled with our non-expert, new but wildly naive ideas concerning chocolate coatings, resulted in some feasible ideas which the problem-owner was pleased to try out.

As with Brainstorming, it is easier on the leader if the group members have equal status or rank, but this is often not desirable for the problem's resolution, and anyway the process and the role of process leader is designed to cope with differences in status. It is also very useful to have a group that contains a couple of people who are 'good' at coming up with wild ideas, and are willing to do so, these people will encourage other members to do the same by setting the cultural norms of the group by example. Synectics Inc. used to have one of their consultants acting as a resource within the group for this very purpose. For the same reason, having some group members already trained in the Synectics process, who know what to do and what to expect, is also advantageous.

7.4   The tasks of group members

Everybody in a Synectics group plays an important part in problem resolution, but the two key roles are those of the client or problem-owner, and the group leader, who is actually more of a problem solving facilitator.

7.4.1   Problem-owner (client)

Ideally the problem-owner should be familiar with the Synectics process, or at least be warned of what to expect, so that he is not alarmed when proceedings appear to run off in a seemingly irrelevant direction. It is only necessary to outline the likely stages of the process, indicating where group members should refrain from criticism, where some unusual measures might be needed to get away from the problem in order to generate some ideas to help us resolve it, and when the client is required to evaluate ideas and offer guidance or direction for future efforts. However, problem-owners should not see this as their sole function; they should also participate as ordinary group members. A trained problem-owner is not a necessity, but if he should know a little about Synectics, it is vital that the leader keeps him 'informed' about what we are doing and why we are doing it as well as telling the group how they should proceed.

7.4.2   Group leader

Chapter 4 showed why using a traditional leader, or chairperson, is not the most appropriate way of running a problem solving session. We will now deal with the practical details of leading a Synectics group.

The role described here is that of a **process leader**, who guides *only* the problem solving process. The leader *should not* get involved with problem 'content' in any way. Leaders should lead the process, not contribute ideas, suggestions or possible solutions, let alone decide the best way of resolving the problem. However, a leader needs to assess how well the group is meeting the problem-owner's wishes, and there is a temptation to do this by 'monitoring' the content (what is being said about the problem). Although not easy to resist, a leader should not become involved in the content even to this extent. A group leader should determine the success of the process by observing, and asking for, the client's reactions to what is going on. If the suppressed desire to be involved in the content affects the leadership of the process, the leader should, with the agreement of the client and group, stand down temporarily and become a group resource, letting another take over the process leadership.

Because the guidance of the problem solving process has been delegated to the leader, the leader needs to maintain the trust of the problem-owner and must be seen as working for the problem-owner, not as a competitor for authority over problem content. The leader also needs to take care of the psychological needs of other group members. We ask the group to say and do some strange things, and therefore must provide the sort of climate (see Chapter 4) which encourages and supports creativity, and ensures that every member is psychologically comfortable with the process.

It is the leader's responsibility to protect members' self-images, so that everyone can win from the situation. Cooperation, mutual trust, emotional support and good communications are the key factors a leader must generate. Prince (1970, pp. 7–8) points out that 'relieved of the burden of self-protection, a member can wholeheartedly devote himself to speculating, imagining, and supporting and considering far-fetched notions – in short, producing the rich variations out of which fresh alternatives and exciting decisions are made'.

Many ideas sessions (*not* truely Brainstorming), appear to fail because they have been initiated and led by an authority figure who fails to appreciate the importance of such factors and why they may not be the most suitable person to lead the session. If a Synectics group leader is seen as serving the needs of the group, she will gain their commitment, enthusiasm and best ideas. If she is seen as serving her own needs, then group members will look after their own needs also and tend not to offer these things.

The group leader is also responsible for: ensuring that group members obey the rules (for example suspending judgement); encouraging speculation; logging all of the ideas; checking with the problem-owner that the group is on the right track; and managing the time. *A Synectics group leader, therefore, needs to be trained.*

7.4.3   Group resources

The rest of the group act as resources offering ideas when requested by the leader. It is likely that they will think of ideas faster than they can voice them or than the leader can record them on the flipcharts. So participants should be encouraged to jot ideas down on notepads until required. When speculation is desired, everyone should be warned to watch out for the operation of their self-censor (see Chapter 4), the culturally ingrained mental block that only permits us to voice well thought out ideas. All ideas are wanted including beginning-ideas, half-formed ideas and wild ideas.

The second most important task a group member performs, after having ideas, is to support everyone else. This can be done by genuinely complimenting them for ideas that are especially commendable for their appropriateness, novelty, practicality, insightfulness, etc., and crediting others when we build on one of their ideas.

Synectics offers useful guidelines to group participants on 'Open Minded Communication', which help towards encouraging cooperation and teamwork. These include:

- Making sure that you understand what has been said (by paraphrasing it back to its author) before you evaluate it.
- Trying to find some value in all ideas.
- Giving your ideas and opinions only when requested.
- Hearing only a positive intent in what other people say.
- Speaking up for yourself and letting other people do the same.

7.5   The planning meeting

Because problem-owners play such an important role in the Synectics process it is essential they are fully committed to the resolution of the problem. 'Planning' meetings are thus essential before a problem solving session takes place. The group leader should check out both the suitability of the problem and the motivation of the problem owner.

Synectics Chairman Vincent Nolan (1989) suggests we should get answers to the following questions (no matter how obvious), before embarking on any problem solving. These should establish whether we have the necessary preconditions for problem solving to take place.

We need to know how many problem-owners we (should) have.

- Who owns the problem? Who is sufficiently dissatisfied with the present situation to consider it a problem that needs to be solved? Who is motivated to solve it?
- Is that person willing to do something new about it or is he just seeking sympathy?
- Is that person expecting someone else to take any consequent action? If so, does the other person see it as a problem that needs solving?

We need to know whether she (and we) can do anything about the problem situation.

- What is the problem-owner's power to act? What can she do to implement a possible solution? What sort of actions is she prepared to take? Does the problem-owner command resources? If so, what are they? Under what constraints does the problem-owner operate?

We do not want to waste our time re-inventing known solutions, or playing 'mind games'.

- Does the problem-owner already have a solution? If so, are they trying to 'check it out' (a candidate for Potential Problem Analysis perhaps, see Chapter 10) or are they satisfied with it and indulging in a misguided commitment gaining exercise?
- Does the problem owner want to find a solution or just prove that one does not exist?

A problem-owner must have the authority and resources to implement a solution when one is found. The exact nature of this 'power to act' can be determined by careful questioning during the planning meeting. More difficult to determine but equally important, is willingness to solve the problem. The group leader should look out for usage, by the problem-owner, of words like 'could', 'should' and 'ought', where perhaps they might have used 'can', 'will' and 'are'.

It is possible that problem-owners perceive limitations to what constitutes a feasible way of resolving the problem. Discovering what these are now need not necessarily restrict our thinking, and should allow us to explore beyond these limitations later without losing the confidence of the problem-owner or causing them any frustration. Knowing we *are* aware of these constraints will reassure the problem-owner about our competence when we do subsequently stray over the edge of the perceived problem domain, particularly if we announce this as our intention – 'just to see what might be possible' or 'to check that we haven't missed any possibilities'.

We should also encourage the problem-owner to explore beyond the problem as originally stated, to see if there may not be more appropriate ways of looking at the problem. This is especially true if the original problem statement is of a general nature, for example, 'How to prepare my company for 1993 and the Single European Market', compared with more specific statements such as, 'How to maintain the current growth in our UK market share beyond 1993'. This process is called Backward/Forward Planning and should give the group leader a better insight into where the problem-owner wants to be at the end of the problem solving session.

7.6   Backward/Forward Planning

Suppose the problem-owner offers the following problem statement:

How to make my colleagues appreciate the need for change?

This problem statement illustrates another potential hazard, which Backward/Forward Planning can help alleviate, which is the fairly typical tendency with people problems, for a problem-owner to express his/her problem in terms of 'motivating others to think or do something'. That is, the problem statement refers to persuading/making someone else change his or her attitudes or actions in some way. This is nearly always a difficult thing to accomplish. The human species seems to be extremely good at perceiving when another human is trying to manipulate them in some way, and invariably reacts to this with an equally effective (and usually total) resistance to this effort, irrespective of whether the change is seen as good or bad.

The problem-owner should be encouraged to rephrase the problem statement in terms of 'How can I change my own attitudes or actions in such a way that this might encourage others to . . .' on the basis that it is much easier (and is likely to be more effective in the long run) to change ourselves rather than to attempt to change other people. Backward/ Forward Planning may help us lead the problem-owner towards this view of the problem situation.

In our attempt to 'expand' the problem statement to include some different perspectives on the situation we first go 'backwards' looking for 'higher' level problems. This is accomplished by asking the problem-owner questions such as:

> If this problem could be resolved instantly by just making a wish, what (higher level) problem would this solve, what would it allow you to do?
> Achieve a total commitment to a common purpose.

The leader would encourage the problem-owner to rephrase responses in a 'I wish/How to' form such as

- I wish I could gain the total commitment of my staff to the organization's mission.

By not having this total commitment, what is it that you are being prevented from doing?

- How to prepare for the challeges of the future.

And not being as 'prepared' as you might be prevents you from . . . ?

- How to ensure that we do not miss any opportunities.

Or perhaps

- How to demonstrate that there are opportunities being missed due to our lack of cohesion.

Then we go forwards looking for additional benefits and 'sub-problems'. For this we ask:

> If the original problem was now solved, and your colleagues appreciated the need for change, what would this mean to you, what additional benefits would come from this?

Some other benefits might be:

- How to use everyone's time more effectively.
- How to reach agreement on and implement the necessary changes.
- How to implement changes more quickly.
- How to redirect our attention to examining the advantages of our new freedom.

Another approach is to ask (very gently) 'What is stopping you resolving this problem?'

- I wish I could convince my colleagues that I have their best interests at heart.
- How to obtain the resources to offer an early retirement package (that no-one could refuse) to those who will never change, who are just hanging on for retirement, or are too high in the hierarchy to ignore, sack, etc.

We now have ten additional possible problem statements. The problem-owner can now decide whether to start with the original one or pursue one of these alternatives. This choice is not critical as yet, since we will shortly generate more ways of looking at the problem before the problem-owner finally chooses which one to use. Backward/ Forward Planning helps counteract the conceptual block of 'tunnel vision' (see Chapter 4) should the problem-owner appear to suffer from this.

Another point for discussion with the problem-owner during the planning meeting is the level of 'quality' desired from the solutions we hope to help them obtain. This is a measure of the compromise that has to be made between the feasibility of a possible solution and its desired novelty or 'newness'. We would be unusually lucky if we achieved a really innovative solution that is also eminently feasible. Synectics assess the 'quality' of a possible solution on three bases, Newness, Appeal and Feasibility. This indication of the problem-owner's expectations can be used at the end of proceedings to gauge the success of group efforts.

The leader of a Synectics-style problem solving session with a group familiar with one another should ascertain in advance whether there are likely to be any professional or personal conflicts between members of the group. Being forewarned of this possibility means steps can be taken at least to ameliorate any manifestations of conflict.

Finally, the planning meeting is a good opportunity for the group leader to give the problem-owner an outline or review of the Synectics process so that they know what is expected of them. We would explain that we will call upon them periodically to check that things are progressing to their liking, and to ask for 'direction' on where the group should most usefully turn its attention next. We should stress that the problem-owner should feel free to (and that it is desirable that they do) contribute their own ideas as if they were an 'ordinary' group member. This is one way in which the problem-owner can provide direction at times other than when specifically asked to do so. We should also explain that at certain stages we will want them and the group to suspend any form of judgement and evaluation, and assure them that there is a reason for some of the 'strange' things that we might ask the group to do. At the same time as this we should be trying to build a sufficiently good rapport with the problem owner so that they trust us to conduct the session in their best interests.

7.7 The Synectics process

To look at the Synectics process in more detail we will now take the 'Slow Coach Ltd' case study (Frame 7.3) through the steps shown in Frame 7.2, while the examples that follow concern people problems. Synectics also excels at research and development problems. The group gathered together for this session might consist of the director (client/problem-owner), two members of the senior management, say the directors of human resources and marketing, two grass roots staff members, a representative from local industry and a couple of clients (students). After greetings and administrative details, the first task for a group leader is to ask the client/problem-owner for a Task Headline (Frame 7.4). Thus, a single sentence describing the problem – sometimes referred to as 'the problem as given', an expression that reinforces that we will not take for granted that this is either (i) the best description of the problem, or (ii) the problem definition we intend to start from. This is written on a flipchart.

The leader announces to the group that the problem-owner will now be asked for some background information about the problem. The group is asked to listen to what is about to be said, not so as to understand the problem (this is not important or even desirable at this stage), but to let what is being said by the problem-owner trigger off thoughts, ideas and reactions in their minds, especially those that suggest alternative and perhaps unusual ways of viewing the problem. The leader says 'Just make a note of any thoughts or ideas that come into your mind. What we would like the most is "fresh" views and ideas, no matter how wild.' Synectics call this 'In–Out Listening'.

The leader guides the problem-owner's exposition of the problem by asking for a *brief* account of the events that led to the recognition of the problem situation described in the Task Headline, ensuring that all the information sought by the following questions is covered, prompting as necessary. If there is a danger of the problem-owner talking at too great a length, the leader should explain why the group does not need to know these details.

───── *Frame 7.3 Illustrative example: Slow Coach Ltd* ─────

Slow Coach Ltd (SC) is an organization working primarily in consultancy and training. Since its inception in 1962, SC has operated totally within the Public Sector education provision. It has been somewhat sheltered from the economic fluctuations and traumas going on in the 'real' world, with the consequence that organizational change is rare and difficult to achieve. SC, along with similar institutions, has just been 'given' corporate status – it can now do more or less anything it likes with the funds it receives from central government and the revenue it generates itself.

For months prior to incorporation and since, the new director has been trying to implement a number of changes in the organization that he believes will better equip it for the future. Sadly, he is frustrated by considerable resistance to many of his ideas. For instance, the organizational structure has been reorganized into easily identifiable cost centres, new senior management posts in functions previously unheard of such as finance, marketing and personnel have been created, and the director now has a company car, but at the 'shop floor' level little seems to have changed. The transition to a private company was guaranteed to have no initial effect on the job security or conditions and pay of the staff employed before incorporation.

His problem was initially summarized as:

SC needs to change dramatically to meet the demands of the future, why can't people see that!

───── *Frame 7.4 Task Headline for Slow Coach Ltd* ─────

Task Headline

'How to convince my colleagues of the need for change?'

Note the rewording of the problem statement from that given in the planning meeting and that despite this and all that was said at the time, it sounds as if there is still an implication in the problem-owner's Task Headline that *he* needs to do something. The leader should be wary of the re-emergence of this attitude as the session proceeds.

- Why/how is it a problem for you?
- What ideas have you tried . . . and thought of?
- What power do you have to implement a solution, if (when) we find one, . . . any restrictions/limitations on what you can do?

- I wonder if you have had any recent thoughts as to how the problem could be solved?
- If by making a wish you could cause your ideal solution to happen, what would this ideal solution be?
- How can we be of most help to you?

In this way the problem-owner reiterates for the group's benefit some of the things discussed during the planning meeting. Let us suppose that the way he relates his problem is as shown in Frame 7.5.

The leader writes up the problem-owner's ideal solution on the flip-chart, underneath the Task Headline. The leader should be careful not deliberately or accidentally to censor, edit or miss this or any other ideas offered. They should also take care with their nonverbal responses (e.g. body language). If an idea needs to be shortened, the contributor should do this; if the leader has to do it, the modification should always be agreed with the idea's contributor.

The problem-owner should not be allowed to describe every intricate detail of the problem situation – particularly in response to questions. If a clarifying question *is* asked by a group member, the leader should immediately try gently to prise out from that person the idea that is likely to be hiding behind the question (see Chapter 5). For example, someone may ask 'How many people work for you?', when what they are thinking is, 'I'd like to know how many people work for you because it would be good if we could pack them all into a pub and have a totally open interchange of ideas and opinions over a few drinks.' Because of this, and because questions can be used to disguise derogatory remarks, Synectics try to minimize questioning during the problem solving session. Questions often have an important place in problem solving, but not here and now (see Chapter 10 — machine problems).

Questions are often asked, not just to check out ideas before they are voiced, but because we feel we need to understand the problem before we can help solve it. A complete understanding of the problem is not likely to help produce novel and innovative solutions. Questions slow down proceedings and stop the flow of ideas. And if group members understand the problem situation in as much detail as the problem-owner they may find themselves too close to the problem and in the same mental rut as the problem-owner.

The next stage of the process has been given various names. 'Goal Orientation' is descriptive because what we are trying to do is view the problem situation in a number of ways, so that we look for a solution in the most appropriate direction. 'Goal Wishing' stresses that speculation/wishing is permitted and desired. 'Springboards' reinforces the idea that we are looking for launching places from which to take off into the problem. Whatever we call it, we are seeking different angles on, or

--- Frame 7.5   *The problem-owner of Slow Coach Ltd* --- *relates his problem*

'When I applied for this post the interviewing panel were obviously looking for someone to lead the organization through "privatization" and into the future. I presumably got this job two years ago on the basis that my ideas concerning the way forward were deemed to be the most appropriate (b).

'The first thing I did when I got here was to go round and see everyone, and asked them how they saw things (c). I asked them for their ideas! When I didn't get any I started offering mine. Since then its been an uphill struggle (d) to implement the changes that I think are necessary. I meet resistance at every turn. I have always believed that I have an open mind, that I can be swayed by a rational argument, but when I did change my mind I was accused of being indecisive (e), two-faced, etc. Now I am just doing what I think is best.

'This is a real problem for me and the organization, because we are wasting a lot of time bickering, when we should be out there looking for the opportunities that I know exist (f), and bringing in more business (g) to put us on a stable footing. People can't seem to understand that corporate status gives us the freedom to do all the things that we have always wanted to do! (h)

'I have tried talking to everybody informally (a), I have set up mandatory "briefing meetings" to keep people informed and to collect their feedback (i) and initiated a "suggestions box" scheme, I have given Heads of Division more autonomy, but none of these things are working as well as I hoped.

'In theory I can as managing director of the new organization do virtually anything (j), subject only to Board approval, and balancing the books next April. I can even fire people (k), something that never used to be possible except in very rare circumstances!

'Things are changing but very, very slowly (l); the only recent thought I have had is to keep on slogging away (m) trying to get my ideas implemented. The government is partially to blame for all this because they haven't (deliberately I think) made things clear enough, and people are always afraid of the unknown (n). I did consider rewarding those who were prepared to address the changes needed (o) by salary differentials, but it seems that I do not have as much freedom in this area as I hoped, the union's attitudes and national agreements from before still seem to be the order of the day.

'I wish I could change the cultural norms of the organization with a click of my fingers!'

redefinitions of, the problem. It is useful to take the problem-owner through the Backward/Forward Planning as a means of starting this stage, writing up their answers to our questions as additional problem definitions.

The group members now report their different ways of looking at the problem. The group leader should stress that they should suspend judgement – not criticize or evaluate any of the suggestions made no matter how strange or irrelevant they seem. In particular they should not evaluate their own thoughts, but just say anything that comes into their minds. Way out ideas often trigger off other ideas in group members. There will be time to evaluate these ideas later. The problem-owner should be reminded that they can offer Springboards to indicate the directions in which they would like the group to go. Finally, the group should be encouraged to offer ideas as short phrases, or 'Headlines', expressed as the 'How to'/'I wish' statements we have seen earlier, followed up with a brief description of where the idea came from. This background information helps other group members see how the connections were made.

Headlining ideas and prefacing them with 'How to' or 'I wish' has several advantages. Summarizing in this clear and succinct way conveys the essence of your idea so that others can start thinking about it and making associations. This also gives the group leader a chance to capture it on a flipchart while you continue with an explanation of what led you to it. The use of the 'How to' preface further conveys positive direction. Rather than 'We have to cut costs', which sounds negative and constraining and could put a damper on ideas that might involve expenditure, expressing it as 'How to find ways of cutting costs' is more positive and less restrictive, implying the need actively to go and look for ways of cutting costs without precluding other ideas. The 'I wish' preface supports and encourages more speculative problem definitions. Following the Headline with the background to the idea is also very important, helping with communications by giving insight into your mind, and often containing 'colourful' material which sparks off other people's ideas.

Initially, Springboards will come from the notes jotted down as the problem-owner described the problem, but once captured and cleared from participant's minds, they will have new thoughts, triggered off by others' comments. Some will be modifications or 'builds' on someone else's ideas. All should be written on the flipcharts, and the leader should ensure the problem-owner also contributes some ideas!. I have referred to Springboards as problem redefinitions. They are far more than this and fulfil many uses. Apart from paraphrasing the problem situation and providing the means for expressing individual interpretations of it, they can also be an 'acceptable' means of challenging restrictions (real or perceived) that seem to have been placed on possible solutions. They can even question the validity of a particular problem definition by allowing an 'airing' of conflicting viewpoints, especially when problem ownership is shared. By using Springboards to 'constructively misunderstand' aspects of the problem situation, to make wishes, to offer intuitive feelings or non-expert opinions, or simply to voice a free association of ideas, we can build up a wealth of material. Finally, if we have already started to 'make connections', we can volunteer a 'beginning-idea' with a Springboard, without the risk that it will be heard as any more than that.

Almost inevitably, there will be *ad hoc* comments between group members: some are disguised criticisms, others are to check if no evaluation was really meant. The leader should try to capture these comments as yet more problem redefinitions. For example:

Susan says: 'I wish I could brainwash my staff.'
John replies: 'Why don't you go the whole hog and give them lobotomies?'
The leader intervenes with something like:
                'John, some of us may have heard that idea as a criticism.'
whilst writing up:
                'I wish we could give all my staff a lobotomy.'

Group members will occasionally forget to give the background to their idea, and the leader should gently remind them.

This is the first time that our 'group of resources' will have made a contribution, and unless they are seasoned Synectics practitioners they will still be unsure or anxious about what they are supposed to be saying and doing. The leader should positively acknowledge first contributions of headlines, background, speculative ideas, or a build on someone else's idea, etc.

In Frame 7.6 I have listed example Springboards for the Slow Coach Ltd case, along with illustrations of what is meant by 'background' to the first few ideas. I have cross-referenced these (a, b, c . . .) with the problem-owner's narrative in Frame 7.5 to give an idea of where my Springboards have come from. Depending on the problem and the mood and experience of the group, up to 50 Springboards are perfectly possible in about half an hour.

7.7.1 Selection

We now have a number of ways at looking at the problem written up around the session room. The problem-owner needs a chance to reflect on these and select two or three that best describe the problem situation. The rest of the group can usefully take a short break at this time. The leader's advice to the problem-owner is to choose problem

Springboards for Slow Coach Ltd ——————— *Frame 7.6* —

- I wish we could have a totally open interchange of ideas and opinions (a).
- How to illustrate that 'traditional' roles/values/attitudes are no longer appropriate?
- How to convince people that my ideas are the best (b)?
    Well if I could, there wouldn't be a problem would there – unless my ideas were wrong!
- How to solicit ideas more effectively (c)?
    I was thinking of someone wandering around the streets of a town asking complete strangers questions, like religious freaks and market researchers do. Some people don't like being accosted in this way, they cross the street if they see someone like this coming, they go all shy and rush off making excuses, give misleading answers – there must be some way of doing it without people suspecting your motives.
- How to turn resistance into support (d)?
    I had this image of schools maths. problems with 'bodies' being pushed or pulled up inclined planes; this led me to thinking of Newton's Laws and the one that says something like 'For every force there is an equal and opposite reaction'.
- I wish my ideas were 'Teflon' coated.
    It's a 'build' on the last idea No. 4, thinking of things without friction, I remembered hearing somewhere that the coatings on non-stick frying-pans were used to reduce friction somehow. Can't we do something to these ideas?
- I wish I could attribute my ideas to someone else.
- How to gain commitment.
- How can I engender 'team spirit' and 'company loyalty'?
- How to be open-minded and decisive (e)?
- How to demonstrate that there are opportunities to be had (f)?
- I wish I could portray the benefits of change! (h)
- I wish I could encourage a positive attitude to change!
- I wish I could brainwash my staff.
- How to minimize the disadvantages of change?
- How to increase revenue? (g)
- How to cut costs?
- How to release more time for Research and Consultancy?
- I wish I could institute a perfect communications system! (i)
- I wish I were Superman, I could make all the changes I feel are necessary instantly, and no-one would question their merit! (j)
- I wish I could fire people with enthusiasm (for change). (k)
- I wish I could sack everybody, and then select a new lot of staff.
- How to bring about rapid and immediate change (l)?
- How to overcome complacency?

- I wish I could shake some of my colleagues into 'life'! (m)
- How to counteract the fear of change? (n)
- How can I discover, encourage and reward the creativity and innovation already taking place within the organization? (o)

definitions that appeal to him and which he would like to develop into possible solutions, regardless of their feasibility. The problem-owner should actually be warned against selecting only those that appear obviously practical, and be advised to choose those that are intriguing, novel and interesting. A practical Springboard will almost certainly lead to a solution, but one which may possibly be ordinary, uninspired or boring. A less practical but more intriguing one, though requiring more effort to develop, may well lead to a really novel solution. If a Springboard appeals to us in this way, we will usually be prepared to put in the effort to see it through to a possible solution. It is permissible for the problem-owner to combine several Springboards into one, and this 'new' one should be written up with the rest.

Whatever is done next with the selected Springboards, the leader should first ask the problem-owner to say what led him to choose them. For instance, 'What good would come out of this if we could solve the problem in these ways?'. The group could also be asked to think of ideas that might lead to possible solutions as they are listening to this. After the problem-owner has made his selection of Springboards, we have one of two possible ways forward. If the Springboard selected implies a specific way of tackling part of the problem, the problem-owner is asked to say how he will pursue this and what additional help he may need to make it happen. Supposing the Director of Slow Coach Ltd had chosen to work with:

> I wish we could have a totally open interchange of ideas and opinions.

or perhaps

> I wish I could attribute my ideas to someone else.

Both of these contain a reference to a specific course of action. The first suggests holding an open forum for ideas, complaints, whatever. Although the staff of SC Ltd number some 300 people, there *are* facilities where they can all meet together at the same time. This already happens once a year, though it is usually a one-sided communication. Our problem-owner might say that he needs additional help over the logistics of running such a 'conference'. The question for the problem-owner here then is 'How to organize a large discussion so as to ensure that everybody has a chance, and feels able, to say what they like?' Although the second is perhaps a bit 'tongue-in-cheek', if the situation is so bad that knowing something is the Director's idea is sufficient to put the kiss of death on it, he may wish to pursue it. In this case the help the problem-owner might need is in finding the most convincing way of circulating 'evidence' suggesting alternative authorship of these ideas.

The leader would asks the group for ideas on how these minor concerns could be dealt with. As each of these ideas is presented, it is evaluated by the problem-owner, but only after he has paraphrased them, i.e. the leader would ask him to explain what he understands the idea to be, to confirm that everyone is talking about the same thing, and then will check back this interpretation with the idea's contributor. It can feel uncomfortable at first apparently echoing what someone has just said, but it pays off in the end (see Chapter 4). After the idea's contributor realizes you are not hard of hearing or lacking intellect, they appreciate the trouble taken to understand what they are saying. We will return to this process and the Springboards selected above later (p. 134).

If no specific action is indicated by the Springboard, the next step is to generate ideas as to how the circumstances it describes might be brought about; possibly by using an Excursion. Suppose the Director of SC Ltd had chosen the following Springboard:

How to turn resistance into support.

and made the following comment about it:

I am really taken by this idea of converting resistance into support. I don't know how you do it, but if we could it would be marvellous. There is so much energy being directed against any changes, that if we could turn this about there'd be no stopping us!

No specific solution is indicated here, so the leader needs to generate ways in which this 'objective' might be achieved. This could be done in the way Springboards were generated, asking the group to suggest different means for achieving this without any judgement being imposed on them. In other words, Brainstorm a number of ways of 'converting resistance into support'. This is the second time we have come across a stage governed by Brainstorming's suspended judgement 'rule'. Note that the group would perhaps be asked only for beginning-ideas that do not need to be 'fully formed' solutions at this time. Again encouragement would be given to ideas that build upon others and everything could be written up on flipcharts.

If this does not produce the 'quality' of ideas hoped for (the desired combination of newness, appeal and feasibility), or if we feel before we start this stage that 'newness' is going to be a key factor in the success of a possible solution, we could use one of the many types of Synectics Excursion, as well as or instead of this Brainstorming session, to generate ideas. My reaction to this Springboard is that if I sat down and tried to Brainstorm this one, I would get a few very ordinary ideas. I therefore intend to take an Excursion in the hope of doing better.

7.7.2   Excursion

Various types of Excursion are used in the Synectics process in order to generate ideas. The one we will use here is an **Imaging** or **Fantasy Excursion**, based on the Fantasy Analogy we came across in Chapter 4. The choice of Excursion depends on the degree of novelty required in the solution, the element of 'risk' the leader is prepared to take and the material we are working on. Another type, the *Example Excursion*, is frequently used (and we will do so later), but unlike the Imaging Excursion it is not universally applicable. The Imaging Excursion is possibly the most unorthodox form of Excursion and can be a potential disaster with a conservative-minded group, though it often works dramatically well when you least expect it. Because of its 'extraordinary' nature the Imaging Excursion is the form most likely to produce innovative ideas.

This stage of the Synectics process, and under these circumstances, is by no means the only place where Excursions can be used effectively. They can be a beneficial exercise whether they produce novel ideas or not. John Alexander of Synectics believes that the positive effects an Excursion has on a group's cohesiveness, open-mindedness and readiness to speculate, can often be as important as its value as an idea-generating mechanism and tries to introduce them as early on in the process as he can.

The problem-owner and the group need fair warning of what we are about to do before branching into an Excursion. I would introduce an Imaging Excursion in this way:

> I think what we need to do now is to try to find some really novel ideas or solutions for this problem, so I suggest we cover up all the material we already have on the flipcharts and try to forget our problem for the moment, get some distance in front of it, in fact get right away from it into something totally different. You all know of people like Archimedes, Einstein, Pasteur, etc. to whom a marvellous idea has suddenly occurred apparently from nowhere, this is what we hope might happen here. We are going to take a flight of fantasy into a 'crazy' story, so as to get as far away from the original problem as possible. Then, when we have done that and collected a mass of colourful and seemingly irrelevant material en route, we will slowly come back to our problem and use this fantastic material to help us find a practical solution.

It is important to involve the problem-owner with this as well.

First a brief warm-up session is needed. A simple 'round robin' word

Slow Coach Ltd: Imaging Excursion ————————— *Frame 7.7* ——

Resistance	Dream
Freedom fighter	Illusion
War	Magic
Peace	Carpet
Pipe	Slippers

Imagine a peaceful suburban Sunday afternoon. Everybody is flat out in armchairs suffering from post-dinner sleepiness. All of a sudden the front door of 42 Acacia Avenue bangs open and a dog comes hurtling out carrying a slipper in its mouth, and runs off down the street with a hobbling middle aged man in a dressing gown in hot pursuit. On reaching the pub on the corner the irrate dog owner gives up the chase and . . .

Meanwhile the dog has scampered off to a nearby recreational ground because it is in desperate need of the sandpit. On reaching it, the dog sees that there are lots of circles in the sand, something is burrowing around it just under the surface. Suddenly, a small blue and yellow snake emerges from one of the circular furrows and riggles sideways to the edge of the sandpit. Then he lifts up his head and hisses at nothing in a frustrated fashion 'Won't somebody get me out of here? I want to go home! Can't anyone hear me?' Then the snake seems to detect a noise, and looks up . . .

The noise the snake thought it had heard is a passing spaceship from Sirius. It is on a reconnaissance mission looking for civilization in other stellar systems. The aliens see the snake and beam it aboard their craft. After five hours of interrogation the aliens conclude that this Earthly life-form, although quite athletic, was not very intelligent, so they eat it.

Back at 42 Acacia Avenue a green VolksWagon is warming itself in the sun. The VW, who is called Spicey, senses the feelings of horror as the snake becomes the first Terran creature to examine, at close proximity, the insides of an alien being. Outraged by this wanton destruction, Spicey quickly opens his engine cover. A thin brilliantly green beam of engine oil sped skywards . . .

The alien spaceship disintegrates instantly into an oil slick that gracefully drifts down through the lower reaches of the atmosphere like black snow, and totally covers a small fishing village in Alaska.

association is usually sufficient (see Frame 7.7). A secondary purpose of this is to help start getting 'away' from the problem. It is usual to start with a word taken from the Springboard the group is working on, such as 'resistance .

We only need carry on the word association for a couple of 'rounds', until things start to get a little 'silly' and laughter breaks out.

7.7.3   Mental imagery

The group is asked to describe a mental picture/story inspired by the last item in the word association, for example, 'slippers'. One person will lead off, and then we want every other group member to add to this story, one at a time. They should be invited to jump in whenever they like and told that the more colourful, outlandish, weird or exotic the story the better. They are given a couple of minutes to think about this image and then someone is asked to make a start. It is usually best to keep the story in the same location if possible as this makes for richer mental imagery. Everybody should try to add about a minute to the story, and then someone else takes over. Change-over points can be left to the storyteller, or be deliberately chosen by the leader at the most 'inconvenient' times.

Our mental imagery for Slow Coach Ltd might have started off as I have shown in Frame 7.8. We should hope to derive some novel solutions from this later.

If the story line stagnates in descriptions of the minute details of one particular image, the leader could ask for description of what is going on in an adjacent location or deliberately ask someone to make something surprising happen. Conversely if images are insufficiently developed because storytellers move on too quickly to other images the leader can 'pin' people to one scenario by asking for more detail.

As mentioned in Chapter 4, as people talk listeners naturally form mental images of what they think they are saying, and this happens during a mental imagery exercise. As the first person sets the scene for our story, we imagine our version of it and cannot help but go ahead of the storyline as we can think quicker than they can describe their mental image. When the storyteller changes, our image is often shattered because it is likely that the new storyteller's image is different from ours and so the story goes off in the wrong direction for us. This can be unnerving, as once a mental image has been shattered like this, we are left with 'nothing' until we build another one.

We may be anxious about doing this mental imaging in public and about our ability to contribute to the story. Psychologists tell us that this 'violent' changing of direction, and our having to build another mental image after the 'destruction' of the first, is precisely what makes the story rich in speculation and evocative images. This is not very reassuring if your mind has gone apparently blank, but don't panic. After the initial shock you will find enough of the old image left (because it was so vivid) to drag the story back your way if you want to and in a few seconds you will start to build a new and possibly better image, perhaps incorporating the best parts of your last one.

Slow Coach Ltd: some 'absurd solutions' ——————— Frame 7.8 —

- I wish we could feed those people who are likely to resist the changes a big roast dinner . . .

  the idea is that with luck they might doze off and sleep right through the actual implementation of the changes.
- I wish we could confiscate the staff's slippers . . .

  in this way we can impair their ability to chase after and stop the changes.
- I wish I could pickle the resistance in alcohol . . .

  I could then put it into an airtight bottle and store it away in a cupboard. I could leave it there out of the way for some time. Then later I can take it out and eat it, it would taste better then perhaps.
- I wish I could get a 'choker' chain for humans . . .

  I was thinking about how you train recalcitrant dogs. It's a shame there isn't a similar thing for people.
- I wish we could cause a distraction that takes people's minds away from the changes we want to make
- I wish we could get all staff to dance around a Maypole . . .

  because as they run around in circles (trying to avoid the changes), the ribbons they are holding will pull them closer and closer together into a tightly bound group.
- I wish I could cover my ears so that the shouts of complaint can be mistaken for the cheers of enthusiasm.
- I wish the people that are resisting the changes could be beamed up and devoured by the occupants of a passing spacecraft.
- I wish I could wash the staff's opposition away . . .

  this came from the idea of washing the VW, I thought of washing clothes and how you can remove stains (old ideas) or change colours with bleach and add stiffness (support) with some starch.
- I wish I could cover the less 'desirable' changes in curry powder so as to disguise their 'distaste'.
- I wish I were a mind reader and could look into my staff's minds
- I wish I could fit a rocket drive to my ideas . . .

  so that no-one can catch up with them (and thus be able to stop them); no-one will even see my ideas if I move faster than the speed of light!
- I wish I could fire my staff through a Black Hole . . .

  because it is suggested by science fiction writers that if you survive this experience you could end up in a parallel universe where certain things are different, perhaps everything is back to front. A universe where change is seen as good, and opposition as support!

- I wish we could bring in the Ghostbusters to dispel the evil phantoms associated with change.
- I wish I could cover my ideas with oil . . .
  they would then be so slippery that other people couldn't grasp hold of them. They would just slip through their fingers.
- I wish I could freeze the resistance to my ideas . . .
  it would then be so brittle that I could crush it into dust and blow it away, or I could sculpture these pillars of ice into my vision of the future.

7.7.4   Absurd solutions

When every group member has had at least one chance to contribute to the story the leader stops the imaging and asks the group to spend a few minutes replaying the story in their minds, and trying to think up some really absurd or impractical solutions to the problem. The problem statement or Springboard the group was working on is then uncovered and these 'absurd solutions' are written up. Again it is perfectly legitimate to modify, combine or build on other people's ideas as they appear. Some absurd solutions of mine for the 'slow coach' problem are given in Frame 7.8.

As with the Springboards earlier, it is helpful if these absurd solutions are offered as a Headline followed by some background thinking (see Frame 7.8). Such background is sometimes unnecessary or obvious, but with really weird absurd solutions we should elicit the background as it may spark someone else's imagination.

Having moved so far from the problem with the Fantasy Excursion it usually becomes desirable to return to the real world and our problem in several stages, the first being the attempt to dream up totally absurd solutions. If a group member immediately comes up with a sensible and novel solution, we are obviously not going to reject it. Some of my absurd solutions are not strictly ways of 'turning resistance into support' but ways of 'diminishing' resistance, but if the problem-owner seems content there is no need to draw this to the group's attention.

The leader now needs to check again with the problem-owner to see if any of the absurd solutions intrigue, fascinate or appeal to them. There should be no problem with picking 'too practical' a solution as there should not be any! After the problem-owner makes his selection the leader asks the group to examine the (chosen) absurd solutions and to try to find a way to change them into something more practical and closer to reality, whilst retaining as much of the original idea as possible. It is not necessary to change them into something practical in one step; it is better to take some time modifying them, because there is a

Slow Coach Ltd: ideas for some possible solutions ——— *Frame 7.9* ———

'Roast Dinner'
I fill the staff up with 'good things': I find out what their 'pet' ideas are and encourage them to pursue these ideas preferably to the benefit of the organization. I offer them all the support and resources I can, in an attempt to channel their enthusiasm in a positive direction, rather than have it being directed against me and the changes I feel I need to make.

'May Pole'
I find a way to 'bind' my staff together against a 'common enemy', perhaps by making a heart-felt plea for their support, stressing the point that everyone has a talent that could be used for the good of all.

'Beam me up, Scotty!'
I transport them off to an 'alien' environment, from which they cannot easily escape, such as one of the many 'country mansion' residential management training centres, where we can thrash out the issues without being disturbed or distracted by other things.
  I 'enhance' and publicize the qualities of my opponents so that they are head-hunted by other organizations, or at least I do my best to support them in finding new positions elsewhere (which I have encouraged them to seek).

'Curry Powder'
I use the newly acquired freedom that incorporation gives me unilaterally to give all my staff a pay rise and/or better conditions of service, thus, by demonstrating some tangible benefits from incorporation, I could perhaps solicit more support for other changes.

'Mind reader'
I invite all staff either to come to me individually and have a 'no holds barred' discussion with me, or if they prefer, to write to me anonimously, to tell me, what they think of the current situation and my ideas, and why they think that way; the things that they are afraid of or concerned about; and the ideas that they have about what they would like to do or see happen.

'Black Hole'
I find and show my staff another organization that is perceived by them to have been in a worse 'hole' than us, but who have been through more 'devastating' changes and come out the other side much better off. Thus showing that the apparent disadvantages of the changes I am proposing can be turned into advantages.

'Ghost Busters'

Invite some people, whose views my staff would respect, and who have been through similar changes, to come and dispel some of the myths about change that are currently being put around.

'Oil'

I describe the less desirable aspects of the changes I wish to make so that their exact nature is somewhat elusive and difficult to grasp, as is understanding their full implications.

tendency to lose the novel feature contained in the absurd solution by 'jumping' back to reality too quickly.

An example of trying to add a semblance of practicality to an absurd solution, without destroying its essence, can be demonstrated with the following absurd solution:

I wish I could freeze the resistance to my ideas.

We might revise this as follows:

I wish I could overcome the resistance by freezing time – by apparently slowing things down.

One of the reasons people fear change is because they believe that it will happen so quickly that they will be unprepared for it.

We then modify it again, and again if necessary, until it forms into a possible solution:

I can 'slow things down' by emphasizing those things which are not going to change in the near future, such as salaries, conditions of service, the bulk of our work, thus reassuring people about some aspects of the future. From this position of relative security, we can then perhaps address the things that do need to change soon

I provide some possible solutions for Slow Coach Ltd in Frame 7.9. Some of the ideas (for example 'Oil') might appear a little underhand. A manager might try this : if he get away with it and people start thinking of change as only having benefits, then half the battle is won and the whole process may snowball from there. Personally, I feel that this action cannot be recommended on the grounds that if the deception is detected, it is likely to make matters worse. However, as process leader I have no right to volunteer such value judgements.

We are now at the stage in the flowchart shown in Frame 7.2 where the two alternative branches come together again. There should now be a number of ideas coming from our group's effort in overcoming the concerns associated with the Springboards that indicated a specific way of addressing the problem (see page 126), our straight 'Brainstorming' idea-generating session (see page 127), or from our Fantasy Excursion. These now need evaluating and developing further. An excursion could of course have been usefully applied to both branches of the flowchart, but it is more likely to be needed when the Springboard we are working on does not suggest a specific way of reaching a solution.

7.7.5   Itemized Response

As noted in Chapter 4, our tendency to classify ideas as good or bad with no degree of merit in between is a mistaken practice both philosophically and practically. In Synectics, there are no binary judgements like this until we get to a possible solution, and even then we can only judge a solution's merits *after* it has been implemented. Nolan (1989, p. 60) comments,

> ideas . . . are only words and pictures – they do not change anything in the real world. So we do not need to make an instant judgement on them; we can explore them in a more gentle, open-minded way. They are neither good nor bad – just more or less interesting and appealing . . .

This belief is a fundamental aspect of the way we handle judgements, and 'goes to the very heart of Synectics'.

For example, how do we classify an idea that we (as problem-owner) like a lot, which has promising potential for developing a possible solution, but about which we have a number of concerns. An 80 per cent good idea or a 20 per cent bad idea? This suggests that a binary judgement is unworkable. Even if we classify ideas on a continuum from good to bad, we would probably attempt to determine an idea's 'position' by trying to pick holes in it. If it survives this, it must be 'pretty good'. Sadly many other 'pretty good' ideas would also be rejected by this same process. Very few ideas come out perfectly formed: they should not be rejected just because of this. Dismissing ideas because they are not perfectly formed is typical of situations where 'hole-picking' is allowed at the outset evaluation.

A related factor is the effect of 'hole picking' on the person who suggested the idea (see Chapter 4). The effort that goes into getting ideas make people quite protective of them. Having withheld judgement earlier, we should not spoil things now, risking the delicate creative climate the group has developed, by hasty and perhaps crude evaluation. Synectics have developed a simple technique, the Itemized Response, that allows a possible solution to be developed from any idea, using gentle evaluation that encourages the ironing out of minor concerns rather than dismissal of the idea. If starts from the assumption that *all*

Frame 7.10   Slow Coach Ltd: Itemized Response

Idea from our Fantasy Excursion

'I use the newly acquired freedom that incorporation gives me to unilaterally give all my staff a pay rise and/or better conditions of service, thus, by demonstrating some tangible benefits from incorporation, I could perhaps solicit more support for other changes.'

Plus points:

- It would be a popular move.
- It would show that there are some good aspects to the changes we are going through.
- I think it could improve morale and hence peoples' motivation.

Major Concern:

'I feel that this idea may have less impact if I am seen to be rewarding those who are not currently pulling their weight.'

Ideas for overcoming the Major Concern

- Make this award only to those deemed to be competent.
- Any doubtful cases have the benefits on a 'probationary' basis.

Response from the director might be:

'What you're suggesting is that I only offer this "new deal" to those that I know are doing a reasonable job, but if there are some doubtfuls, we could offer it to them on some conditional basis. (Paraphrasing the idea)

'That's great, that might well work, it also partially overcomes another concern that I had which was the cost, but if we could do this on the promise of an equivalent increase in "production", I won't be worsening conditions and so I should be OK with the unions. I am concerned about one other matter, that is, there are supposed to be some national salary negotiations coming up shortly, I'm scared of "giving away too much".'

Idea to overcome second Concern

- Offer these benefits for six months at a time, renewable subject to a satisfactory review, or a change in the national conditions.

ideas have value, and thus before any 'flaws' and 'imperfections' in the idea are pointed out, first some of the good points about it (say three) are listed. This reinforces the value of the idea, and justifies the additional time that will be spent overcoming our concerns about it. Further, it gives a sense of satisfaction to the idea's contributor and makes it easier for them subsequently to accept any shortcomings the idea might have.

The problem-owner is asked to identify practical, helpful or attractive aspects of an idea, giving reasons wherever possible. It may be helpful to let the group contribute to this also, since they may see benefits not immediately apparent to the problem-owner. Then the leader asks for the problem-owner's major concern with the idea, expressing this as a 'How to/I wish' in order to give the group a direction for the further development of the idea in order to overcome this concern. The leader then gathers ideas from the group and writes them on the flipcharts while asking the problem-owner to paraphrase the suggestions to ensure understanding. If the group comes up with a suggestion that only partially overcomes the concern the Itemized Response process is repeated with this latest suggestion. As the idea develops in this way it becomes more difficult to get three 'new' good points each time, but the time spent trying is usually worthwhile.

Hopefully having resolved the major concern, the group now tackles any other concerns the problem-owner may have regarding the original idea, always taking them one at a time. This is often the most difficult thing for an inexperienced group to do, due to what seems to be a natural desire to dump all the concerns on the table at once, particularly with multiple problem ownership. The leader needs to be strict about this to avoid often circular arguments about which is the most serious concern, which invariably results in the idea being thrown out as an easy means of ending the argument. When working with more than one problem-owner the leader's ultimate aim is to achieve consensus (see Chapter 5); opting out like this is not the way to achieve it.

It may appear that we are running the risk of spending an inordinate amount of time going round in circles, resolving concern after concern, trying to make something of an idea of little or no potential. In practice Itemized Response is not a long-winded process. First, the problem-owner selects the idea to take through Itemized Response on the basis of its interest and appeal; the group would not spend time on ideas of little value to the problem-owner. Secondly, as the major concern is being tackled, the minor ones often dissipate or are resolved at the same time. An illustration of part of the Itemized Response process for the Slow Coach problem in given in Frame 7.10.

This process continues, gradually homing in on a possible solution, a course of action which the problem-owner can implement without further help from the group. The leader then writes up the possible solution.

7.7.6   Possible solution

On nearing a possible solution we need to check again with the problem-owner that the process is fulfilling their expectations. If the problem-owner reports no need for further help from the group with the possible solution, it can be compared with the NAF (Newness, Appeal and Feasibility) rating discussed during the planning Meeting, asking:

- Is it feasible?
- Is it appealing?
- Does it have newness/novelty?

If the problem-owner responds favourably, the leader can start them towards implementation of the solution by asking whether the problem-owner is beginning to form a plan of action. It is rewarding for group members to hear what the problem-owner sees as the next steps in the solution's progress and also ensures that the problem-owner does not go away with a solution and no idea what to do with it. The meeting is usually adjourned after these 'Next Steps' are written up.

Concluding thoughts

We leave Slow Coach Ltd with a couple of fairly 'concrete' Ideas for Possible Solutions that require very little additional development, plus the idea that we have just taken through the Itemized Response process.

   If it is felt that we have left the Director of Slow Coach in a slightly 'unsatisfactory' way, because, for instance, we may be thinking something like 'Well if it had been me, I wouldn't have started from there', this is understandable. For as we are about to see in Chapter 14, in order to gain other peoples' commitment to an idea or change, they really need to feel part of it, to have been in there from the start. Our Director is trying to gain commitment 'after the event', but that *is* his problem, and we had to start helping him from where he was.

   Now that we have been through all the stages of the Synectics process, a timely warning: because the 'opening up' stages are great fun, there is sometimes a desire to open up the problem further and further so that eventually we have hundreds of fairly specific ideas, none of which is developed enough for the problem-owner to use. Letting the group do this is sometimes rationalized on the basis of 'trying to cover all the possibilities', and protecting the creative atmosphere and well-being of the group. The leader should guard against this and 'close the problem down', going into the evaluation/development phase when the time is right. Ultimately the group is trying to help someone solve a problem, and, despite feeling that we may 'be missing something' by going into evaluation/development earlier, we can often end up in the same place. For example, earlier we had the following, quite specific)

Springboard, 'I wish we could have a totally open interchange of ideas and opinions'. If our problem-owner had said: 'That is precisely what we need, but how do I go about it? I need help on the practical details', it is not inconceivable that spiralling through the Idea-Paraphrase Itemized Response sequence several times could have given us an ide very similar to the one which came from our Mind reader solution (Frame 7.9). If this was exactly the sort of thing the problem-owner was looking for, we would not have had quite so much fun, but would have resolved the client's problem quicker.

It is usual for the problem-owner to be presented with all the sheets of paper from the flipcharts, carefully sequenced, or better still a typed but unedited version of the same, so that he can look back over the session to see where ideas have come from. More importantly, these sheets will contain many different aspects of the problem and probably several other half-formed solutions which the problem-owner may want to pursue at another time.

Leading a Synectics-style session is not easy, but it is invariably exhilarating!

7.8   Multiple problem ownership

In the real world few problem situations have just a single problem-owner. The Synectics approach (only a part of which we have so far seen) makes an even more significant contribution to multiple problem-owner situations. It helps us sort out who actually 'owns' which bits of the problem situation and provides us with the means for separating the consequential problems (where my actions may directly impinge on what other people do and cause difficulties for them) from irrelevant 'second opinions'. The following is only one of several days Synectics deals with the complexities of real world organizational problems. We are now going to look briefly at another example which illustrates how the Synectics process can be modified to cope with more than one problem-owner (the Synectics Consensus Meeting) and another type of excursion, the Example Excursion, which is based on the Direct Analogy (see Chapter 4).

Where two or more people are concerned with the same problem situation, what we can do is to go through the stages discussed earlier in an attempt to solve the problem as far as one person is concerned (during which time the other problem-owner(s) acts solely as a group resource). When we have done this, the solution for the first client becomes the starting point (problem) for the second client and we repeat as much of the process as is necessary to make this a solution for them as well. This is not as circuitous a procedure as it sounds.

Abstract examples have limited utility as a practice exercise for the material in this chapter owing to the lack of a real and involved problem-

Frame 7.11 Illustrative example: Northcliffe Sands

Task Headline

'How to increase revenue from tourism without "spoiling" the location?'

Frame 7.12 Northcliffe Sands: the problem

Northcliffe Sands is a small seaside town of approximately 10 000 people. The only road into the town competes with the River Froam for the limited area of flat land in the Froam valley. Unbelievably, Northcliffe Sands with its wooded estuary, picturesque harbour and its golden sands has only just been discovered by tourists.

Over the last ten years the number of summer visitors has increased from just the occupants of a couple of guest houses and a trickle of passing touring caravans, to a steady stream of many thousands of visitors during the peak months, so much so that they at times out-number the indigenous population.

David Eastman describes his problem as follows:

There is considerable concern amongst the local residents that the town's amenities and things like the roads and sewers are rapidly becoming unable to cope with this number of people, and that their environment is suffering accordingly. There are always traffic jams in the narrow streets, cars and motorcaravans are parked everywhere, and fishing boats unloading and some vans deliver-ing to the shops contribute to the chaos! And then there are the dinghy sailors driving through town with trailers: one reason for this sudden increase in visitors is that Northcliffe Sands seems to be ideal for sailing.

Those in business have got used to the increased profits the tourists bring, and some of them are greedy for more. Other locals believe that this desire for more and greater profits is destroying their community. It's our job to run things the way people want us to, but everything we do is wrong! To give you one example, we had a scheme to make some of the lanes near to the harbour into a pedestrian precinct. Our aim was to try to keep traffic out of the middle of town, and restrict access to the harbour: for everybody's benefit we thought. We were accused of pandering to the tourists and the retailers' lobby, at the expense of curtailing the move-ments of the locals by one pressure group, and attempting to reduce or disrupt trade by keeping passing motorists away from the town centre and restricting where their delivery vans could load and unload by another.

At first all the local trades-people and hoteliers welcomed the extra business that the increase in tourism brought to the area; now even some of them are beginning to realize that this may come to a premature end if the attractiveness of the location is destroyed. They are also worried about the interest recently being shown in the area by large national retailers and hotel chains.

This problem has come up at many recent Town Council meetings, and also a number of special public meetings organized by the various pressure groups, but very little agreement has been achieved as to how best to proceed. The Town Council have devised a number of plans to improve roads, car parks, and amenities, but they have invariably been thwarted by local opposition. Also, large expenditure needs sanction from the County. There is also a growing number of influential 'semi-retired middle-class newcomers'. Their viewpoint is not one of only resisting further expansion in tourism, they want to return to a situation that existed before many of them ever came to the area!

I wish we could get just the tourists' money but not them. We could then carry on living in the way we have grown accustomed, and we could return things to the way they used to be.

Northcliffe Sands: some possible Springboards ———— Frame 7.13 —

- I wish we could get just their money.
- I wish we could attract only rich tourists.
- How to justify increasing all our tariffs?
- How to create and maintain a relative exclusivity?
- I wish the Froam valley was an 'assault course', only the best tourists can get through it.
- I wish we had a toll bridge on the Froam Valley Road.
- How to make tourists pay for the new infrastructure?
- How to limit the number of guest houses?
- How to attract only tourists that are conservation minded?
- I wish we could attract only those tourists who respected our environment.
- I wish it would always rain on the undesirable tourists.
- How to make a lot of people seem to be less?
- How to lengthen our holiday season?
- I wish we could push all traffic (jams) off the harbour wall.
- I wish we could persuade retailers to take deliveries only on certain days/at certain times.
- I wish we could institute a 'sailboat' tax.
- I wish we had more than one slipway.
- I wish we could stop arguing.

- How to promote the idea that the quality of life is more important than profits?
- How to 'educate' the retailers/hoteliers?
- How to show that the suggested improvement schemes are for the benefit of everybody, not just the tourists?
- I wish we could show the benefits of a pedestrian precinct.
- How to persuade the big retailers not to come to Northcliffe?
- I wish we could please everybody.
- I wish I could demonstrate the unfairness of the 'no expansion' policy of the 'new-comers' to the long-standing local residents.
- I wish we could enforce our local bye-laws.

owner to select and evaluate ideas, and to offer direction at the appropriate moments. It would be better to practise the Synectics process on one of your own problems. However, since there is a need for this second illustrative example, I have tried to choose a problem situation that most readers will be acquainted with and probably have opinions about. The scenario I have chosen is 'the degradation of holiday resorts as they become more popular' and concerns the mythical seaside resort of Northcliffe Sands.

We have been asked by David Eastman, the chairman of the Northcliffe Town Council, to process lead a small group of interested parties who wish to tackle the problem as stated in Frame 7.11. The group consists of representatives from both the Hoteliers' and the Retailers' Associations, the Chief County Planning Officer, a spokesman for the local fishermen, a couple of residents and a distant relative of Eastman's, in Northcliffe on his annual holiday with his family.

In Frame 7.12 you will find a brief description of Northcliffe Sands, and David Eastman's account of the problem situation as he sees it.

For the purposes of illustrating the two additional aspects of the Synectics process mentioned above, we will assume that the planning meeting with David Eastman has already taken place and that we have started to open the problem up with some Goal Wishing on the background information to the problem (Frame 7.12). Anyone wishing to see further illustrations of Backward/Forward Planning can find an indication of what might have been said in Appendix 2. I have included in Frame 7.13 some of the Springboards that I thought might have been generated by Goal Wishing.

7.8.1   An Example Excursion

We are trying to solve the problem first for the chairman of the Town Council, David Eastman. He has been asked to select a few of the Spring-

┌─ *Northcliffe Sands: the chosen Springboard* ──────── *Frame 7.14* ─┐

The Springboard we are going to work with is . . .

   How to make a lot of people seem to be less?

David Eastman says: . . .

That sums up our problem in a nutshell. I have absolutely no idea how we might actually resolve the problem in this way, but if you could somehow accomplish this we would get the best of everything. A lot (more) of people means increased revenue to pay for the improvements we need to make, and if we can make them seem to be less in the effect they have on the community of Northcliffe we remove the biggest immediate threat temporarily, and this will give us the chance to get together and perhaps agree on how to sort out the best way to 'repair' the damage to our environment that we perceive has happened.

boards that have just been generated. As group leader, we are aware that a number of sensible ideas have already been suggested and rejected, and although we have produced some quite speculative Springboards, we have also noticed differing and even contradictory opinions being shown by some of these. We have concluded that our best policy might be to take the group on an Excursion, not just to get more speculative ideas, but also for the 'bringing together' effect that Excursions often have.

Look at Frame 7.14 to see which Springboard our problem-owner has chosen to work with and the comments he had made about its appeal.

An Example Excursion would be introduced in a similar way to the Fantasy Excursion on page 128, as a means for getting right away from the problem, a means of generating some apparently irrelevant material that we may be able to 'connect' with the problem situation in order to find some innovative solutions. We now cover up everything to do with the problem so far, and ask the group for examples of 'things that seem a lot less than they are' from the world of biology. As usual we write up all these ideas, and encourage group members to explain their sources if not volunteered. Some examples can be found in Frame 7.15.

The choice of appropriate 'worlds' depends largely on the leader's experience of which particular worlds have worked well in the past. Biology is a good resource for Direct Analogies (see Chapter 4); using organic analogies for inanimate objects and vice-versa is also a good idea. Some of the alternative 'worlds' used by Synectics are given in Frame 7.16.

Frame 7.15   Northcliffe Sands: Example Excursion from the world of biology

Locusts
  all you see is one black cloud
Raspberries
  they tend to hide under the plant's curling leaves
Trees in a wood
  there are probably a lot more than you think when you look at say a
  wooded hilltop from a distance
Oil-seed rape
  there must be millions of plants in a field but all you see is this vivid
  mass of bright yellow, it's pretty too
Stick insects
  we have a dozen of them in a jar at home, big ones and little ones,
  but they are very difficult to see amongst the privet twigs unless
  they move.

'I'm sorry, its not an example, but I've got this image of a holiday-
maker-eating Triffid in my mind that I need to get rid of.'

Sky-larks
  you can hear them but seldom see them because they fly so high.
Honey bees
  a friend of mine has a handful of hives, but you very rarely see the
  bees in his garden. I don't know why this is, perhaps they are
  scattered far and wide or are in the hives most of the time making
  honey
Bats
  I know they only come out at night, but they are so small and so
  quick that you tend not to see them either, until they nearly bump
  into you

It often happens that when encouraged to think of 'strange' things or
images, a compelling idea comes to our mind when we do not particularly want it. My 'Triffid' in Frame 7.15 was such an image and was
stopping me from making other connections. I became almost obsessive
about trying to fit in this solution where I did not really want one, until
I was able to exorcise it in this way. Since this is known to block further
ideas, it is perfectly in order for a group member to 'dump' ideas like
this. Far from doing any harm to the flow of Examples, voicing an idea
like this is likely to encourage imagination.

Having generated a number of Examples, we return to the Springboard we were working with by uncovering it, and ask the group to try
to make connections between the Excursion material and the problem.

'Worlds' and 'Careers' for Example Excursions ——— Frame 7.16 ——

[Organic]		[Inorganic]
biology	archaeology	physics
anthropology	medicine	palaeontology
sport	science fiction	crafts
fashion	computing	chemistry
music and dance	models	mathematics
warfare	agriculture	electronics
history	space travel	astronomy and astrophysics
mythology	acoustics	engineering

A variation on the Example Excursion is to try to imagine how you would think of, or react to, a problem situation if you found yourself in a totally different role in life. This is called a Career Excursion. Typical roles that the group leader might assign to the group members in this situation are:

traffic warden	undertaker
coal miner	politician
brain surgeon	ornithologist
pilot	teacher
farmer	astronaut

These (edited) lists of typical 'Worlds' and 'Careers' have been reproduced here by kind permission of Synectics Ltd.

This stage is called the Force Fit. Some ideas that our Northcliffe group might have come up with are given in Frame 7.17. Note again the use of Headlines and Background.

We now ask the problem-owner to select from these ideas, and we then proceed into the Itemized Response phase of the process to develop and evaluate those ideas which he selects. We shall skip this stage and move straight to a possible solution for our first problem-owner, to see how things continue from there. Before we do, you might like to consider what plus points and concerns you would have come up with in David Eastman's position of trying to develop the idea 'I wish we had a multi-screen cinema', assuming that Northcliffe already has a small but financially secure cinema. Appendix 3 contains an illustration of my thoughts on the way such an Itemized Response might proceed. In actual fact I am going to let David Eastman settle on a different solution, since the one above is likely to be too specific an idea fully to resolve his problem, though it could form part of a 'total package'. In Frame 7.18 I have described briefly how the final stage of the 'closing down' part of this problem might have occurred for our first problem-owner.

—— *Frame 7.17   Northcliffe Sands: Force Fit ideas* ——

Create more shopping arcades

> I was thinking of the leaves of raspberries curling around the fruit and hiding it, and that reminded me of the entrance to the 'Mall' – you can hide tourists in shopping arcades.

Provide better access to North Beach

> I liked the idea of lots of things looking less from a distance, you know, the trees in the wood; oil-seed rape plants are the same really, but their yellow made me think of a beach. Very few people use North Beach, even though it's a lovely wide long beach, because you can only reach it around the headland. It's also some distance from the town centre!

I wish we could camouflage the tourists

> Thinking about the stick insects and how well they are hidden by their camouflage I thought, let's make it a bye-law for everyone to wear sand coloured T-shirts, shorts and swimming costumes on the beach.

Suggest that the boatyards should consider running flotilla cruising holidays

> A friend of mine has a really nice 30-foot cruising catamaran called 'Sky Lark'. I'm always very envious when I see him sailing out of the harbour to wherever. That made me think that, if we could persuade our day sailors to take up cruiser sailing, we could sell them a week's supply of food and drink and then pack them off to sea. This way we *could* have their money and not them!

I wish we could lock the holidaymakers in their rooms

> I was thinking of the bees being shut up in their hives busily making honey.

Let's open a casino

> This is building on the last idea, the association honey–money led me to thinking about shutting people up in a room where they (or rather we) could make some money.

Get the Northcliffe Bus Co. to run more organized bus tours

> I was thinking about bees as well, but about them being 'invisible' because they are so dispersed. Let's spread our tourists all around the area with organized bus tours.

I wish we had a multi-screen cinema

> That one about bats and not seeing them in the dark appealed to me, and something someone said earlier about shutting people up in a room and taking their money, then I thought, so why not a dark room?

Northcliffe Sands: 'closing down' for one problem-owner ─────────── Frame 7.18 ─────

After selecting several of the Force Fit ideas, and developing them using Itemized Response, David Eastman announces the following:

> I can see something definite forming in several of those ideas, what I might call 'dispersement'. Presently, everyone tries to get in and out of the town centre at least a couple of times a day. If we can encourage them to do this less often, by making this less necessary or more attractive not to do so, I believe we can meet my initial objectives, which was to relieve the immediate pressure.
>
> I can see lots of ways we can do this; some are very long term, like encouraging the sailing fraternity to make a move towards the idea of flotilla cruising, but there are also a number of things we can do now. For instance, Fred Johnson has wanted to build a proper campsite behind the 'Dog and Duck' for years, but we keep refusing to let him expand because of our fears of increasing the number of campers. If we let him do that, and then enforce the prohibition of camping/caravaning, etc. from the vicinity of the town . . . , we could even run a regular minibus service up to Fred's pub.
>
> Another thing we could do is provide parking and picknicking areas up in the woods, perhaps even set up some woodland walks, etc. Proper access and a car park at North Beach should also discourage the current tendency for beach-goers to dump their cars on or around the harbour, so as to gain access to the beach by walking around the cliff path, etc. A slipway on the estuary we could do almost right away; I know where we could build it at very little cost – we'll still charge for using the harbour slipway though!
>
> I am content for the moment; I have got some things I can pursue. My only outstanding concern is, as always, I need everybody's agreement to go ahead with them. I know that we are now going to try to resolve the problem for the rest of you, and I feel that this may develop later as we do that, along with perhaps some more ideas.

7.8.2   Returning to the problem of a problem shared

To get a workable solution for Northcliffe we need to get everybody's agreement and commitment to some form of plan. We know that the Town Council has considered restricting access to vehicles, more car parks, improved road systems, etc. and now our first problem-owner has several more new ideas. He says he is content for the moment. He knows that if the worst happens and no consensus is achieved his turn

——— *Frame 7.19   Northcliffe Sands: Itemized Response from* ———
                 second problem-owner

'I can see that tourists out of the town centre and on the beach will certainly ease congestion in the centre and make things more civilized.'

'I have always said that we could do with a local minibus service to help the elderly get around, perhaps we can combine the two ideas.'

'I also think that this idea may incur little or no loss in income for the retailers and hoteliers, that's always their complaint against my ideas.'

'My major concern would be that it could "back-fire". By providing ways of "dispersing" the tourists we might eventually end up attracting even more of them!'

will come around again, and so we are able to take his 'dispersement' possible solution and offer it to our next problem-owner as an idea.

This is Mrs Eleanor Smyth-Wilson, representing the views of the 'semi-retired middle-class newcomer' faction. We could ask her to do an Itemized Response on the 'dispersion' idea – ask her for some features about it that she considers to be good, and then ask for her main concern. Let us suppose her reactions are as indicated in Frame 7.19.

We would now ask the group to generate ideas for ensuring that the 'dispersion' policy works, and then ask our second problem-owner (Eleanor Smyth-Wilson) to select, paraphrase and perform an Itemized Response on her favourite idea(s). We would continue spiralling through this process until she is content with our solution so far. After our second problem-owner has a possible solution, we offer this to the third problem-owner (Peter Frith) as a starting idea, and so on (see Frame 7.20).

Our next step would be to ask the group for ways of overcoming our third problem-owner's concern. I believe that we have pursued this story long enough now to show how the problem is 'handed over' from one problem-owner to another, so I will stop at this point. However, for the sake of completeness, Appendix 3 contains a couple of ideas we might offer Peter Frith.

When we have been right through the problem-owners in this way we should return to the first (David Eastman) to see whether he is still happy with the possible solution. Although he is unlikely to be totally opposed to his initial 'solution' now that it has been modified by the other problem-owners, additional concerns may have arisen which he wants the group to address. If need be we must go right around the circuit of problem-owners again. It is very unlikely, however, that this process could develop into a never ending circle. Each problem-owner

Northcliffe Sands: the third problem-owner —————— Frame 7.20

Let us suppose that we have satisfied Mrs Eleanor Smyth-Wilson that any additional amenities, such as camp sites, car parks, beach access roads, slipways, etc., can be provided at the same time as strict restrictions on similar features are enforced elsewhere, i.e. it is possible to 'relocate' or disperse tourist activity in this way. We have even managed to incorporate her minibus hobby-horse, and her enthusiasm for conservation issues into the grand plan as well. She is (presently) well pleased, and so this possible solution for her is offered to our next problem-owner.

Our third problem-owner might be Peter Frith, the manager of Northcliffe's biggest food shop, and there representing all the other retailers in the town. After remarking that he can see a number of merits in our second problem-owner's 'solution', including the fact that, with the reduction in traffic congestion which the revised 'dispersion' policy should ensure, his delivery loading/unloading difficulties would disappear, he might state his major concern as follows:

> I am worried about the possibility that, with the tourists scattered all around the nearby countryside and coming into town less often, my trade could suffer if 'fringe' retailers set up in business where the tourists actually are.
>
> I don't care whether my customers come in to my shop once a week or every day, as long as they purchase the same amount of stuff overall. In fact once a week could make my staffing problem easier to handle by reducing the number of 'rush hour' periods I have to try to plan for. I never seem to have the right number of people on duty to cope with the number of customers I get at a given time! But if someone like Fred opens his own 'camp-site' shop in competition to the town, it could have a serious effect on us!

knows that they will have an opportunity to offer their ideas and voice their concerns and their own chance to develop a solution. This tends to 'relieve the pressure' and encourage the participants to reorientate themselves from attacking other people's ideas which they see as threatening to their pet solutions, to where they actively and readily support other peoples' ideas and wholeheartedly help to find a mutually acceptable way of modifying them to everyone's benefit. Finally, when we seem to have arrived at a consensus solution we should ask whether any group member still has any outstanding concerns, and deal with these appropriately.

7.9   Other uses for elements of the Synectics process

I have mentioned above that Goal Wishing is an effective way of sharing perceptions of a given situation, a 'safe' way of airing differences of opinion, and also that an excursion can be used in isolation to generate a mass of unusual and innovative ideas. I should add to this that Itemized Response, apart from being a method of developing and evaluating an idea, is valuable in taking stock of situations, presenting proposals, and in conflict resolution and appraisal situations.

7.10   Meetings, bloody meetings!

The Synectics 'philosophy' has implications for how ordinary 'agenda' type meetings, as opposed to problem solving sessions, can be improved. This involves having separate agendas for each meeting participant published on flipcharts around the room, which can be added to or amended as the meeting proceeds. Each item on a person's agenda should have a personal priority attributed to it (in case of time pressures), the estimated length of time that person believes is required to deal with it adequately, and what type of item it is. For instance, the owner of the agenda item may wish to give information, collect information or ask the group to assist in some problem solving (though this may be best deferred to a separate meeting).

The process leader (who again has no dealings with, or interest in, the likely content of the meeting) should go around the meeting participants dealing with one item per person at a time, and recording the actual time spent on a particular item. Even if several members of the meeting wish to bring up the same issue, this is recorded on each agenda and dealt with as individual items as they will be seen from different viewpoints. If we did have several people with the 'same' problem we would doubtless call a separate problem solving session to tackle it (much as we did with Northcliffe Sands). The meeting starts on time and runs for no longer than the previously agreed duration, unless the meeting unanimously agrees on an extension.

I intend to leave Synectics for now but just as we came across Synectics and their ideas long before this chapter started, we will encounter Synectics concepts again later.

7.11   Cognitive Mapping

Determining exactly what the problem is, or deciding the initial direction(s) we should go in to search for ideas and possible solutions, is often the most crucial stage in problem solving, particularly when we are helping other people solve their problems. Cutting through the tangled mess of information we have relating to the problem and seeing the problem situation through the 'camouflage' of our own and other people's opinions and attitudes is not particularly easy. This is what the Backward/Forward Planning and Goal Wishing stages of the Synectics process seek to achieve. This difficulty with problem identification has also inspired the development of a relatively new technique called Cognitive Mapping. In simple terms, this technique is an extended and more systematic version of these early stages of the Synectics process.

The originators of Cognitive Mapping like many others in the field believe that in trying to resolve a problematical situation our perception of it is shaped by our particular mental framework of beliefs, attitudes, hypotheses, prejudices, expectations, values and objectives. They offer their technique as a means of 'capturing' these concepts, describing it as:

> a modelling technique which intends to portray ideas, beliefs, values and attitudes and their relationship one to another in a (diagrammatical) form which is amenable to study and analysis. (Eden *et al.*, 1983, p. 39)

By attempting to 'map out' these concepts and showing the interrelationships between them, Eden *et al.* believe the process of problem identification is facilitated. Cognitive Mapping seems to be particularly useful in uncovering and identifying the essence of a problem situation with multiple ownership.

Because problems are not 'objective entities', but actually belong to someone, our starting point when helping others to resolve problems should ideally be 'an empathetic understanding' of the problem as that person sees it. Eden *et al.* suggest that we achieve this by listening to the 'language, descriptions, theories and beliefs that are expressed' as the problem-owner describes the problem situation. In the first instance, the map we are building shows we have been listening carefully and we are making an attempt towards empathy.

To construct a Cognitive Map we start from a 'label' of the problem as given, for example 'low morale', written in the centre of a large sheet of paper, then in discussion with the problem-owner(s) we 'map' out various perceptions of the problem situation showing their causal interconnections with arrows. We solicit these perceptions by asking questions such as:

'Why does . . . matter?'
'What reasons come to mind as explanations for . . . ?'
'Why is . . . like that?'

For the question 'Why does low morale matter?' we might get the answer, 'Because of it our productivity has fallen right off'; to 'What reasons come to mind as explanations for the low morale?' we might get 'It's the result of poor leadership'. For each of these perceptions we

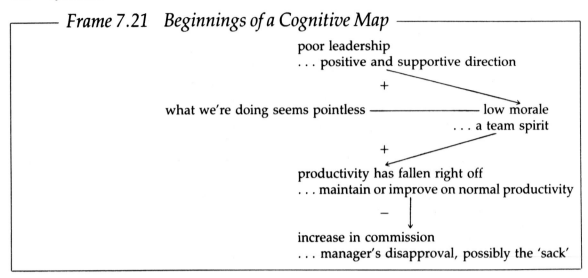

Frame 7.21   Beginnings of a Cognitive Map

poor leadership
. . . positive and supportive direction

+

what we're doing seems pointless ——————— low morale
. . . a team spirit

+

productivity has fallen right off
. . . maintain or improve on normal productivity

−

increase in commission
. . . manager's disapproval, possibly the 'sack'

try to write down beneath them what the problem-owner considers to be a 'satisfactory alternative to this circumstance'; and gradually our map builds, as in Frame 7.21. The plus and minus signs on the arrows show whether the problem-owner believes a direct or an inverse relationship exists between the first item in each pair of concepts. Eventually, we should be able to discern 'clusters' of perceptions within the map we have been building that indicate main area(s) of concern.

Often, during discussion with the problem-owner we encounter phrases with the same or a linked meaning, or that describe attributes of a particular concept rather than being causally related to it. These connotative links can be shown on the map with non-arrowed lines or depicted separately in attribute diagrams. The 'discovery' of these links is important because they provide us with a better appreciation of what a person means by that particular concept. For example, 'low morale' may be so linked with 'what we're doing seems pointless'.

Once a map has been drawn it can be examined for 'loops', some of which will be self-stabilizing (negative feedback loops), while others indicate the manifestation of vicious circles (positive feedback loops). Individuals caught up in the latter are usually only too well aware of being so, but seeing it shown on the map makes it clear to everyone concerned that an untenable position exists and helps us to find ways of breaking free by revealing the outcome we might expect from 'breaking' any one of the links in the circle.

In a multiple problem-owner situation, Eden *et al.* advise that we first produce a separate map for each problem-owner and then form an aggregated map showing the group's perception of the situation. As we study 'completed' individual maps, we may notice that the same or similar concepts appear on different maps, which may indicate that certain perceptions of the problem situation are shared. However, great care must be taken when attempting to 'merge' concepts such as these. We must ask the contributors whether they really do mean the same thing, even if they say the same thing. When combining maps in this way, it is best to do it in a group situation so that all the contributors can check with each other on the meaning of similar concepts, perhaps using Synectics-style paraphrasing. By comparing individual maps we get an idea of the diversity of viewpoints and discover potential areas of conflict, as well as determining which perceptions are shared.

There is obviously far more to Cognitive Mapping than this, for example a good rapport needs to be built between the problem solving facilitator and the problem-owner(s) in order to gain answers to our questions (see Chapter 12). Anyone interested in learning more about Cognitive Mapping should read Eden's book, which uses an extended case study to present the difficulties of helping other people decide on what their problem is and then resolving it.

CHAPTER

8

Introduction to logical thinking

Virtually all of the explicit training we receive in problem solving skills through our educational system is in 'logical thinking', What precisely is this? Does it include 'common-sense'? And how can we apply this to real-world problems? The term 'common-sense' can mean anything from something which is intuitively sensible to something which is rationally sensible, or logical.

By doing something logically we normally mean that we are methodically working through a rational series of steps in the hope of systematically converging (by a sort of process of elimination) on our desired objective, for example, the solution to a problem. If there is any choice along this route, decisions we have to make regarding which of several possible directions to go in next, the appropriate choice can normally be inferred from what has gone before, and the facts we have established en route. Logical thinking, whilst systematic, rational and mainly 'convergent' in nature, is often referred to as analytical thinking. Analytical thinking, the main tool of scientific research and mathematics, is usually thought to involve finding ways of separating a given phenomenon (the object of our interest) into its component parts, so that by studying these we can make guesses (hypotheses) about their nature which we can then test out and modify as necessary. The hope is that all this will ultimately help us to discover and establish some underlying principles that explain the nature and/or behaviour of the phenomenon we are studying.

The split between creative thinking and logical thinking is often paralleled with that between divergent and convergent thinking. This is not quite a perfect match, as creativity is thought to include some convergent/logical (evaluative) processes. But analytical thinking *is* predominantly convergent and so the bulk of this chapter concerns strategies of this type. However, while we draw somewhat artificial boundaries between creative and analytical thinking, this should not be allowed to divert our attention from the fact that most of the time we need *both* for effective problem solving.

In their introduction to logical thinking skills, Peter Grogono and Sharon Nelson (1982) differentiate between 'strategies' and 'tactics'. Tactics are specialized methods which are very likely to work with a certain limited set of problems, whereas strategies are more universally applicable, but can in no way be guaranteed to solve any one particular problem. Strategies are more of 'a method worth trying' when you do not know which specific tactic you 'should' be using.

We will consider only logical techniques that would be referred to in this classification system as 'strategies'. In the way of general advice, Grogono and Nelson say we should state the problem clearly and under- stand it. We need to identify what we know with regard to the data that we have, and the restrictions or limitations that are imposed on the situation, some of which may not be explicitly evident. This under- standing also includes having a clear idea of what constitutes a solution; we should not attempt to solve a problem *by logical means* until we are sure that we know exactly what it is that constitutes a solution. If we do not know what the problem is exactly or have no precise concept of what form a desired or acceptable solution might take, we should first be using the methods described in other sections of this book in order to help us establish what these might be, or at least in what directions we might best look to find them out, not rushing off trying to find a solution.

8.1   Logical strategies

Grogono and Nelson offer a number of different logical strategies which are described below.

8.1.1   *Abstraction*

Expressing the problem in abstract terms assists us establish what we do know about the problem. It is also useful for cutting away super- fluous information (but we must make sure that it *is* superfluous, rather than just 'difficult to fit in' with the rest of the information that we have. To implement this strategy we need to select an appropriate method of notation, the building blocks of our abstract model. For instance, should we express the problem algebraically, diagramatically or verbally? This choice is important, because as we have already seen, one of our con- ceptual blocks is 'an incorrect choice of language problem solving strategies'.

Let us suppose that, from an annual summary report derived from company personnel records, we know that, of the 17 qualified engineers

Figure 8.1 *The Engineers problem: fill in the missing numbers.*

Experience		Petro-chemical		
		Y	N	Totals
Civil	Y			10
	N		3	
	Totals	6		17

Figure 8.2 *The Engineers problem: where do we put the other 14?*

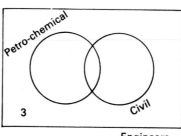

Engineers

working for us, 6 have experience of the petro-chemical industry, 10 have been involved with civil engineering contracts and 3 of them have worked in neither of these fields. And now we want to know how many have worked in both. We could express this problem in an algebraic form, but it is also possible to express it in tabular form (see Figure 8.1), or in a more visual form similar to the drawing in Figure 8.2. The answer is that 2 of our engineers must have previous experience working in both fields (see Appendix 3).

You may have been able to visualize the problem without a diagram or a table; you may have used mental arithmetic or perhaps trial and error. You probably did not have to call all 17 engineers into your office, or go back to the personnel files (that is, solve the problem without abstraction) to find out who had worked in both fields. When faced with a situation like this most of us will use some method of abstraction – one that we are happy to work with *and* one that suits the problem situation. The art is knowing which one; when in doubt, try several!

As I have already said, when using abstraction we are generally forced to sort out the relevant information from the superfluous variety, but often we are obliged to go further than we might wish and work with a *simplified* abstract model. We should always be aware that with most complex, real-world problems, our abstract model is very rarely an exact representation of reality.

8.1.2   *Progress by inference*

This is what most people think of as logical thinking. The problem statement will contain or imply certain facts, and possibly indicate the rules we may apply to these facts. From these we can infer the truth or validity of other facts and rules that will hopefully come closer to determining the unknown thing which is our problem. In the Engineers problem above, from knowing that three engineers out of the 17 had no previous experience in either of the fields, I was able to infer that 14 engineers must have experience in at least one. A byproduct of this process is that it can identify any missing data which we should attempt to find.

There are actually two types of inference. Deductive inference (deduction) is trying to infer from what is known to be true or valid about things (objects, people, situations or events) generally, that it is also true or valid for a specific example of them. Inductive inference (induction) is attempting to infer from what is known to be true or valid about a specific example (or from a 'pattern' perceived in a number of particular examples) some thing that is also true or valid for these things generally. The former is the more reliable process and tends to be the most used; the latter is often in practice little better than an inspired guess.

8.1.3   *Break the problem into sub-problems or stages*

We may be able to resolve a relatively complex problem by dividing it into parts and solving each part in turn, paying due attention as we do so to the dangers inherent in restructuring problems. This can be done both in a vertical fashion (assuming that the problem situation was originally structured so as to permit this), and also in a lateral direction by considering the problem as a succession of sub-goals to be achieved. For example, if our problem is to produce reliable forecasts of the demand for one of our products or services, an appropriate sub-goal might be to find some economic indicators that show a good correlation with the unit sales of that product or service.

8.1.4   *Working backwards*

If our goal or objective is clear, but we cannot see how to get to it from where we are, we may find it easier to work logically backwards from the solution until we get to our present situation. At each backwards step we would ask ourselves something like 'What has to be or needs to be done just before this, in order to make it possible?'

8.1.5   Look for 'stock' solution methods

Grogono and Nelson stress the importance of our past experience in problem solving. Each 'new' problem need not be treated in isolation: we are likely to have recollections of previously solved problems that have a direct relevance to the new one. Our first line of attack should always be to establish whether or not there are any standard solution methods available for this category of problem, for example, using linear programming to determine the optimal production mix of a manufacturing plant.

8.1.6   Consider similar problems

If no stock solution is applicable, we could look at whether a modified version of a method we had previously used successfully on a similar problem might work in the new situation.

8.1.7   Investigate special/more general cases of the problem

In simple terms mathematical induction is a process by which you first attempt to prove that a special case of something is true, and that if the something is true for one case it must be true for another. Real life is never quite as easy as this, but we can often get hints and clues about how to go about tackling a more general problem by considering how we have solved a special case of it. The converse of this can also be helpful. If we believe that the current problem can be thought of as a special case of a wider family of problems, for which a particular solution method has been found to be generally useful, we might consider trying this method. For example, Network Analysis, has been found to be a useful tool in many planning and scheduling situations; it might be a useful technique to use are next time we need to plan something.

8.1.8   Transforming the problem

In its simplest form this is the same as abstraction'. We do not like the form the problem is in so we change or transform it into another form, a new frame of reference we find easier to work with. Expressing geometric problems in terms of algebra appeals to some people! Taken to its 'illogical' conclusion this idea spans a range of possibilities from a change of notation to a Synectics Excursion.

8.1.9   Checking for validity

Finally, and commensurate with the philosophy of the logical approach, after carrying out one or more of these strategies and having arrived at a solution, we should then check both our solution and our argument for validity.

Part of this method is in direct contradiction to methods described elsewhere in the book. Sorry! The art of effective problem solving is knowing at what point in our problem solving we should be thinking logically, and when we need to cast this aside temporarily and do some creative thinking.

8.2   Danger! Logical thinking

Logical thinking invariably starts from a set of 'facts' and 'rules', some assumptions or premises we make about the problem situation. It should be obvious that if we start our logical thinking from a false premise, making incorrect or inappropriate assumptions, we will end up logically and systematically deducing an incorrect or inappropriate solution. This should place considerable responsibility on the problem-solver to ensure that any logical thinking starts from the right place. Often, in practice, such considerations are not made or at least not made carefully enough. The cavalier attitude some people adopt towards the formation of assumptions seems to indicate a belief that the logical process will compensate for any 'minor deficiencies' in this respect. It will not.

Worse than this sloppy use of logical thinking is its deliberate abuse. Because we believe in its potency and effectiveness, a semblance of logical thinking can be used to justify, legitimize or give credibility to what might be perceived as an inappropriate decision or solution. This is not just the use of an apparently rational argument to cover up unsatisfactory decisions and solutions, although this does happen and we need to be watchful for it. It is also the deliberate intent to disguise (managerial) prejudice, by surrounding it with a screen of false rationality, covering a favoured idea or course of action, which may have no rational or generally approved justification, with a camouflage of pseudo-logical netting. If we believe *intuitively* that something is the right thing to do, then we should declare it as such; most people will respect us for our openness. It is usually only those who are aware that their view is highly prejudiced, or have ulterior motives, that find it necessary to justify their case with false logic.

It has been argued by Buchanan and Huczynski (1985) that technology can be used as a political tool by management and this provides a good illustration of the abuse of logic. Management wishing to tighten up or change work practices might argue 'We have to do things differently now so as to meet the requirements of the new computer system we have installed. This will improve the way we allocate and utilize our resources and ultimately our profits and your rewards in our new profit sharing pay scheme.' The faults in this 'logic' are relatively easy to see;

the unquestioned assumption that a new computer system and considerable re-organization *will* improve profits. Those intent on abusing logic in this way often do so much more skilfully than this.

8.3   When to be logical

Given the 'Health Warning' above, perhaps I should now suggest when we should consider the use of a predominantly logical or analytical approach to our problem solving, remembering that this means doing some logical or analytical thinking, *not* just using a systematic approach. Systematic usually means 'closely following a set of logical steps'. By this definition all the problem solving strategies in this book can be called systematic, because they all contain steps or stages, and the originators of these strategies would maintain that the steps are organized the way they are because of some underlying rationale. There is nothing wrong or inherently limiting in being systematic, so long as we remain flexible as well. If our problem solving is not systematic, then it is difficult for us to learn from our past experience of problems how to improve our problem solving skills. Some strategies require mostly logical/ analytical thinking, others involve mostly creative or systemic thinking.

In most problem situations there will be times when we will want to 'open' things up – gathering information, getting different perspectives on the situation (redefining the problem), generating ideas, developing possible solutions – and shortly after each of these we may wish to perform some sort of selection or evaluation. And, of course, eventually we seek 'closure', we want to converge on to some possible solutions. It is during these 'convergent' phases that logical thinking is likely to be appropriate. However, if the problem situation is well defined and we have a clear idea as to what will constitute an acceptable solution, then a predominantly logical approach is likely to be the order of the day. For example, if everyone concerned is in agreement that we need to find ways of altering our present distribution system in order to reduce transport costs, then employing operational research techniques in a logical and systematic manner may well be the best line of attack. If our problem is essentially diagnostic in character, such as a machine fault, then a predominantly logical approach in the form of Kepner and Tregoe's Problem Analysis is likely to be most appropriate (see Chapter 10).

8.4   Concluding comments

Despite the fact that we are dealing with tame, logical problems here, Grogono and Nelson also emphasize the need for 'insight', the sudden realization that using certain symbols, a particular notation, considering a 'special case', or transforming a problem in some way, is the key to the solution of the problem in hand. We are talking about the same 'connection-making' process as with creativity, but this time the raw material comes from theoretical knowledge, rather than apparently irrelevant perceptions and memories.

The classic text by Polya (1957) on logical problem solving delves into these concepts in greater depth and would be useful to any reader with an interest in this or mathematics. The next two chapters will look at how some of the ideas summarized above are applied in practical problem solving strategies.

CHAPTER

9 Structured opportunity searches

Morphological Analysis (MA) is an extremely pretentious name for what can be a simple and effective way of making a systematic search for new (usually product type) ideas. There are several morphology techniques described in the problem solving literature, but they are all founded on the same basic theme, namely, the use of some form of n-dimensional grid to permit a systematic and logical search for ideas. First of all we will look at an example of MA in its original form (Zwicky, 1969).

When looking for an idea for a new product, we chose two or three independent attributes that the product must have, and represent these on the axes of a two- or three-dimensional grid or matrix, subdividing each of these into several independent ways in which the attribute can be accomplished. The result is a diagram consisting of cells or boxes, similar to those shown schematically in Figure 9.1. Each of the cells represents one of the many possible combinations of the subdivisions of each attribute.

There is no reason why we should be limited to three attributes, except that more than three aspects is virtually impossible to represent diagramatically in this particular way and almost as difficult to manage by any other means. This last point is also why the number of subdivisions is normally restricted to a small number, say, six.

9.1 Inventing a totally new way of doing something

Superficially, the process of MA is similar to the full Attribute Listing technique mentioned in Chapter 6. Both start off by trying to list the main features or attributes of the item we are trying to invent. When using Attribute Listing to design, say, an improved hammer we would note that it has a metal lump, with a flat face on one side, a rounded one

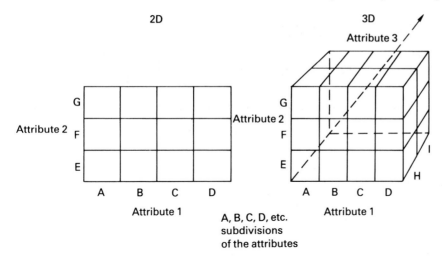

2D

3D

Attribute 3

G

Attribute 2

F

E

A   B   C   D

Attribute 1

G

Attribute 2

F

E

A   B   C   D

Attribute 1

I

H

A, B, C, D, etc.
subdivisions
of the attributes

Figure 9.1 *Grids showing schematic way of representing the essential attributes of a possible new product.*

on the other, and a hole for inserting a round wooden shaft, and that it is heavy, and then we would think of ways of modifying each attribute. For example, we might think of replacing the rounded face of the hammer head with a nail-removing claw or a cold chisel blade, or having a hollow metal shaft with a nail storage compartment in it. If we are using MA to help us design a totally new way of inserting nails into wood, we need to think in far more general terms about the attributes we desire. We would not derive them from observing an example of the latest state of the art hammer. Instead of the attributes suggested in the previous paragraph, our attributes would probably be something like, some sort of driving force (to push the nail into the wood), a method of holding and/or positioning the device, a means of gripping nails. Our starting position 'a new way of inserting nails in wood' is necessarily more generic as well.

Once we have chosen the main attributes, we need to generate various ways in which these attributes can be provided. For instance, the driving force of the nail inserter could be compressed air, explosive force, mechanical leverage, elastic potential energy (for example, compressed springs and stretched strings), electro-magnetic repulsion or angular momentum of a heavy weight (simply, swinging it around your head like you do with an ordinary hammer). The holding and/or positioning device could be a free-standing structure, something that adheres to the surface (for example, suction pads), a (horizontal) surface-skimming mechanism (for example, rollers, air cushion), a hand grip appendage (for example, D-shaped hand grips on the side, or a pistol grip, or even a long round shaft). And the means of holding the nails could be fingers, a built-in 'spring' clamp mechanism, or a groove/gun barrel attachment.

Figure 9.2 *Main attributes for a new device for inserting rails into wood shown on a three-dimensional grid.*

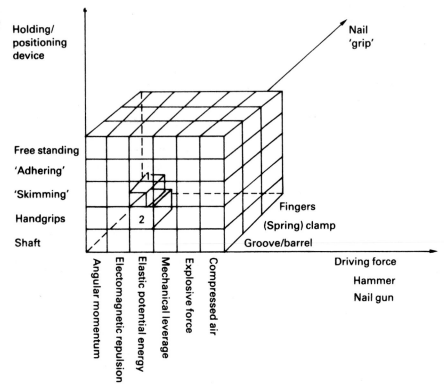

We now need to represent all this information on a three-dimensional grid (see Figure 9.2). Then we explore the cells, systematically looking for presently existing ways of inserting nails into wood, and new ways of doing this which are worth pursuing.

Figure 9.2 shows two existing products:

- the hammer (angular momentum, a long round shaft, fingers);
- the nail (staple) gun (elastic potential, a hand grip, groove/barrel).

As we look through the cells, we are bound to find some that we feel we cannot do much with, for instance, explosive force, a long round shaft and fingers. But do not give up on them too quickly. We should give every cell, or combination of attribute subdivisions careful consideration, just in case there is a possibility there. If it is unusual, and we can make it work, we could be on to a winner. There should be many cells that offer new ideas for getting nails into wood, though some will be more practically and/or commercially feasible than others.

I wonder if anyone has thought of:

- a nail crossbow (elastic potential energy, a pistol hand grip, groove/barrel);

- a lever-operated nail-inserting tool (mechanical leverage, a D-shaped hand grip, groove/barrel) (similar to a device for getting wine corks into wine bottles);
- a nail-inserting tool based on the principle of the linear motor (electro-magnetic repulsion, a pistol hand grip, groove/barrel);
- a 'shooting stick' nail gun (elastic potential energy, a long round shaft, groove/barrel): you push a nail into a spring-loaded shaft until a clamp with a quick release mechanism grabs the nail head; useful for getting into recessed places;
- a cross between a roller skate and a stapler (mechanical leverage, surface skimming, spring clamp) which would be foot operated and would hold the nails in a magazine clip (as in rifle) on the skate, and take the back/knee ache out of nailing floorboards;
- a miniature pile driver (explosive force, free standing, spring release clamp): a small internal combustion engine drives a cam that raises and releases a weight that drives large nails into really hard wood.

The first idea come from the same cell as the nail gun. This indicates that I have not thought carefully enough about my subdivisions. There would seem to be two 'energy source' categories here rather than one: perhaps I should have compressed springs and stretched strings/wires as two different ways of producing the driving force. In my initial attempt at this problem my holding and/or positioning device attribute (which in the first instance was just a holding device) had D-shaped hand grips and pistol hand grips as *two* different subdivisions (along with a long round shaft). I soon realized that it was going to be extremely difficult to think up ideas for a particular power source and nail holder in *both* of these (layers) which would represent substantially different tools! They would be basically the same apart from having different grips. Perhaps, then, either a holding device is not a very important attribute or the choice of subdivisions for that attribute has not been sufficiently thought through.

Realizing these subdivisions were not independent, I tried to be more inventive with them. Revising the 'holding device' attribute's sub-divisions, I began thinking about the 'positioning' aspect of it because I saw simultaneously several possible ways of improving the present technology:

- some form of nail gun (on rollers) tracking along a metre ruler (possibly with an L-shaped cross-section for butting up to the edge of a piece of wood) that would facilitate the insertion of a number of nails at equal spacings;
- a (height adjustable) free standing nail gun that would make the nailing of vertical wood panels a little easier.

Then I started thinking of whether the concept of positioning should include the use of some sort of artificial sighting device for situations where the bulk of the tool prevented us from seeing the nail's point in order to line it up. We could even stretch this idea of a sighting device further and include a nail gun with a built-in metal detector – no more nails through pipes and cables. The idea of a gun made me wonder if you could fire a nail as you would a bullet, and whether using the principle of a rifled barrel it could be used with screws as well.

Forcing myself back to my grid I eventually got to the 'pile driver' idea and realized I could do similar things with an electric motor. Should I have included electrical power? I managed to convince myself that this would probably be turned into some form of momentum, so I left my attributes as they are now.

There are many possibilities, so we need to think carefully about our choice of attributes and their subdivisions before we compile a grid and start searching through it for ideas. MA is a powerful technique for generating ideas as long as we work at trying to do something with the combinations of features it suggests. With the nail inserting problem there are theoretically 90 combinations in total. If we manage to get ideas from most of them, our productivity is comparable to what might be expected from a Brainstorming group session.

9.2 Systematic search for unexploited opportunities

Instead of letting the axes of a grid represent two or three attributes of a product, they can represent two or three aspects of an organization's operations. For example, a manufacturing company might analyse its operations against the three variables:

- manufacturing processes available;
- raw materials used;
- markets for its products.

This way of using an MA grid is illustrated by the manufacturing company WC Louis described in Frame 9.1.

With what we already know about WC Louis, the raw materials they currently have to hand and the manufacturing processes they are equipped for, the first thing to do is to help them think of possible market segments that appeal to them and which they might be able to move into, say, household products and leisure. Next, we should think about the processing capabilities WC Louis possesses. Often, just listing the different processes involved in the manufacture of the products (drilling, cutting, shaping, painting, colouring, engraving, electro-plating, making ceramics, grp moulding, etc.) and representing all of them as subdivisions along a process axis is not too helpful. This often produces no go areas on our grid because some of these processes are specific to certain raw materials. For instance, one would not apply grp moulding technology to metals, electro-plate clay, or put a plastic item into a

Illustrative example: WC Louis Ltd —————————— *Frame 9.1* —

WC Louis manufactures and sells bathroom 'furniture', using 'wood' composites, clay, plastics, glass and some metals as raw materials. They have processing facilities for cutting, drilling and shaping metal, wood and glass; for applying decorative finishes (paint, colouring, engraving, electro-plating, etc.) in or on most of the raw materials they use, and for moulding of ceramic and plastic shapes including the production of glass-reinforced polyester (fibre-glass).

At present they have only one market, 'bathrooms', although this could be split down into builders' merchants, and retail D.I.Y. outlets. They are particularly interested in expanding their product range and diversifying into new market segments, but do not wish to invest a lot more of their funds in new manufacturing processes or stocks of new raw materials.

We have been asked to assist them in the task of thinking up some new ideas in products and markets.

kiln. It is also necessary here to rationalize the production processes to prevent a lot of 'repeat' cells containing the same ideas. For instance, products made from certain materials for certain markets will require drilling, cutting *and* shaping, and would thus occur in three cells. It is usually best to think of the processing capabilities of the organization in terms of generic areas of expertise. In the WC Louis example one area is applying decorative finishes. Another is moulding/curing. Drilling, cutting and shaping can be put together. Implied expertise can also be included; because of the products that they manufacture, WC Louis must know a fair amount about waterproofing and insulation.

We can now build a three-dimensional grid, with Raw Materials, Manufacturing Processes and Markets as the axes and fill in on this grid the extent of the company's current operations, as shown in Figure 9.3. The grid has been drawn differently this time, as three separate planes as opposed to a three-dimensional box: an easier arrangement to work with. There are a lot of open spaces on this grid which might contain opportunities for expansion and diversification. The main use of this variation of MA is to show companies how they can easily (minimum cost and disruption) and safely diversify. Initially, we examine the 'home' layer, the market that WC Louis knows best – bathrooms. Then move up to other layers, the markets identified earlier as possibly suitable for expansion into. Frame 9.2 contains some possibilities for new products.

These possibilities would have to be evaluated very carefully. WC Louis would need to perform a careful analysis of the present use of

Frame 9.2   WC Louis Ltd: Possibilities

Bathrooms

- WC Louis might apply their moulding/curing expertise to the production of aluminium replicas of Victorian cast iron baths.
- Their expertise in moulding and shaping glass products might allow production of smaller bathroom products, for example, soap dishes, toothbrush holders, splash backs and many household products as well.

Other markets

- With their supply of plastics materials and their existing grp production facilities they could allow a venture into the leisure industry, making surf boards, dinghies and canoes.
- They have the appropriate raw materials and processing facilities to make large ceramic items; perhaps they could move into smaller household items such as cups, plates or even 'old fashioned' jugs, wash basins, potties, etc., which are now very popular.
- Ceramics in the leisure industry – clay pigeons?
- Applying moulding techniques to wood laminates could open up possibilities in furniture production.
- Not really a household product in the usual sense, but they have the necessary expertise to manufacture gutters and drainpipes, etc. (this idea could be found in a number of cells, for example, moulding-plastic or decorative-plastic); I put it only in the cell where I first thought of the idea, because I wanted to leave the other cells blank to force me to think up additional ideas for them.
- A variation on the theme of No. 2; drilling/cutting clay might allow production of parsley pots and the like.
- Another possibility might be waterproof 'plastic' clothing, bags or enclosures generally for use in connection with water sports.

their production capacity, do some costing, and attempt to assess the likely share of the new markets they could realistically attain. In other words, they need to do a full feasibility study on the most promising ideas. After they have collected some of this data they may determine the most likely candidate for a new venture using the Grid Method (see Chapter 6, or the more sophisticated Kepner–Tregee Decision Analysis (see Chapter 10).

When considering moving into a new market, two questions should be asked: how familiar are we with the market; and can we exercise some control over it? For example, WC Louis is probably better off con-

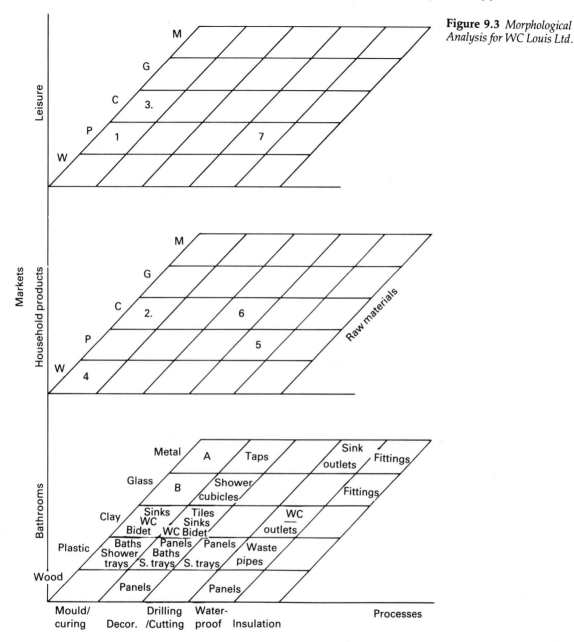

Figure 9.3 *Morphological Analysis for WC Louis Ltd.*

sidering Household Products than Leisure because the behaviour of the former is far more akin to their present market, the market for leisure products being highly seasonal and subject to rapid changes in fashion. They probably already have connections with distributors and retail outlets operating in the Household Products market. Only after investigating known territory that is currently not exploited, should areas further afield be looked at, first considering new materials, then new processes and avoiding materials and processes that are not understood. Clearly, a process similar to this can assist with the development of corporate strategy.

9.3   Morphological Forced Connections

We are now back to the search for new products. Although based on exactly the same principles, this variation (Allen, 1962; Koberg and Bagnall, 1974) on the use of morphology (the study of shape, form, pattern) does not have a cell on the grid for every combination of attribute subdivisions. Instead of each axis representing an attribute, all the attributes are represented on *only one* axis. The two-dimensional grid has the attributes written across the top columns and the ways these attributes can be accomplished written in the cells beneath. A combination is represented by a line linking a cell from each column. A grid set up to generate new ideas for a garden refuse carrier is shown in Frame 9.3.

It is important to specify the object of the search in generic terms. Using MA on a problem such as designing a new bed would lead to finding just a few 'cosmetic' attributes, like shape and construction material. These attributes would probably only enable you to identify some new styles of bed, although if we were really lucky we might come up with a minor improvement such as a three-legged bed. The reason for this general lack of success is that the fundamental bases of the objects concerned are not being questioned.

What we should do is define our problem as 'design a new item of furniture for sleeping/relaxing on'. This starting point would suggest far more significant attributes such as:

'method of bodily support'
(air, water, foam, springs, fabric, the structure itself)
'type of surrounding structure'
(rigid frame, folding frame, non-rigid free-standing, none, so that the 'method of bodily support' can be rolled up, etc.).

With these attributes and the cosmetic ones (shape and construction material) we should be able to come up with some really innovative ways of fulfilling the functions desired.

The fundamental attributes of a garden refuse carrier are how we fill and unload it, and the mechanism by which we transport the device from one place to another. If you immediately think of a wheelbarrow the way these things are done is taken for granted: if we start from a narrow description of what we are looking for in a new product we could well 'miss' important attributes. A list of attributes for a garden

To find a new form of garden refuse carrier ——————— *Frame 9.3* ——
by Morphological Forced Connections

Material	Shape	Method of filling	Means for transporting	Method of unloading
Plastic	Open box	Throw in at top	Carrying handle(s)	Tip-up one end
Polythene sheet	Flat bed	Suction	Wheels/rollers	Opening door
Metal	Cylinder	Scoop	Skids	Turn upside down
Wood	Envelope		Air cushion	Lever-operated ejection system
Ceramic	Inverted 'cone'		None	Lift (push) off
Glass				

refuse carrier and some suggested subdivisions of them can be found in Frame 9.3.

It is more difficult to progress through all the possible combinations but try. Once again, do not dismiss the apparently 'impossible' combinations too quickly. They can sometimes be very fruitful.

In this sort of grid it is often useful to build in the option of 'none' where this seems appropriate. We should be careful, however, not to use this 'none' option as a means of avoiding selecting from a certain column just because the combinations might give are difficult to do anything with. There is also a temptation to incorporate an 'other' category or subdivision in certain columns, just in case we think up some wonderful idea using a category we do not have half way through our analysis: a better ploy, under these circumstances, is simply to add this new category into the list and then deliberately try to make some more connections with it.

In frame 9.4 some existing garden refuse carriers are listed, with a couple of new ideas.

This variation of MA is intended for situations where we wish to consider more than three attributes. If we had had only two or three attributes for our 'garden refuse carrier', we could have drawn up our grid in exactly the same way as before.

─────── *Frame 9.4   Garden refuse carrier: existing products and new ideas* ───────

Existing products

Metal/Box/Throw in at top/Wheel/Tip up on one end = Wheelbarrow.

Plastic/Inverted frustrum/Throw in at top/Carrying handle/Turn up side down = Bucket.

Polythene sheet/Flat/Throw on to/None/Tip up one end = 'Grass mat' (a small groundsheet that you throw grass cuttings on to and which you then drag along the ground by two of its adjacent corners.)

Wood/Flat bed/Throw on to/Wheels/Lift (push) off = Wooden trolley (with skids instead of wheels, we have a sledge being put to good use in the Summer.)

Polythene sheet/Envelope/Throw in at top/None/Turn upside down = Dustbin bag

New ideas

Wood/Cylinder/Throw in at top/None/Turn upside down – I envisage something like a wooden barrel one of whose ends is removable. You stand the barrel upright on its 'fixed' end, throw stuff in it, and replace and fasten the removable end. Moving it is achieved by pushing it over on its side and rolling it to its destination, whereupon we undo the removable end and tip the whole thing upside down.

Plastic/Box/Suction/Air cushion/Opening door? – a converted hover mower, that can reverse its thrust to suck small bits of garden debris into some receptacle – a bit like a vacuum cleaner. It would then be pushed easily to its destination in normal hovercraft mode. I decided to settle for a mundane method of unloading – a door in the side of the receptacle, but perhaps we should think of trying to persuade the air to go in one of *three* different directions and get this device to blow its contents out in the right place.

9.4   Analysing problems using MA

Whilst we have used MA for idea generation when searching for new products and opportunities, it can also be used effectively for other stages in problem solving. MA can be especially useful when making initial attempts to analyse a problem situation – at those times when we are trying to find some structure in it, or to get some 'handles' on a mass of confusing data.

9.4.1   Selecting attributes

Probably the most difficult part of any form of MA is the finding and selection of the attributes (or the 'dimensions' of the problem, if we are employing it for problem analysis) that are to be represented by the axes of the grid, and the subdivisions (or components) that we need to break these down into. A good method for improving your ability to select attributes is to take a problem, select some attributes, *fail* (unintentionally) to get much out of the subsequent analysis, and then force yourself to do it again, this time remembering to:

- express the problem and/or the attributes in generic terms;
- use your imagination when choosing attributes – do not let yourself be constrained by images of existing products and services;
- ensure that your chosen attributes/subdivisions are independent – trying a few experimental grids should reveal if they are not.

Another idea (M. S. Allen, in Gundy (1988)) is to collect all the information we can relating to the problem without any consideration at all of its importance. Each bit of information is then written on a separate card and these are gathered together at random into groups of say 12. Study all the cards carefully, and then go and do something else for about 30 minutes. On returning to the cards regroup them in such a way that all the cards in a particular group are related in some way. Give a title to each group (a provisional attribute name) and write the titles on a different set of cards, each of which is placed with its appropriate group. Repeat this process, but this time working with the groups as units – in other words, group the groups rethinking the group titles. Try to end up with between four and seven final groups. With the attributes thus decided upon turn to the original cards associated with each of them, and rationalize these down to about seven subdivisions per group. All this can take a little time, but it can be a useful exercise, if we have no clear idea what our attributes and their subdivisions should be.

9.5   Concluding remarks on systematic searches

It is not just the ability to make inspired connections between apparently unrelated things that can lead to new ideas and profitable ventures. There are a number of known sources of opportunities, relatively mundane situations, which many of us tend to overlook or fail to realize the full potential of. Many a successful entrepreneur has been able to take advantage of such opportunities. It seems appropriate to finish this section with a list of these sources. If you are looking for a business opportunity, it is worth periodically going through this list systematically.

- What problems do other people have? Can you offer them a solution?
- Are there any changes in legislation imminent? How can you take advantage of them?
- Can you foresee any social changes, for example, crazes?
- What new technologies have recently been announced? Can you think of an application for any of them?

- Is it possible to copy and/or improve something that someone else is doing/making?
- Can you do anything with local raw materials and/or peoples' skills?
- Can you make something different from somebody else's 'sub-assemblies'?
- Can you do something with other people's waste materials?
- Does anybody require a particular service in your area?
- Can you capitalize on any gluts or scarcities?

The 'common-sense' (Rational) approach

In the late 50s and early 60s, Charles Kepner and Benjamin Tregoe studied examples of both good and bad management, looking for ways of thinking that could differentiate between them. They concluded that the best managers, or those considered by other managers to be 'the most effective and successful', used 'variations of four distinct routines or patterns of thinking, in handling problems and decisions' (1981, p. vii). In the first instance (1965) the Kepner–Tregoe approach to problem solving and decision making (KT); their philosophy of **rational management** was a set of guidelines on good thinking practices for managers, a 'leader's guide' for the team manager rather than advice for those working in a team. Whether you are managing others or not, many of these ideas offer useful guidance for **self-management** as well.

In *The New Rational Manager* (1981) they concede that teamwork is important in organizational effectiveness. Their view is that teamwork will improve if everyone has been trained in KT, because KT serves as a 'common language' providing a rational description of the cause of a problem or the outcome of a decision. There are no misunderstandings, no possibilities for bad communications, no 'moving goal posts'. There is, however, more to building an effective team than this; good communication is a necessary but not a sufficient condition. They also support the view that people are resistant to change and need to be 'sold' its advantages. They maintain that the introduction of KT, and the development of teamwork, is best encouraged and implemented in a 'top-down' fashion.

10.1 An overview of rational thinking

The four patterns of thinking identified by Kepner and Tregoe are exemplified by the following questions managers ask every day (Kepner and Tregoe, 1981, p. 20).

Frame 10.1 Four Patterns of Thinking (Kepner and Tregoe, 1981)

Situation Appraisal

- assessing and clarifying situations;
- sorting things out;
- breaking down complex situations into manageable components;
- achieving and maintaining control of events.

Problem Analysis
'Cause and effect' thinking:

> accurately identifying, describing, analysing and resolving a situation in which 'something has gone wrong without explanation'.

Decision Analysis
Making choices between courses of action:

- determination of the reasons for and purpose of making the decision;
- consideration of the available options;
- assessment of the relative risks of each option.

Potential Problem Analysis
Anticipating the future:

- what might be and what could happen;
- what problems might occur;
- what decisions will have to be made.

(Charles Kepner and Benjamin Tregoe, 1981, pp. 21–6)

- What's going on?
- Why did this happen?
- Which course of action should we take?
- What lies ahead?

These four patterns are called Situational Appraisal, Problem Analysis, Decision Analysis and Potential Problem Analysis and are summarized in Frame 10.1. We will look at each in turn.

10.2 Situation Appraisal

Situational Appraisal is being aware of what is going on around you, knowing what needs to be done in situations likely to occur, and being able to carry out effectively one or more of these tasks at a time. It is knowing when it is necessary to make a decision, have a problem solving session, prepare contingency plans, or just carry on 'looking around' to make sure we have not overlooked something which we should have seen as a concern. Kepner and Tregoe frequently refer to 'concerns' which they define as 'any situation that requires action and for which you have full or partial responsibility' (1981, p. 166). It is important not just to be able to handle problem situations as they occur, but actively to 'go out' looking for things that need to be done; *not* creating work for work's sake, but being proactive rather than reactive.

By adopting a proactive outlook, we tend to discover the opportunities that the reactive person seems not to have time to consider. We tend to detect problems when they are still quite easy to deal with, saving us time we can use for our Situation Appraisal. Situational Appraisal consists of continuously cycling through four separate but interrelated tasks, that help us evaluate our circumstances and select when and how to apply the rest of the KT process appropriately:

- recognizing concerns;
- separating concerns into manageable components;
- setting priorities;
- planning the resolution of our concerns.

These tasks are not necessarily sequential. We can seldom complete a whole circuit without back-tracking, because the situations that we have to deal with are invariably confused, multifaceted, overlapping and fragmentary.

10.2.1 Recognizing concerns

Kepner and Tregoe recommend a four-pronged attack to this task, not all of which needs to be accomplished at the same time.

- We can make a list of
  (a) all the situations that are not quite as we would like them to be, i.e. likely candidates for some problem solving;
  (b) situations we see as threatening to our well-being or that of the organization;
  (c) what we see as possible opportunities.
- We can compare our progress with existing activities to what we had previously planned. In doing this we may well discover items that we need to add to our list.
- We should do some forecasting – start planning ahead for the consequences of what we are working on at the moment: decisions which we will have to make, solutions that we will have to implement. And we should also be on the look-out for 'surprises'.
- Finally, we look for ways of improving the things we are currently doing and our methods for doing them, i.e. improving both the product and the process.

We should not expect these to be four separate tasks; they are inextricably interlinked, as reviewing our progress on one problem inevitably indicates previously unforeseen problems and opportunities. Creative thinking is vital to the effective execution of Situation Appraisal. Successful appraisal of any situation depends on sensitivity, serendipity and synergy (Parnes's three S's, see Chapter 4). It may also be that indulging in some Goal Wishing is not only a good means of exploring the situation, but also helps to ensure that we do not waste time resolving the wrong problem.

10.2.2   Separating concerns into manageable components

When performing this task, we must remember the dangers involved in attempting to restructure problem situations to make them more manageable. Things are seldom as simple as they first seem, and what appear to be totally disconnected phenomena are often related in some way. We should ask the following questions in order to discover if we should, and how best to, break a complicated situation into a number of smaller concerns we are capable of dealing with.

- Do we think one action will really resolve this concern?
- Are we talking about one thing or several things?
- Are we agreed as to the reason we are concerned about this?
- What evidence do we have that says this is a concern?
- What do we mean by . . . ?
- What is actually happenning in this situation? Anything else?
- What do we sense that tells us we must take action?
- What is there about the way we handled this situation that should be improved?
- What is really troubling us about this situation?

The asking of these questions in a group session can reveal that people within the group possess different viewpoints on, or information about, the situation under discussion. Done separately to any problem solving, this should lead to few complications, but we should keep in mind that others (Synectics, see Chapter 7) maintain that questioning can have undesirable effects. If such questioning does uncover a number of concerns where there was only thought to be one, we add these to our list of problems to be resolved.

10.2.3   Setting priorities

To decide in which order we should tackle our concerns we prioritize them on the basis of their seriousness (impact), their (time) urgency, and an estimate of their likely growth. This can be done by asking questions such as, 'What will be the consequences if we postpone consideration of a concern?', 'Will a problem get worse if we do not deal with it for a while?' The importance and hence the priority of a concern may be determined by any or all of these factors. Assessing the importance of an activity and assigning it an appropriate priority with as little subjectivity as possible, is a difficult process. The human mind is very good at justifying why we are doing something that we should not be doing. We all prefer activities that we enjoy to those we do not, and thus tend to give them a higher personal priority by inflating their importance, justifying doing them, and perhaps doing them *first*, no matter how important we *know* other activities to be.

If we discipline ourselves to assess the things we have to or want to do on the basis of their seriousness, urgency and probable growth, it makes it more difficult to attribute inappropriate priorities to them than if we assign an arbitrary degree of importance to them without considering these contributory factors. Once we have organized ourselves a little better so as to have more time for *all* our tasks, we can use the doing of the preferred (but less important) activities as a reward for accomplishing some of the less desirable (but important) activities.

We are still left with the problem of combining the seriousness, urgency and growth factors into an overall importance rating. This process has to remain fairly intuitive, in the sense that it cannot be prescribed for, each situation will need to be judged on its own merits. However, in many cases urgency will be contained in either seriousness or probable growth, seriousness often being the slightly more significant factor.

In all this we must guard against any tendency to procrastinate, whether caused by the daunting number of tasks piled up ahead of us, guilt, self-pity, or whatever. Get on with something, anything! Preferably the truly important tasks.

For an attempt at prioritization to be effective, it is essential to break a complex task down into its component activities; these activities, not the task, should be given a priority. This is because it is usually difficult to differentiate between the perceived inportance of the relatively few *major* tasks we are involved in. However, the component activities, once identified, will at any given moment in time have very different priorities from each other. Although we have already separated our concerns into manageable proportions, it is probably worth reviewing these in order to ensure that they could not usefully be considered as a series of even 'smaller' activities before we assign priorities.

This process of considering a major task or project as a series of component activities, together with the estimation of the likely time each activity will take and the determination of possible interdependencies of activities, is the basis of **Critical Path** or **Network Analysis**. This is a fundamental part of **Project Management**. There are several software packages available which produce (Gantt) charts that show how activities should be or are progressing with time, (network) diagrams that show interdependency, and tables that help us determine whether activities are time-critical or can be delayed without affecting the total project time. These packages can also help with the costing, resource allocation and monitoring of a project's implementation.

10.2.4   Planning how to resolve our concerns

Having determined and assigned priorities to our concerns, we must decide how to tackle them and what depth of treatment is appropriate. Do we need to make a decision, have a problem solving session, prepare contingency plans, or just make sure we have not overlooked something which we should have seen as a concern? The depth of treatment will depend on the circumstances. A decision may have to be made now, or we may at present only need to think about the criteria we will use to assess the options at a later stage. Do we need to call people together for a full problem solving session, or do we only need to schedule an uninterrupted hour to do some lone thinking about problem identification?

We need to plan what has to be done, think about who ought to be involved and determine how much of a particular process we need to perform. Situation Appraisal is an on-going activity, where we continuously check to see whether something needs to be done.

10.2.5   The effective use of time

An extremely helpful way of improving the handling of prioritization and planning in the Situation Appraisal cycle is to adopt one of the better-known **Time Management** philosophies, such as James Noon's (1985) 'Business Time/System' or that of 'Time Manager International'. Both systems have much to commend them, containing 'self-analysis' exercises and some truly useful guidelines on making the most of our time. Both are based upon the premise that many of us do not spend enough time on the things most important to us and our work – the high priority activities. Though their terminology varies, they suggest that we determine what is important to us by breaking key performance areas into key factors/tasks and then performance objectives/activities. They offer advice on how to plan that sufficient time is available for these activities, for running the time-management system and for dealing with the inevitable interruptions. As with setting priorities, considerable self-discipline is involved in both planning our time *and* protecting it for its intended purpose.

Business Time/System aims at improving the way managers organize their work by concentrating more attention on 'high priority' tasks. Extra time is made available by attempting to eliminate work stress, procrastination and other time wasters. It also offers advice on related issues, such as communications, leadership and delegation. Time Manager International, on the other hand, is intended to help us place some structure on the whole of our lives, not just the time we spend at work.

It encourages us to clarify our goals in life and helps to identify and plan the tasks and activities that we need to perform. By regaining control over our time, TMI believes, we are empowered to do more of those things that *we* want to do. These techniques could be seen as a method of regulating every second of your waking life, though I believe them to be ways of making life more satisfying and enjoyable. However, you do have to spend some time on them in order to appreciate their aims and set them up in a way that works for you.

Everyone can benefit from some form of time management 'system', even if it is only a 'Don't forget' list and a notebook to jot ideas down in.

10.3   Problem Analysis

Kepner and Tregoe believe that people at any level within an organization will not only accept problem solving tasks, but will actually seek out problem solving situations, so long as the following four conditions exist:

- They possess the appropriate problem solving skills needed.
- They experience success in using these skills.
- They are rewarded for successful problem solving.
- They have no reason to fear failure.

The converse of this is also true:

> People will avoid problem solving situations when they are unsure of how to solve their problems, when they do not experience success after trying to solve a problem, when they feel that their efforts are not appreciated, and when they sense that they have less to lose either by doing nothing or by shifting responsibility. (1981, p. 33)

Problem Analysis is a problem solving process which assumes that by a thorough and logical analysis of the problem situation we should be able to identify certain changes between before the problem existed and now, and from these deduce the cause of the problem. It is not sufficient to know all the things that could have caused the problem and then attempt to solve it by rectifying the most likely cause. This way of resolving problems can waste a lot of time and money, as many car repair bills confirm. This is connected with the tendency to assume that a given problem is so similar to a previous problem that the appropriate remedy must also be the same. This approach is particularly noticeable when it is important to get a quick solution. Problem Analysis can help us avoid these pitfalls.

10.3.1   Overview of Problem Analysis

Kepner and Tregoe believe (1981, pp. 36–7) that problem situations are typified by 'a deviation between expected and actual performance'

┌───┐
│ *Frame 10.2   Problem Analysis*
│
│   • Definition of the problem.
│   • Description of the problem in four dimensions:
│   **Identity** – what it is we are trying to explain;
│   **Location** – where the problem is observed;
│   **Timing** – when the problem happens;
│   **Magnitude** – how serious and widespread the problem is.
│   • Use of this key information to generate possible causes.
│   • Testing for the most probable cause.
│   • Verification of the true cause.
└───┘

and that problem solving consists of 'a search for a specific change' that has caused this decline in performance. Despite this tight definition of a problem, they believe that many different sorts of problem can be thought of in this way and that this strategy can be used to deal with both 'machine' and 'people' problems. An outline of the Problem Analysis process can be seen in Frame 10.2.

It may not always be necessary to complete every stage of the Problem Analysis process before a solution is found, nor always essential that the full analysis is written out. Shortened and/or 'informal' Problem Analyses are often necessitated by situations which lack sufficient information for a 'full' analysis. The one type of problem that does not seem to fit this description is the 'ever since we installed that new machine it has been totally useless' situation. Kepner and Tregoe refer to this as a different but similar type, that they call a 'Day 1' problem. We use the same process as with any other problem except that we compare the actual poor performance with what we believe should have happened instead of the performance observed before the problem was noticed. There are dangers in comparing present performance with some sort of ideal performance; we should guard against setting our expectations of what should have occurred too high, or too low.

Although Problem Analysis is normally thought of as an individual problem solving process, there is nothing preventing it from being employed by a team of people. It is absolutely essential for one problem solver to have technical expertise bearing directly on the problem content, but the team should include a member with no such technical expertise and they should lead the process questioning. This helps prevent the team getting bogged down in the technicalities of the problem situation and being blinded to the consideration of an unusual occurrence. Kepner and Tregoe encourage us in certain circumstances to speculate about possible causes of the problem situation.

Frame 10.3 gives a description of a problem at Lowlands Distilleries, which we will attempt to solve using Problem Analysis. Before we start

Illustrative example: Lowlands Distilleries Ltd ——— Frame 10.3 —

Lowlands Distilleries are makers of rye whisky, who occasionally perform commercial distillation for other companies in the food and drinks industry. One Monday morning, a couple of hours after the stills had been started up after the weekend break, a leak was reported in the main Still Room. This was the first problem with the stills for many months. A quantity of liquid, which after a cursory inspection was deemed to be mostly ethyl alcohol, had been found on the floor underneath the condenser.

From the diagram of the Still Room it can be seen that there are six stills altogether. Each still has a retort which is heated from below and into which the liquid to be distilled is pumped periodically. The temperature is carefully monitored to ensure that only the appropriate vapours are allowed to pass out from these retorts up and along a network of pipes (individual to each still) and through the condenser. From here the liquid whisky is piped to the collecting vat. The flow of water used in the condenser can be controlled by a valve on the exit pipe.

The maintenance crew check the vats, piping, etc. every Saturday morning, after operations shut down for the weekend. They check for leaks and rectify them once found and also examine the equipment thoroughly and carry out preventative maintenance. Last weekend, Robert Jones, who had joined the maintenance crew three weeks ago, had replaced a section of the piping on No. 2 still between the condenser and the collection vat because, he had reported, it was showing early signs of corrosion.

The No. 1 and No. 2 systems are considerably older than the others, being the first stills operational. The other four have been added sub-

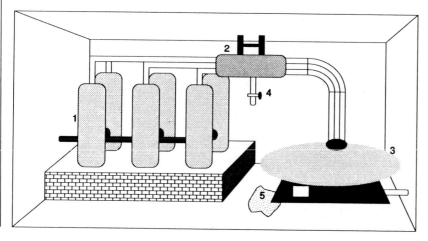

Key
1 Stills
2 Condenser
3 Collection vat
4 Cooling water
   control value
5 Spillage

sequently as demand for rye whisky has increased. The connectors joining the pipework used in these stills are of the 'compression' type. In the newer stills longer 'runs' of pipework have been used that precluded the need for these connectors. The maintenance crew have continued to use compression-type connectors on these old stills to make it easier to maintain and replace the ageing pipework when needed. A new batch of compression connectors had been delivered last month.

The spillage was cleaned up and the system carefully observed. After a close inspection of the pipework it was found that the leak appeared to originate from the vicinity of the replaced section of piping on No. 2 still. There was certainly liquid running down the outside of this pipe from the connector where it emerged from the condenser. This liquid was then running around the collection vat, and dripping off there on to the floor. The stills had continued to operate throughout Monday, with frequent mopping up operations.

The maintenance crew were asked to check the new pipework on No. 2 still on Monday evening. Robert Jones drew the short straw. Jones, still finding it inconceivable that anything he had done last week could been wrong, removed all the new piping and joints he had put in last week, and replaced them with more new items.

It is now Tuesday 11.00 a.m. The Still Room supervisor has just been called to the Still Room to inspect what appears to be a patch of liquid on the floor similar to that found yesterday.

analysing this problem situation, make a note of what you think is the cause of the leak.

10.3.2   Definition of the problem

The first step in Problem Analysis (PA) is to write up our 'Deviation Statement', a brief problem definition. Bearing in mind the warnings given in Chapters 4, 6, 7 and 12 about assuming that we know what the problem is, this may seem to be a retrogressive step. In Problem Analysis, however, describing the problem as a deviation (or decline) in performance from some norm or expectation is not quite the same as the problem definitions elsewhere in this book, as here we are merely attempting to describe a problem's symptoms. We will not hypothesize about what the problem is or its cause, until we have performed a careful analysis of the problem situation. This may be the best approach to a 'machine' type problem.

To ensure that we do not start from a position where we know what the problem is Kepner and Tregoe suggest we formulate the Deviation Statement as follows. Having written down something we ask whether

---

Lowlands Distilleries Ltd: Deviation Statement ——— *Frame 10.4* —

There is liquid running down the outside of the pipework on No. 2 still, apparently leaking from the new pipework.

Problem specifying questions ——————————— *Frame 10.5* —
(Kepner and Tregoe, 1981)

Identity
   What is the unit that is malfunctioning?
   What is the malfunction?
Location
   Where is the malfunction observed (geographically)?
   Where on the unit is the malfunction observed?
Timing
   When was the malfunction first observed?
   When has it been observed since?
   When in the operating cycle of the unit is the malfunction first observed?
Magnitude
   What is the extent of the problem?
   How many units are affected?
   How much of any one unit is affected?

---

we can give an explanation of the problem as currently stated, if so we can back up one stage at a time until we get to a Deviation Statement that we cannot explain.

In the example, the problem could have been defined as 'Distillation products found on the floor'. This is a problem for somebody as they have to keep cleaning it up, but a Deviation Statement worded this way is explainable: There are distillation products on the floor because distillation products are dripping off the side of the collection vat. Furthermore, distillation products are dripping off the side of the collection vat because there is a *leak* in the distillation apparatus up above and the leaking fluids are running down the pipework. This leak cannot presently be explained so this is where we start. We should phrase our deviation statement carefully and precisely, because all that follows is logically dependent on it.

10.3.3   Description of the problem in four dimensions

Kepner and Tregoe next recommend that we collate information about the problem in four 'dimensions': Identity, Location, Timing and Magni-

Table 10.1 *Problem Analysis for Lowlands Distilleries Ltd*

	Deviation Statement: Specifying Questions	Performance Deviation IS	COULD BE but IS NOT	DISTINCTIONS between what IS and IS NOT	CHANGES suggested by DISTINCTIONS
Identity	WHAT is the unit with the malfunction?	Still No. 2	Stills Nos. 1, 3–6	No. 1 repaired by Robert Jones	New and perhaps inexperienced maintenance engineer
	WHAT is the malfunction?	A leakage of distillation products	Water, incorrect distillation products	Distillation process, & condenser, OK	Nothing
Location	WHERE is the malfunction observed?	On the floor by collection vat	Elsewhere	Likely source of leak is above there?	Nothing
	WHERE on the unit is the malfunction observed?	The new pipework	Other pipework, condenser, collection vat	Replaced recently	New pipe and connectors
Timing	WHEN was the malfunction first observed	Late Monday morning	On the previous Friday and before	A maintenance check on Saturday	Nothing additional to above
	WHEN has it been observed since?	Continuously ever since	N/A	N/A	N/A
	WHEN in the operating cycle of the unit is the malfunction first observed?	Whenever the stills are operating	When stills are not operating	Pipe only contains distillation products when in operation	Nothing
Magnitude	WHAT is the EXTENT of the malfunction?	Half a litre/hour	More or less than this amount	Commensurate with badly fitting connectors	New batch of connectors last month
	HOW MANY units are affected?	Only still No. 2	Stills Nos. 1, 3–6	As 1 above	Nothing additional to the above
	HOW MUCH of any one unit is affected?	New pipework	Rest of pipework on Still No. 2	New connectors	As 8 above

Lowlands Distilleries Ltd: distinctive features ———— Frame 10.6

The distinctive feature about the fact that the leak is coming from the pipework of still No. 2 and not any of the others, is that the pipework on still No. 2 has been replaced recently. This in itself is nothing particularly unusual but it suggests a change; this is the first time that Robert Jones, a new maintenance engineer, has done a repair in the Still Room and perhaps his inexperience has caused the leak.

tude (see Frame 10.2). The method for determining this crucial information concerning the problem situation is probably the single most important contribution that Problem Analysis offers us with regard to the solution of machine problems. We elicit this information by determining the answers to ten questions which can be seen in Frame 10.5.

With the Lowlands Distilleries problem we would probably answer 'What is the unit that is malfunctioning?' with 'Still No. 2', and 'What is the malfunction?' with 'A leakage of distillation products'. The rest of the answers for the Lowlands Distilleries example are given in the Problem Analysis chart (Table 10.1). Complete the whole analysis yourself before looking at this.

Having gathered our information, we now look for a similar situation or machine that *could be* exhibiting the same symptoms but *is not*. This comparison allows us to reduce the number of possibilities and hence the size of the search area for our cause. For example, the leak appears to be coming from the pipework of still No. 2, but not stills Nos. 1, 3–6. You may notice that stills No. 1–2 are older than the rest, and link the problem to that. We have now established that still No. 1 is all right whereas still No. 2 is not, meaning that 'age', though perhaps a contributory factor, is not the significant cause of our problem. We need to look elsewhere, but have at least narrowed the field of possible causes by one.

10.3.4 Generating possible causes

After doing the above for as many of the answers to the Specifying Questions as we can, we look at our two sets of answers, those that say what, where, when and how the problem, or performance deviation, *is* and those that describe what, where, when and how the problem *could be* but *is not*, searching for any **distinctive feature** that may help us unearth changes that have taken place which might have caused the malfunction. We are beginning to look for possible causes. As we note these distinctive features we should also note any changes that occur then we go back through our distinctive features specifically looking for as many additional *changes* as we can.

Frame 10.7   *Lowlands Distilleries Ltd: possible causes*

There are two possible causes of our problem:

- Robert Smith's inexperience has led to him bungling the repair job on the pipework.
- There is something peculiar about the new batch of connectors that arrived recently.

When you have completed this analysis for all four 'dimensions' of the problem definition, compare your results with Table 10.1.

10.3.5   Testing for the most probable cause

Once we have determined some possible causes in the changes we have uncovered, we test whether they would give rise to *all* the symptoms (the answers to our problem specifying questions) that we noted. We do this by logical questioning of each symptom in the following manner:

If Robert Smith's inexperience is the cause of the problem then how does this explain *why* only still No. 2 was affected?
Because it was the only one he worked on.

We repeat this process for any other possible causes we have, eliminating some because they cannot account for all the symptoms. Both possible causes summarized in Frame 10.7 pass this test.

10.3.6   Verification of the most likely cause

We now need to verify the true cause of the performance deviation that constitutes our problem. If possible, an obvious method is to swap the offending article (or person) with the identical counterpart in a working system. We could get another maintenance engineer to replace the pipework on still No. 2 for the third time, or we might investigate whether Robert Smith did use one of the new connectors and if so determine what difference there was between these and the older variety.

In this example Robert Smith is absolved: the problem was later verified as due to the new connectors being made to metric specifications, whereas the older ones were imperial sizes. They were similar enough to be used as equivalents, but the slight discrepancy in sizes, coupled with the old pipework, led to the leak.

10.3.7   Problem Analysis and people problems

Though a good strategy for dealing with machine problems, Problem Analysis has been criticized since its introduction as not really suitable for dealing with people problems. Kepner and Tregoe (1981) have addressed this point, though whether they consider that all people problems can be expressed in terms of performance is not clear. They seem to use the term people problem synonymously with human performance problem and obviously still believe that Problem Analysis is an appropriate way of dealing with problem situations in which people are not doing what is expected of them. They do warn us to apply Problem Analysis differently with people problems: unlike machines, people have self-esteem, and identifying their shortcomings may not have positive results.

They also admit (1981, p. 186) that the cause of a person failing to perform as expected is usually rather more complex than with machines and that managing human performance problems by finding a 'reasonable adaptive action' to improve a problem situation, as opposed to solving the problems, is perhaps a more realistic expectation. This 'adaptive' action may not always be good enough, as it can misfire and hurt innocent bystanders if the cause is not thoroughly checked out before the adaptive action is taken. For human performance problems the specifying questions have been rephrased in less mechanistic terms and reduced from ten to six questions:

Identity
Who is the person (or group) about whose behaviour we are concerned?
What specifically is that behaviour?
Location
Where is the behaviour observed?
Timing
When did this behaviour first become apparent?
When since that time did we observe this behaviour?
Magnitude
What is the extent of the behaviour?

However, they remain to some extent immaterial, since you will either judge them as appropriate and acceptable or not. This places great importance on the verification process.

Kepner and Tregoe go on to suggest that often when the precise nature of a person's underperformance is specifically stated in the Deviation Statement, the cause is readily identified by all concerned as being a simple misunderstanding of what performance level was actually expected. Kepner and Tregoe also argue that the specifying questions give us real data, factual differences in circumstances, which are better than mere speculation in determining the causes of poor performance. The availability of this information during the testing and verification processes is what ultimately *protects* us from management building a case that supports a preconceived notion such as 'He's just an awkward. . . .!' by possibly providing contradictory evidence undermining such a preconceived notion.

It is also important when gathering information on the four dimensions of Problem Analysis that the things that people say, as well as the things they have or have not done, are recorded, no matter how distasteful to the manager or the organization these comments may be. These remarks will contain clues to the speaker's behaviour.

My main concern in using Problem Analysis on people problems is in starting with too precise a problem definition. Whilst it may be appropriate to start a machine problem with a statement such as 'There is liquid running down the outside of the pipework on No. 2 still', the Deviation Statement 'John Smith's attitude to his manager has been getting worse and worse over the past three months' does not seem so helpful. It suggests the possibility that a value judgement has been made and that the fault lies squarely with John Smith. It is the systematic and objective use of the specifying questions that is supposed to reveal the true cause of the problem, but this is not as reliable at rooting out real problems as the early stages of the Soft Systems approach (see Chapter 12) or Synectics' Goal Wishing. Both of these problem solving strategies have elaborate ways of ensuring we are solving or managing the right problem by forcing us to look at the situation from many viewpoints.

Whether or not human behaviour is basically rational, I question whether one person can reliably assess the rationality of another's behaviour. Attempting to deduce something logically from another person's behaviour is to me a very dubious enterprise.

Kepner and Tregoe believe that their technique is an objective process and conclude that the questions of Problem Analysis when asked with 'skill and courtesy . . . cannot help but improve matters for everyone concerned. . . . The important thing is to treat people fairly and honestly, making full use of all relevant information' pp. 206–7). However, Vincent Nolan (1989, p. 86) comments that, 'It does nothing to encourage (indeed, it tends actively to discourage) creative and imaginative thinking, and completely ignores the human factors which are such an important component of most "real world" problems.' Moreover, the actual use of Problem Analysis on people problems has often been associated with the worst aspects of Scientific Management, the principles of management advocated by F. W. Taylor and others at the beginning of this century, and which was still prevalent until relatively recently. This was mainly due to Problem Analysis' rational method and behaviourist connotations.

Comments such as 'Managing human performance problems calls for a compassionate, considerate approach' and, 'Few things hurt productivity more than having people think they have been dealt with unfairly, arbitrarily, or without the intention of understanding their views and positions' seems to suggest that perhaps we may have misjudged them by this association. But as David McHugh reminded me recently the use of Problem Analysis on people problems (i.e. most real world problems) *is* essentially Taylorist in effect, if not in intent also. Simply attaching a few Human Relations-style prescriptions as caveats does not change this, nor does it make it any more acceptable than other Taylorist practices. We are both by no means alone in having reservations about using Problem Analysis on people problems.

Kepner and Tregoe (1981) give many accounts of the application of Problem Analysis to a variety of both 'machine' and 'people' problem situations.

10.4   Decision Analysis

Kepner and Tregoe maintain (1981, p. 85) that good decisions depend on the *quality* of:

- our **definition** of the specific factors (criteria/objectives) that need to be satisfied by the chosen course of action;
- our **evaluation** of the available alternatives;
- our **understanding** of the consequences of these alternatives.

Their method of decision making is an extension of the common-sense approach that has been around for some while, and which is also the basis of the simpler Grid Method used in Chapter 6.

Many people believe that decision making is not a problematic process, and that decisions are simply a choice between several alternative courses of action, one of which may be to do nothing. In taking this stance we have to assume that we have a sufficient number of alternatives of an appropriate quality. It is difficult to define these terms precisely, other than to say that if they are not met then the decision may be difficult to make. The first problem with decision making is the acquisition of these alternatives in the first place. The only real guidance that can be given about this is that the problem solving session that generates them must be carried out to the best of our abilities.

Having decided what the decision is that we must make, we must select the criteria which will be the basis for our choice, the factors which we feel we must consider in assessing the relative merits of the alternatives. These will consist of the objectives we believe to be important to our overall aim (the purpose of the decision) and which need to be satisfied by the chosen course of action. This selection of criteria can also be a problem in its own right.

The Decision Analysis process involves six steps (see Frame 10.8), and the two 'problem solving' stages, namely the selection of the criteria and the generation of alternatives, are thought to be part of this whole process. Whether the problem solving is done chronologically within the

---

Frame 10.8   The Decision Analysis process

- Decision Statement.
- Establish objectives.
- Classify objectives into MUSTS and WANTS.
- Generate alternatives.
- Evaluate alternatives.
- Compare and choose

. . . balancing alternatives with potential risks.

---

sequence shown or beforehand is immaterial, what is important is that we recognize the existence of these problem solving stages and do not attempt to mix the evaluation stage with the determination of the alternatives and criteria. Failure to do this usually results in thinking and meetings that go round in circles.

It can be argued that decision making in meetings or groups will generally be inferior to individual decision making. Conversely it is argued in Chapter 6 that if a group can argue its way to a consensus opinion, the resulting decision is often better than either a decision based on an average of individual opinions (such as can be obtained by voting) or that from any one individual.

Harold J. Leavitt (1978) believes that the factors which can make a group decision better are:

- the group can bring more information to the decision making process,
- the group is able to analyse the information critically and with more 'objectivity', and
- a strong commitment to the group and its success develops amongst its members.

If an individual can obtain all the information needed, is capable of processing it, and the quality of a decision is important, Leavitt says that individual decision making may be the best means of proceeding. However, if commitment to the decision is the over-riding issue, a group decision is essential.

Before we look in detail at Decision Analysis, it is worth pointing out that the term is used not only in this context, but also to describe a branch of mathematics that deals with uncertainty. It is now also gaining popularity as a means of describing a genre of computer software packages that assist in the process about to be described.

10.4.1   The Decision Statement

The first step is to state the decision we intend to make: the type or kind of action we intend to take and the results we are hoping for. Once again the wording of the Decision Statement must be considered carefully as the rest of the process derives from it. In particular we should include guidance on the level at which the decision is to be made, otherwise we may not compare like with like and our decision analysis will be impaired. An example of the level at which the decision is to be made can be illustrated by supposing we wanted to make a decision on 'How to improve our company image'. Some alternatives that spring to mind are:

- Redesign the company logo.
- Change the company name.
- Improve the presentation of correspondence, catalogues, lists, etc.
- Conduct a nationwide 'Lifestyle' TV advertising campaign.
- Move the company's office to a better district.
- Acquire some prestigious brands.
- Sell off all our diversified subsidiaries so that we can concentrate/ specialize in one area.

This is deliberately a disparate and incomparable list of alternatives. The budget required to implement all but the last of these alternatives varies from a few thousand pounds, up to perhaps tens or hundreds of millions of pounds. We need to impose some limitation on the range of alternatives that should receive our consideration. This is what must be included in our Decision Statement. We could impose these limits later on when declaring which features our alternatives must have, but by then we would have wasted time arguing over which criteria we should use for assessment, because of the difficulty of selecting criteria that can operate effectively across such a diverse range of options. The last alternative might actually be a cost saver in the long run, releasing funds for other expensive options such as a TV advertising campaign.

The details of the process of Decision Analysis will be shown by using an illustrative example concerning a fictitious magazine *Life's Alternatives*. The decision situation we have is described in Frame 10.9.

10.4.2   Selection and classification of objectives

The next couple of steps involve the selection of the objectives or criteria we are going to use to compare and evaluate our alternatives, and the classification of them into MUSTS and WANTS. MUST objectives are mandatory, that is, alternatives must meet this requirement. We use our MUSTS to make the initial screening of our alternatives – those not satisfying the MUST criteria are rejected. In order to perform in this way a MUST criterion must be measurable; even a very important item may have to be used as a WANT criterion because it is not measurable. For example, a very important characteristic in a new employee might be

Frame 10.9   Illustrative example: Life's Alternatives

Life's Alternatives is a monthly magazine of interest to such people as organic farmers and fruit and vegetable growers, smallholders and private individuals who feel that there are better and healthier ways of producing food and living our lives than the predominant methods and lifestyle current today.

Life's Alternatives, currently only available by subscription, at the moment has some 50 000 subscribers. The cost of subscription, now £20 per annum, has had to increase several times recently to keep up with printing costs. The publishers of *Life's Alternatives*, GIP – a non-profit making organization, will shortly be faced once more with the need to generate additional income if the publication is to continue to exist. However, they fear that raising the subscription again, despite the upsurge in interest in 'Green' issues, will not necessarily yield the needed increase in revenue if the number of renewed subscriptions falls as a result.

The magazine currently survives because it receives good and informative articles, from well-known people in the field, at little or no cost. Most of the contributors write for the magazine either because of their belief in, and commitment to, its aims, or because they believe that they will personally benefit from their contributions to the magazine in other walks of life.

The publishers are pleased by the reputation the magazine has acquired for the quality of its articles and its independence of viewpoint. *Life's Alternatives* does not carry any advertising.

GIP believe that the alternatives open to them are:

- Increase the subscription by 10 per cent.
- Cease to be subscription – only and 'go public' – this will entail accepting as much advertising copy as they can get.
- Seek sponsorship from government or private agencies.
- Accept limited (and selected) advertising to 'top up' the existing subscription revenue.

All but the first of these alternatives are seen as potentially compromising of editorial independence. Another fear is that a more commercial orientation might at best encourage the present contributors to seek payment for their articles, and at worst, the possibility of editorial interference from sponsors or advertisers may cause some of them to decide they no longer want to be associated with the magazine.

Decision Statement

Select a method for generating an additional £100 000 revenue p.a.

Life's Alternatives: weighting of objectives ——————— Frame 10.10 ———

MUST
  produce an additional £100 000 revenue p.a.

WANTS	Weight
little effect on editorial independence	5
unlikely to 'offend' contributors	5
increased circulation	4
even more revenue	2
retain non-profit making status	1

'being a good team member', but measuring this is difficult (and subjective) and so it cannot be used to select alternatives for further consideration. We would need to use something like 'minimum qualifications' or 'years of experience', although these too are not always a good guide.

WANT objectives are the features that we would like each alternative to possess, and which we can use to distinguish between the relative merits of the alternatives. It is quite reasonable for a criterion to be both a MUST and a WANT. For example, in our recruitment example above, we could insist that a potential employee has, say, five years' experience in the business, and use the number of years over and above that as a means of differentiating between applicants.

If the criteria are being chosen by a group of people we should be watchful that the final choice of criteria does not favour one particular viewpoint.

The final task at this stage is to determine the relative importance of the WANTS criteria and allocate them a weight accordingly. For example, 'editorial independence' may be seen by the publishers of Life's Alternatives to be of paramount importance, deserving a maximum weighting of 5, whereas bringing in additional revenue over the necessary £100,000 would be nice, but of less importance, perhaps deserving a weighting of 2. Kepner and Tregoe, although saying that the precise values we use for weighting and scoring are immaterial, always use 1–10 for both weights and scores. I often find this too 'wide' a range and it exaggerates the differences in merit between the alternatives. I generally use 1–5. Let us suppose that the objectives (MUSTS and WANTS criteria) for the Life's Alternatives decision and the weightings they have been given are as shown in Frame 10.10.

We should never look upon WANTS criteria as of secondary importance, as they are used for a different purpose, namely, to differentiate and decide between the alternatives selected by the MUSTS criteria. In summary, it is the MUSTS that decide who plays the game, but the WANTS that decide who wins. Appendix 4 gives decision alternatives which might be appropriate for part of the Northcliffe Sands case in Chapter 7.

10.4.3   Generating and evaluating alternatives

If we find that one of our 'promising' alternatives is unable to give us all the MUSTS that we want, we should reject it. If we are reluctant to do this it suggests we need to review our MUSTS criteria (and perhaps the WANTS as well) to see whether we have chosen the best criteria, given the purpose of the decision. It is often useful if this does happen, because it causes us to think again about our assessment criteria. You have to feel right about a criterion if you are going to use it to reject a favoured alternative, and this element of doubt invariably sharpens our choice of MUSTS and WANTS. This does not mean that we can or should amend the criteria so that they give the decision we think we want, just that the surprise of seeing a favoured alternative facing rejection concentrates the mind on our choice of criteria.

The first alternative in our *Life's Alternatives* decision – increase subscriptions by 10 per cent – might fail to meet the MUST criteria if a drop in subscriptions subsequently occurs, however I have 'kept it in' for the moment since we will deal with that eventuality when we come to discuss the consequences of the various alternatives.

After we have checked that our alternatives meet the MUSTS requirement we assess how each of them satisfies the WANTS criteria, awarding a score of 0–5. The scores are given as follows: Alternative X satisfies the objective – totally 5, very well 4, by more than half way 3, some 2, only a little 1, not at all 0.

For each alternative we multiply the score it obtains on a certain criterion by the weight we have given to this criterion, and then we sum these products to obtain a total (see Frame 10.11). The alternative with the highest total score will be our tentative decision. It is useful to record comments by the scores so that the rationality of the score is obvious

───── *Frame 10.11* *Life's Alternatives: evaluating the alternatives* ─────

Decision Statement

Select a method for generating an additional £100 000 revenue p.a.

Alternative
Increase subscriptions by 10 per cent

	Weight	Score	Weighted score
MUSTS			
produce an additional £100 000 revenue p.a.		Yes, if no fall off in subs.	

WANTS

WANTS				
little effect on editorial independence	5	No effect	5	$5 \times 5 = 25$
unlikely to 'offend' contributors	5	No change	5	$5 \times 5 = 25$
increased circulation	4	The opposite possibly	0	$4 \times 0 = 0$
even more revenue	2	None	0	$2 \times 0 = 0$
retain non-profit making status	1	Yes	5	$1 \times 5 = 5$
		Total		55

Evaluating the other alternatives in the same way produces the following scores:

'Go public'

	Score	Weighted score	
Considerable – readers 'dictate'	1	5	
Half the contributors will leave	1	5	
Could be considerable increase in circulation	5	20	
Could be considerably more revenue	5	10	10
Not viable	0	0	
		40	40

Sponsorship

	Score	Weighted score
Possibly a little	4	20
Fairly acceptable to most contributors	4	20
Not much, if any	1	4
A possibility	1	2
Would need to probably	5	5
		51

'Top up' advertising

	Score	Weighted score
Inevitably some	3	15
It would depend on who the advertisers were	2	10
Not much	2	8
Some extra revenue	2	4
Doubtful if this is possible	2	2
		39

Frame 10.12   Life's Alternatives: the final decision

In our *Life's Alternatives* example, 'going public' might have been seen as having a high risk of seriously compromising both editorial independence and financial security, had it scored higher. As it is, 'increase subscriptions by 10 per cent' may be thought of as having at least a medium risk of causing a 'fall off' in subscriptions (and hence failing to increase revenue), and may thus be rejected in favour of 'sponsorship'. This latter may only give a low risk of frightening away contributors, which is not considered quite so adverse as the possibility of having to close down the magazine due to additional funds from subscriptions not being forthcoming.

---

and can be appreciated by others. This is particularly so if the decision has to be justified to a third party, not involved in the decision making, at a later date.

We should be wary of scores which are all high or all low. The former indicates the possibility of unrealistic expectations for our alternatives or that we have chosen undemanding and perhaps inappropriate objectives. The latter may suggest that we have included unimportant details amongst our criteria. We should also be cautious about an alternative that stands out above all the rest as this could indicate that the criteria have been (unconsciously?) rigged to favour this alternative.

10.4.4   Comparing and choosing our alternative

When we have reached this tentative decision, we should vent our most destructive, negative and pessimistic thoughts and feelings about each of the alternatives in turn, starting with the best. We need to determine the **adverse consequences** of the choices and rate them according to both the **probability** of them occurring and the **seriousness** of the consequences if they do. Kepner and Tregoe recommend (1981, p. 100) asking at least the following four questions in our attempt to discover the potentially unpleasant consequences of the alternatives:

- What are its requirements for success?
- What factors could harm its acceptance or implementation?
- What kind of changes (both inside and outside of the organization) could harm its long-term success?
- What kinds of things tend to cause problems in implementing this type of decision?

It is possible that the highest ranking alternative on the previous analysis could be rejected at this stage in favour of another, because it has a high risk of incurring serious adverse consequences, whereas another option does not (Frame 10.12).

10.4.5   Are all decisions the same?

Kepner and Tregoe identify several types of decision in their accounts of the use of Decision Analysis. I believe these to be variations on only two themes. First is the type where there *are* several alternatives to compare and where the process described above is eminently suitable. When such a decision is complicated by the amount of detail known about the alternatives and the number of criteria involved, it is usually beneficial and easier to compare each alternative with an 'ideal' alternative rather than with each other.

The second type is where only one alternative is under discussion, such as making a decision whether to do something or not, to change something or leave it alone, or deciding whether one alternative is good enough. If suitable criteria can be found to permit an objective comparison between doing something or not then we can proceed in the normal fashion, with just these alternatives. The danger exists that the criteria may be stacked against one of these options; indeed the usual approach adopted is that of simply criticizing the 'do' option. The other way of proceeding here, particularly when no viable alternative is available for comparison, and it is agreed that change is necessary, is again to compare our one alternative with an ideal course of action. With this procedure we must beware of not making our ideal too difficult or too easy to attain.

Finally, Kepner and Tregoe include a 'How to find the best way of doing . . .' type of decision, in which there are no alternatives presently available for consideration, not even an ideal one. In this situation they advise using creativity to generate a number of alternatives, something very like a Creative Problem Solving session, culminating in a 'Grid Method' assessment of the generated alternatives.

10.4.6   Some final words on decisions

When the Decision Analysis is complete we should have the best decision that we could make based on the criteria chosen; what we might call the most rational decision. Sometimes the outcome may be a surprise to us; on rare occasions we may not like it. If we feel strongly that the decision given is wrong we need to reassess the situation totally. We need to think again about the purpose of our decision making and the best criteria for assessing the various courses of action we could take.

Decision Analysis can contain a learning element as far as decision makers are concerned. Whilst we should not manipulate the criteria to give the decision we desire, quite often the criteria may need some fine tuning. If done with integrity, some adjustment of the criteria may be considered to be a normal part of clarifying objectives. If we are still unhappy with a decision, it is likely that our list of alternative courses of action is lacking in quantity and/or quality. All this assumes that we are rational beings, I for one have made irrational decisions that I have never once regretted!

10.4.7   Decision Analysis computer software

A few years ago half a dozen software packages for IBM PC compatibles which claimed to assist in the evaluation stages of Decision Analysis came on to the market. They did not claim to make decisions for us, unlike some Expert Systems, but simply to provide tools to help with our decision making. After being given a description of alternative courses of action, the selection criteria and their relative weighting, the main function of these packages was to take the user through the process of scoring each alternative against the criteria, and then calculate the 'best' alternative on that basis. Apart from the benefits of speed and accuracy, another advantage of using a computer for this is that we can play 'What if' games with our decision quickly and easily. For instance, we can see whether our best choice is affected by a different weighting of our criteria, allowing us to assess the validity of our decision under different circumstances.

Three packages offered other useful individual features:

- Assistance with the selection of criteria, achieved by presenting back a randomly selected subset of the alternatives entered (usually three at a time) and asking whether any difference (a potential criterion) could be identified between any one and the other two, and at the same time checking against the possibility of two differently named criteria apparently identifying the same thing.
- The ability to incorporate several people's weightings for the chosen criteria and to produce an 'average' group weighting of the criteria, or alternatively to indicate clashes of opinion between group members, and to accept the same people's individual scores for the alternatives and merge these into a group decision showing the degree of consensus attained.
- The ability to enter sub-criteria and sub-sub-criteria, using an indexed 'thought outliner' facility which can also detect 'duplicate' entries occurring at different levels. This can help us sort out our various proposed criteria, allowing us to check for any overlap or any major difference in level (importance), particularly with more complex decision situations.

Other minor features typically offered were friendly user interfaces, and the ability to edit the results of the decision analysis, adding titles, etc., before the final report is printed out. While little is heard of these packages at present, they may well return to prominence again in the near future as part of some new 'personal productivity' software package.

┌─Potential Problem Analysis ─────────────── Frame 10.13 ─

- Identify the vulnerable areas.
- Identify the specific potential problems within these areas, whose negative potential is sufficient that it merits taking action now.
- Identify the likely causes of these potential problems and any preventative action that can be taken.
- Identify any contingent actions that can be taken if either preventative action is not possible or if it fails.

10.5   Potential Problem Analysis

> Change is what life is all about. Success and survival depend on being able to anticipate change, and to avoid being swallowed up by its negative effects (Kepner and Tregoe, 1981, p. 141)

The fourth pattern of thinking employed by the effective manager can be described as trying to determine what might conceivably go wrong with the implementation of a problem solution or decision, and preparing contingency plans against these possible occurrences. This deliberate planning for successful implementation is something that many of us neglect.

Kepner and Tregoe (1981, pp. 139–141) describe Potential Problem Analysis (PPA) as a systematic process for uncovering and dealing with potential problems that are reasonably likely to occur and therefore worthy of attention. They believe that this process remains fundamentally 'an individual activity, whose results are guided primarily by individual motivation and concern' (1981, p. 139), but once again, as with Problem and Decision Analysis, we will benefit collectively from using a common methodology. The basic questions we must ask are: What could go wrong? What can we do about it *now*?

There are four stages in the PPA process, as shown in Frame 10.13, but they are not necessarily sequential. Preventative action is designed to remove completely or partially the likely cause of a potential problem. Contingent action is intended to reduce the impact of such a potential problem, particularly if it cannot be prevented.

When deciding what actions can be taken, we must weigh up the cost (not just in financial terms) of performing them, against the cost of the potential disaster they are helping us to avoid.

What these vulnerable areas are likely to be, and how we recognize them, will of course vary from one situation to another. Kepner and Tregoe suggest two approaches to determining the vulnerable areas. One is to rely on our experience of similar situations and our common sense, which is fine as long as it is not a totally new situation. We could try individually to Brainstorm all the things that could go wrong and then identify those having the most potentially serious consequences; this is really wrapping two steps together. The second way involves carefully going through the implementation of our solution chronologically, listing all the things that must be done from start to finish. As we do this, potential problems should become obvious. Some common potential problems listed by Kepner and Tregoe (1981, p. 145) are:

- anything that has not been done before;
- overlapping responsibilities – 'I thought Joe was handling that one';
- tight deadlines;
- any activities that have to be carried out, or coordinated from, a long distance away;

to which I would add:

- anything involving machines (particularly computers);
- interdependent activities; and
- acts of Nature, God, etc.

Having identified the vulnerable areas, we need to look within these for specific potential problems.

To provide an example to illustrate PPA, let us suppose we have decided that we will hold an exhibition of products and services connected with the application of information technology in business. How would we use Potential Problem Analysis to ensure that we minimize the risk of anything going wrong with the holding of our exhibition?

The best way of determining possible vulnerable areas would be to gather together the people concerned with the organization of the exhibition (plus, if possible, potential exhibitors and visitors) and Brainstorm all the things that could go wrong. We were told first to look for the main vulnerable areas, and then look for specific problems within these areas. The Brainstorming group leader should consider possible vulnerable areas, to ensure that the group addresses all of these areas. However, group members can go in directly at the specific potential problem level, it being difficult to keep a Brainstorming group at only one 'level' anyway. After the Brainstorming session the problems can be grouped into main vulnerable areas if so wished. For instance problems referring to power cuts, lack of plugs, fuses, power points, etc. can be considered together under 'facilities'. Frame 10.14 gives some possible responses that we might get in such a session. They are grouped under some possible categories of vulnerable areas, after they were generated.

Once we have established *what* might go wrong, we need to consider the *where*, *when* and the *extent* of these specific potential problems. This should indicate their likely causes and help us decide what can be done about them. For example, traffic problems are only likely to occur at the start and end of the exhibition and in the near vicinity. The forecasted

Illustrative example: The Great B.I.T. Exhibition ——— *Frame 10.14* ———

What can go wrong?

People related:
- no visitors turn up;
- too many people turn up;
- difficulty finding the venue;
- traffic jam outside the venue;
- minor accidents;
- illness of visitors/exhibitors;
- food poisoning;
- other emergencies;
- fire.

Administration:
- tickets printed wrongly;
- wrong date advertised/printed on ticket;
- planned media coverage fails to appear;
- another popular event held on the same day;
- lose money.

Facilities:
- milk for refreshments goes off;
- bar/caterers do not turn up;
- public address system fails;
- no spare plugs/fuses;
- inadequate power/lighting;
- major power cut;
- inadequate food/refreshments;
- not enough parking space;
- toilet blockage.

Activities:
- exhibitors do not turn up;
- exhibitors cannot get access to the venue to set up their stands;
- guest of honour/speakers do not turn up;
- not enough exhibition space.

Anti-social behaviour:
- everyone gets drunk;
- theft of exhibits before exhibition opens;
- theft of exhibits during exhibition;
- vandalism;
- political demonstration;
- civil riot;
- bomb scare;
- World War III.

Natural disasters
- weather-related problems;
- earthquake, storm, flood;
- Act of God.

attendance suggests that we may get a tail-back in either direction perhaps a couple of miles long (worse for those turning right into the exhibition site), which will take some half an hour to an hour to clear. The cause is obvious – volume of traffic – but things could be considerably worsened if our jam coincides with the normal rush hour traffic.

A major power cut could happen at any time. It could be an internal fault due to overloading circuits with all this extra equipment, or it could be due to external influences. In this latter case, it is likely to be coincidental with a thunderstorm, hurricane, or heavy snow fall. So perhaps we should consult a local weather forecast. Another potential problem is people not turning up; the cause might be wrong dates or an ambiguous venue printed on the tickets or in the advertisements, or possibly a rival event.

10.5.1   Likelihood and seriousness of potential problems

As well as specifying their details, looking for causes and starting to think what can be done about them, we need to consider both the seriousness of the potential problem and its likelihood. The traffic jam is very likely, but not necessarily serious; a prolonged power cut at *certain* times of the year is unlikely, but could be devastating at an exhibition of information technology.

We might ignore fairly trivial potential problems, unless they were extremely likely, in which case we might want to guard against them being the last straw, particularly if they are easy to prevent. The traffic jam does not quite fit into this category, because people can find them very annoying, even if they expect them. The simple expedients of starting the exhibition at say 9.30 or 10.00 a.m. after the rush hour and informing the police so that they can assign extra men to traffic duty are *preventative* actions worth considering. It may also be viable to open up another entrance to the site. The only preventative action against the unlikely occurrence of a power cut would be to hire a heavy duty mobile generator. We need to weigh up the cost in time and money of taking preventative action against the likelihood and seriousness of the potential problem.

The potential problem of people not turning up could be equally disastrous, but it is easy for us to double-check the dates and venue on the tickets and advertisements before they are released. We should also try to ensure there is no other event being held on the same day which is likely to detract from our possible attendance.

Regarding the seriousness of repercussions, we should not just consider the *direct* significance of a problem, because it is usually possible to obtain insurance against weather, theft, financial losses, etc. People who attend events of this kind tend to remember the minor things. They may be prepared to accept that their favourite beer is not available at the bar, but inadequate toilet facilities is another matter. Such things contribute to the quality of service experienced by our customers.

10.5.2   Can we realistically do anything about it?

If unable to prevent a potential problem we need to develop contingency plans to alleviate its possible effects. For the potential power cut problem, if it is impractical to have a second full source of mains power, we should at least ensure that the emergency lighting works, and perhaps borrow two or three generators to provide enough extra light to examine key exhibits, to power essential computers, slide or overhead projectors and the public address system, so that our main lectures and presentations could carry on as planned.

There will be some potential problems we can realistically do little or nothing about. For example, precluding the disruption of the event due to a bomb scare, except that presumably we have evacuation arrangements planned in case of a fire, or the possibility of food poisoning, apart from ensuring that we are using competent caterers, and that we have an ambulance crew standing by anyway to take care of any minor health/accident problems. It is very difficult to know where to draw the line.

One final piece of advice is to be alert for the little everyday things, which we often take for granted, but which might have serious consequences. For example, suppose a regular fire alarm test was planned for the day of our exhibition, and we had overlooked this common occurrence. Our visitors would hear it as a genuine fire alarm, and unless we could get to the public address system quickly and announce that this was only a practice, our carefully planned exhibition could degenerate very quickly into a situation of total disruption and panic.

10.5.3   The 'mechanics' of PPA

I have now described all the stages of PPA and if you are left with the feeling that these were not as clear cut as with Decision Analysis and Problem Analysis, it is because they are not. It is therefore a good idea to commit your PPA to paper as it develops. Starting with a brief 'Action Plan Statement' of what you are planning to implement, we need a document that also indicates to anyone concerned how far we have progressed in the investigation and in forestalling any potential problems. I envisage a large sheet with classified specific potential problems listed down the side, and headings across the top as follows: Likelihood, Seriousness, Can we realistically do anything?, Preventative actions, Person responsible for carrying them out?, By what date?, Other people that need to be informed, Contingent actions, Effectiveness, 'Trigger' mechanism, Other comments. If this were implemented on a computer we would be able to sort potential problems by likelihood, seriousness or person responsible.

In this document we should also have an account of the procedures for triggering our various contingency plans – who is responsible for initiating it, and under what conditions should plan A, B or C be brought into play, etc. These plans should be widely publicized among the organizing team.

10.5.4   Concluding comments on PPA

To be effective at PPA, as with anything else, we must be motivated to do it. You have to *want* the thing you are planning to be a success, and even then you may not always win. A half-hearted attempt gives no more than a false sense of security. I conclude by offering two well-known sayings, just in case I have not convinced you of the need for good PPA. Remember:

> What ever can go wrong, will go wrong, but not only that, it will do so in the worst possible way at the most inconvenient time.

> The more complex a system is, the more likely it is to go wrong.

Kepner and Tregoe (1981, p. 161): 'PPA is not a negative search for trouble. It is a positive search for ways to avoid or lessen trouble that is likely to come in the future.' They maintain, not without justification, that PPA is a most rewarding experience.

10.6   The KT approach: Conclusions

Kepner and Tregoe intended their approach to be a complete system of rational thinking that would help managers become more effective problem solvers and decision makers. Whatever the disputes over whether or not this is the case, to gain any benefit from the process, it must be applied systematically. Because of the 'rigidity' associated with the idea of a systematic and logical method for doing anything, the implementation of a KT approach could be criticized as inflexible. It need not be. More significantly, the approach's systematic nature could make it vulnerable to external pressures, such as constraints on time, lack of information, availability of support staff, distractions, disruptions and crises, not to mention the effects of intra-organizational politics. If we are planning to use the KT approach (or any part of it) we need to be aware of these things.

To an extent, the process should be 'self-correcting' in regard to some of these pressures. Situation Appraisal involves a trouble-shooting element and, indirectly, time management considerations aimed at providing extra time for operating the approach or dealing with the inevitable disruptions. Potential Problem Analysis is also intended to help us minimize the number of unexpected events and crises that might happen.

The claimed benefits of the approach are that we will feel 'secure in knowing that all necessary questions are being asked, all critical information considered, and all bases covered', and that from this condition of security we will be free 'to work imaginatively and creatively in pursuit of the resolution, choice, or plan that is not only safe and correct, but perhaps unusual or outstanding as well' (Kepner and Tregoe, 1981). Whether or not these claims are valid, the external pressures mentioned above have the potential for wrecking any such sense of security.

For this reason Kepner and Tregoe seem to prefer the adoption of their approach on a 'top-down', *organization-wide* basis rather than by individuals within the organization. However we need to remind ourselves here of the view that while solutions to problems are rational, the process of finding them is not. In any quest to develop our problem solving, communications and teamworking skills, we have to look some way beyond the KT approach. It is not a total problem solving/decision making package, and as a method for managing others, I have severe reservations about it. However, there is still much to commend in the KT approach if it is viewed as a 'bundle' of practical common-sense advice intended to improve our self-management skills and the way we organize our own individual tasks.

11 A system by any other name

This chapter essentially supports the explanation of the systemic approach to problem solving that we shall look at in Chapter 12. Although we are now about to look at problem situations as systems, we should not forget the importance of creativity in *any* problem solving situation. 'Since creative thought is the most important thing that makes people different from monkeys, it should be treated as a commodity more precious than gold and preserved with great care' (Hall, 1962).

The first objective of this chapter is to introduce some basic systems ideas, the understanding of which will be assumed in the next chapter. Secondly, through a critical evaluation of 'traditional' (or 'hard') systems thinking as a problem solving tool, I hope to show how Soft Systems thinking preserves the best aspects of systems thinking in general, whilst remedying the deficiencies of the 'hard' systems approach. And thirdly, I shall attempt to clarify the systems terminology I will have to use in tackling my other two objectives. An immediate example of this terminology is that the word 'systemic' does not mean the same thing as 'systematic' (usually defined as closely following a set of rational and logical steps or procedures), but simply 'using "systems" ideas'. Before our exposition of systems ideas in detail, a brief description of how and why the Systems Movement came into existence will provide a frame of reference for these ideas.

11.1 The origins of the Systems Movement

For many centuries, scientists have tried to establish a set of laws that would explain (and ultimately allow us to predict) some of the mysteries of life and the universe. This is a rather large endeavour, and there has been a tendency arbitrarily to break these investigations down into several fields of research, namely, physics, chemistry, biology, and more

---Systems ———————————————————————— *Frame 11.1* ———

A system is . . .

> . . . a group, of people, things and/or ideas connected by some common reason or purpose, that is clearly differentiated from its surroundings, and which has attributes or properties that are different from those its members have individually, and the belonging to which alters those members in some way . . . as perceived or conceived by an individual human being.

Systems thinking is . . .

> . . . the process of trying to use this (systemic) image (with the properties that we have attributed to it), to help us understand the real world.

We may think of the following as systems:

- a sunflower
- the solar system
- an Apple Macintosh microcomputer
- physics
- humanism
- Total Quality Management
- The National Health Service
- The United Nations

recently psychology and the social sciences. But, looking back over the development of the sciences, the nature of these subdivisions does seem to possess some form or coherence. The various sciences did not just happen simultaneously, but developed sequentially.

This sequential emergence of the sciences seems to parallel the degree of complexity of the things being studied. These fields of study, our arbitrarily contrived scientific disciplines, now appear to fall into a hierarchy based on this complexity, and also on the way in which one science presupposes the laws of another. For example, chemistry tells us how elements react (which physics does not) but relies on physics to explain their atomic structure, biology tells us how living things procreate but depends on chemistry to describe the workings of DNA. Attempting to classify the sciences like this reminds us of their fundamental inter-relatedness. This is necessary in that as our knowledge increases and, with it, the complexity of the things we wish to study, the tendency is to break down our fields of research into even more specialized areas of investigation, such as, astrophysics, nuclear physics, organic chemistry and marine biology. This tendency could, however, lead us to miss some significant connections and inter-relationships. Our ignorance or neglect of the complex inter-relationships between the components of our world, for example, means it may no longer be possible to control some of the (eco)systems that we have tampered with. But this is not our only problem.

Coincidental with this expansion of the sciences and our consideration of things of greater complexity has been the realization that the main method of scientific research, that of the application of systematic and objective analytical thought, becomes less effective and appropriate. Using the three Rs (Reductionism, Repeatability, Refutation), that is, analysing a complex situation in order to find ways of breaking it into small enough bits (reductionism) for us to design experiments (that can be validated by virtue of their repeatability) to test (refute) hypotheses that we have formed concerning certain specific aspects of this situation, does not seem to work as well in studying human behaviour as in investigating, say, the way heated inanimate objects cool down in various environments. The failure of operational research techniques, and management science generally, to deal with problems of managing an organization is an illustration of this.

The more complex a situation becomes, the less easy it is to find ways of isolating suitable little bits of it on which we can design and conduct appropriate experiments. And even if we could do this, the potential dangers we encountered earlier (in Chapter 1), when discussing the consequences of restructuring a problem situation (that is, the possibility of missing the crucial issue because it falls between two fragments of the problem situation), would be equally applicable to our planned set of experiments. Specialization further compounds this problem.

The increasing complexity of the entities now studied, the spreading awareness that they may also be intricately related and form part of much wider systems and the fear of the results of increased specialization, have prompted some scientists to consider the feasibility of a holistic approach, that is, taking the problem situation as a whole and adopting a systems approach. In view of this it is perhaps not surprising that among the pioneers of the systems movement was a biologist, Ludwig von Bertalanffy. It was the realization by people like him that the entities they studied seemed to be collections of interrelated parts, that each entity had attributes or properties different from those of its constituent parts, that it had some sort of purpose – a reason for its existence and was itself part of another collection, that led to the creation of the concept of a 'system'. As Peter Checkland puts it (1987a, p. 2), when it comes to trying to understand the world we live in, systems ideas are 'potentially useful since our intuitive knowledge of the world suggests that it is densely interconnected'. And so the Systems Movement has evolved. A fuller and more rigorous account can be found in Checkland (1981).

The study of systems — Frame 11.2

One of the aims within the systems movement has been to devise a (General) Systems Theory, an abstract meta-science, which would be 'above' all the other sciences in the hierarchy mentioned earlier and would thus (hopefully) contain a set of laws that would explain and generally 'sweep up' all the awkward phenomena found in the other sciences. To some extent this has been quite successful, but there is still a long way to go to the realization of this aim, if indeed it is attainable! But the use of systems concepts (that is, systems thinking) does appear to be a viable (and many people would now say more appropriate) alternative to analytical thinking when we are delving into areas where the latter experiences some difficulties. It certainly helps us understand and deal with many situations on which analytical thinking falls down. Peter Checkland (1981) believes that eventually systems thinking along with analytical thinking will be thought of as 'the twin components of scientific thinking'.

Systems Engineering — Frame 11.3

The seven stages in the process of Systems Engineering identified by A. D. Hall (1962) are typical of 'hard' systems methodology:

- Problem definition – essentially a definition of a need.
- Choice of objectives – a definition of physical needs and of the value system within which they must be met.
- Systems synthesis – creation of possible alternative systems.
- Systems analysis – analysis of the hypothetical systems in the light of their objectives.
- System selection – selection of most promising alternative.
- System development – up to the prototype stage.
- Current engineering – system realization beyond prototype stage and including monitoring, modifying and feeding back information to design.

11.2 Systems thinking

A system is a **totally abstract mental construct** that we have invented in order to understand the real world that much better. It does this by providing us with a means of modelling our perception of things in the real world. The system itself does not actually exist in the real world, although there is some confusion because we now tend to use the word 'system' to describe everyday things which we do and which are often tangible entities that can be sensed. For example, 'the minister announced today that there will be further cuts in the educational system'; 'the company's newly installed computer system "crashed" again today'; or even 'Voyager 1 has now left the Solar system and is heading off into outer space'. These things may have some of the properties of a system, and could no doubt be usefully *thought* of as systems, but they are not systems in the sense that we speak of them here.

Checkland argues (1987a, pp. 7–8) that the reason why we now use the word 'system' too casually and perhaps incorrectly, in our everyday language is due (at least in part) to the success the original concept achieved as a model of perceived reality. Although there may appear to be no real harm in using the same word to describe both the thing that exists in the real world and the mental concept that we use to help our understanding of it (so long as we always remain aware of this difference), this confusion has already made systems thinking more difficult to understand, inhibited its development and slowed its attainment of more universal acceptance as a useful learning and problem solving process. This is particularly so in regard to human affairs, for as Checkland has said (1987a), the confusion caused by the dual usage of the word 'system' is important because

> it constrains and limits systems thinking, without this being noticed. The constraints are not too damaging in relation to the use of systems thinking to conceptualize objects in the natural world – such as frogs and foxgloves – nor in relation to the design of man-made objects such as cars and cow sheds. But the confusion is very damaging in relation to attempts to use systems ideas in trying to understand the phenomena of the social world, since it restricts the application of a systems approach there to a crude form of functionalism.

This differentiation may seem pedantic, but it is necessary if we are to understand and apply the useful findings of the systems movement effectively. If we persist in thinking that the thing 'out there' is a system, we may inadvertently and probably incorrectly attribute to it the properties of a system. For instance, the organization whose problem we are trying to help resolve may well be 'a collection of people, things and ideas'. But are they necessarily 'connected by some *common* reason or purpose'? It is doubtful if they have a major problem, and even if they are, are we sure that this organization has all the necessary control processes and feedback that it needs in order to survive the changes taking place in the environment around it?

A secondary consequence of this is that we may fall into the trap as some systems analysts have of assuming that the thing we are studying does have some sort of integrity. It is often referred to inadvisably and perhaps wrongly as the 'original system', when it is at best an *implementation* of a system, and could in fact be the implementation of an idea that has no systemic coherency at all. Having made this mistake we are likely to analyse only *how* it is doing something, then, noticing anomalies with this, we 'patch them up' in an attempt to improve its performance. During this however, we may have failed to consider whether this activity should actually be done in the first place or to question the very purpose of the thing's existence.

Although a 'system' was always intended to be an abstract concept, there has been a certain ambiguity in the writings of systems thinkers. If blame for the spread of this confusion is to be apportioned anywhere, however, then some of it must lie with those people who ported systems ideas during the 1950s and 1960s from science into the area of human affairs.

11.2.1   'Hard' systems thinking

Having said that the perceived need to view things holistically came with the realization by some scientists of the complexity that pervaded everything, including ourselves, I should add that it was not long before other people applied systems ideas to the planning, appraisal and execution of complex human endeavours, typically those which evolved out of a desire to translate the discoveries being made in scientific and technological research into realized applications that would benefit mankind by fulfilling *some defined need*. These people, however, tended to think that systems *could* exist 'out there' in the real world, and that the (system) models which they built were representations of something that did or would exist in it. All that was then necessary, they believed, was to take a systematic approach to the 'engineering' (contriving and modifying) of these systems. From the 1950s onwards there were many attempts to provide this systematic way of conceiving, designing, evaluating and implementing these projects. This began what is now called 'hard' systems methodology, or at least one strand of it, which in essence reduces problem solving to: define the system; define the system's objectives; engineer the system to meet those objectives (Checkland, 1985).

There would appear to be three main 'strands' in the development of 'hard' systems thinking: Systems Engineering (SE), (RAND) Systems Analysis (SA) and Operational Research (OR), although these have evolved into a number of variants. A statement of the nature and purpose of OR has already been given in Chapter 1. Checkland describes SE and SA as:

> Systems engineering comprises the set of activities which together lead to the creation of a complex man-made entity and/or the procedures and information flows associated with its operation. Systems analysis is the systematic appraisal of the costs and other impli-

cations of meeting a defined requirement in various ways. (1981, p. 138)

OR is different from the other two primarily because it was intended to help with *tactical* decisions concerning *existing* 'systems', as opposed to SE and SA whose origins are in research projects and planning respectively and are thus concerned with *strategic* issues and *not yet existing* systems. Although having slightly differing aims, there is much similarity between them, particularly with regard to their underlying assumptions, as Checkland (1981, Chapter 5; 1983) has argued. Consequently Frame 11.3 uses only the steps involved in SE to serve as an illustration of the 'hard' systems approach.

All these methodologies assume that the problem situation can be expressed as a need and our objective is to find the best way to satisfy this need. Here is Checkland talking about SE and SA:

> The words differ somewhat but the thought is always the same, that at the start of the study it is essential to know, and to state, what end we want to achieve, where we want to go. Given that definition, the systems thinking then enables us to select a means of achieving the desired end which is efficient, if possible economically efficient. (1981, p. 139)

Although he later (1978, 1981) revised his views on problem 'solving', Ackoff (one of the pioneers of OR) writing in 1957, similarly summarized the essence of 'hard' systems thinking by saying that 'All problems ultimately reduce to the evaluation of the efficiency of alternative means for a designated set of objectives.' In other words, 'hard systems' thinking assumes that **goal seeking** is what we are about.

Another key feature of the 'hard' systems approach was the belief that not only was it quite reasonable to strive for optimal solutions, but that such things could actually be attained. This was until Herbert Simon pointed out (see Chapter 3) that this was seldom possible in practice, and that we should be content with a solution that **'satisfices'** – one that is the best we can presently manage under the circumstances.

Because of some initial successes in areas where a specific need had been identified, people tried to apply 'hard' systems thinking to less well-defined situations such as 'people' problems, where it met with considerably less success, partly due to the imposition by the methodology of the limited form of functionalism mentioned above. (Ironically, the attempts to introduce this form of systems thinking into the social sciences came at a time when the limitations of functionalism were encouraging a search for better alternatives.) 'Soft' systems thinking was intended to salvage the best aspects of the 'hard' systems approach whilst providing a more adequate means of tackling open-ended 'wicked' real-world problems. So what exactly was wrong with the 'hard' systems approach?

11.2.2   The problem with 'hard' systems thinking

Probably the most important shortcoming of hard systems thinking is summarized by Checkland thus: 'SSM was developed because the methodology of systems engineering, based on defining goals or objectives, simply did not work when applied to messy, ill-structured, real-world problems. The inability to define objectives, or to decide whose were the most important, was usually part of the problem (1985, p. 763).'

Checkland (1983, p. 667) and others believe that with most real world problems, especially those in which several people have a stake, defining the objective will always be a problem because everyone involved will see the problem situation from different perspectives and are thus likely to have different objectives. It will seldom be obvious whose objectives we should be addressing. 'Hard' systems thinkers do not see this as a problem. For the RAND analyst or the systems engineer there is no question as to whose value system we should use when selecting our problem definition. It would be the real world decision taker who has the decision problem, or the originator of the specification for the SE team, respectively. That the 'hard' systems approach does not consider that 'the likely victims of the system in question, those who decree its creation, its designers or, indeed, any other group with any interest in the outcome of the study', may have a valid view of the problem situation is, to Checkland, a major weakness.

11.2.3   Fundamental differences between 'hard' and 'soft' systems thinking

The difficulties in defining objectives in real world problem situations involving people led some systems thinkers to doubt whether 'goal seeking' was an appropriate description of them. Sir Geoffrey Vickers (1965, p. 33) is known for first questioning whether human systems should be thought of like this:

> To explain all human activity in terms of 'goal-seeking', though good enough for the behaviour of hungry rats in mazes, raises insoluble pseudo-conflicts between means and ends . . . and leaves the most important aspect of our activities, the ongoing maintenance of our ongoing activities and their ongoing satisfactions, hanging in the air as a psychological anomaly called 'action done for its own sake'. (1965, p. 33)

The problem with means and ends occurs if we think of ends as being goals, then, no end can ever be more than a means. We almost invariably strive for particular goals because we perceive that through their attainment we can establish or maintain some on-going process, for example, the continuing satisfaction of certain needs. A better description of what human (activity) systems are about, Vickers believed, was **relationship maintaining**. The idea that we continuously seek to attain one goal after another is fallacious and based on the assumption that we desire objects rather than relationships. 'No one "wants an apple". . . . [we] may want to eat it, sell it, paint it, admire it, conceivably even merely to possess it – a common type of continuing relation', in other words, what we want to do is 'to establish or change some relation with it'. Any goals that we do seek are to do with 'changes in our relations or in our opportunities for relating; but the bulk of our activity consists in "relating" itself' (Vickers, 1965, p. 33).

Another contribution Vickers made to the development of Soft Systems thinking was to stress the importance of realizing and accepting that people perceive problem situations in different ways, and that their individual system of values and beliefs affects this perception.

> Appreciation manifests itself in the exercise through time of mutually related judgements of reality and value. These appreciative judgement reflect the view currently held by those who make them of their interests and responsibilities, views large implicit and unconscious which none the less condition what events and relations they will regard as relevant or possibly relevant to them, and whether they will regard these as welcome or unwelcome, important or unimportant, demanding or not demanding action or concern by them. Such judgements disclose what can best be described as a set of readinesses to distinguish some aspects of the situation rather than others and to classify and value these in this way rather than in that. I will describe these readinesses as an appreciative system. (1965, p. 67)

This concept of an **appreciative system**, would seem to be an elaboration of what has been called 'mental set' in Chapter 4.

It was from these beginnings that Checkland developed his Soft Systems Methodology (SSM), which can be seen as 'a formal practical expression' of the idea of appreciative systems. A problem solving strategy designed (amongst other things) to incorporate various people's perspectives of the problem situation and their differing objectives, thus overcoming the second 'weakness' of the 'hard' systems approach. Because of the importance that the 'soft' systems approach places on this, they are never so presumptious as to assume that their systems are models of the real world. As Checkland (1985, p. 764) says, 'the models of human activity systems in SSM do not pretend to be models *of* the world, only models which embody a particular stated way of viewing the world'. These are models such that by comparing a number of them with the real world situation, we hope to gain a better understanding of what is going on 'out there' and how things perhaps should be if we are to improve the situation from those perspectives.

'Hard' systems thinking assumes that we know where we are going, and hence what sort of changes are required in order to improve the situation, so all we have to do is affect these changes in the most efficient way. 'Soft' systems thinking on the other hand accepts that we do not always know what changes are needed, but believes that by considering the situation from these various viewpoints we will discover the changes we need to make. We have found a way by which learning can effectively replace optimizing or 'satisficing', our implied aim when we left Chapter 3. This learning process is in theory (and probably in practice) a cyclic and never-ending one. There will be no 'final solution' with 'soft' systems thinking, but that is not necessarily a bad thing.

11.2.4 A reprieve for 'hard' systems thinking?

Having criticized the 'hard' systems approach it seems appropriate to conclude this section on a positive note. As stated earlier (Chapter 1) it is not that OR, or the 'hard' systems approach generally, is no longer of use and should be replaced, but that it is only suitable for a certain subset of problems. Where there is nothing problematic about the purpose of the organization, division or section we are investigating, and there is agreement over what needs to be done to resolve the problem situation, hard systems thinking can help us, as it did with projects intended to satisfy specific human needs in the early days of SE.

Checkland (1985, pp. 765–6) says that 'soft' systems thinking should be seen as the general case, of that which 'hard' systems thinking is 'the occasional special case'. He goes on to say that at a 'basic operational level there is very often a complete consensus on what needs to be done and what constitutes efficiency in doing it'. In these situations, when we have a well-defined problem and our objectives are clear, for example, a mail order company which is unable to satisfy its orders within a reasonable amount of time because of an inadequate stock control 'system', the use of the powerful techniques of OR, SSADM (Structured Systems Analysis and Design Methodology) etc., are appropriate and can assist us in resolving our problem. But equally there will be many other situations, such as deciding what products are to be offered in our mail order catalogue, which will be different matters altogether with many differing views of them and requiring an entirely different treatment.

In an attempt to 'balance' the score, this final quote comes from Geoff Cults, an exponent of one aspect of current 'hard' systems thinking, 'It is essential to only consider the use of SSADM in an environment which is predominantly well-structured' (1987, p. 14).

11.2.5   More systemic thoughts

If we look again at the definition of a system at the beginning of this chapter, you will notice that it finishes with ' . . . as perceived or conceived by an individual human being'. Many 'definitions' fail to emphasize this point. Whether or not there is any need to make the distinction between perception and conception is debatable, because in everyday usage we tend to use the words 'perceive' (become or be aware of through the senses, get knowledge of by the mind, understand, discern) and 'conceive' (form in the mind, imagine or think about, understand) almost interchangeably. This is particularly so with regard to 'understanding' things, which is essentially what systems are all about. Perception is so intimately linked to intentionality (the way the mental processes of consciousness are 'directed' at whatever we are thinking about) that the whole process can be viewed as one of conception, some might even say that perception is no more then the mechanism of conception. But to use just one word (and it is usually 'perceive' that occurs in those definitions of a system that do stress this point) might seem to preclude the other.

What happens when we do some 'systems thinking' depends to a certain extent on whether we are trying to make sense of something we have seen, heard, etc., or are dreaming up (designing) something new. When we look at the public sector provision for educating the young in our country, with a view to trying to improve it, we may think of it as a system. That is, there is educational provision 'out there' somewhere, we have this concept of a system in our minds and we use this concept to help us order, structure and generally make sense of our perceptions of this provision. When we are designing something which is 'new', say the setting up of a desk-top publishing facility for a small manufacturing company, we may also wish to view this as a system. It is likely that for this, we will be using a different system (but again a mental construct) to help us organize our recollections of the company's needs and our previous experience of similar installations. Thus systems thinking can involve both perceiving and conceiving something as a system.

We have not as yet said exactly what is involved in systems thinking. John Beishon and Geoff Peters (1981, p. 14) describe systems thinking as 'looking at situations, topics, problems, etc., as a complex of interacting parts which can be divided into specific systems and within these, subsystems, and if necessary into sub-subsystems, and so on. Identification of these various systems is followed by an examination of the relationships among them, including the flows of influences (or information), materials and energy and the routes these take among and within the systems involved.' Before taking it any further than this (in Chapter 12), we need to consider whether there are different types of system, and to look in more detail at the properties of a system.

11.3   Classification of systems

The universe may be thought of as being made up of systems within systems. Various attempts have been made to classify these systems. One such effort, by K. E. Boulding in 1956, did this on the basis of complexity. Starting with static structures, such as crystals, it went through various types of 'mechanical' and organismal systems and finally culminated with Man, socio-cultural systems and transcendental systems. Another by N. Jordan; in 1968, attempted to classify systems according to three 'dimensions', Structural (static) v. Functional (dynamic), whether or not they are Purposive, and their Connectivity. The latter is when some elements (or the connections between them) are changed, removed or destroyed and the remaining elements will also be affected or not. Essentially this is a distinction between organismal and mechanical systems. But as yet there is no agreed way of partitioning the Universe like this.

Checkland (1981), however, has suggested the following minimal classification of systems types as being sufficient for our purposes here:

- natural systems, e.g. a molecule, the universe;
- designed physical systems, e.g. a hammer, the lunar module;
- designed abstract systems, e.g. mathematics;
- human activity systems, e.g. British Airways, Greenpeace;
- transcendental systems, e.g. God.

If we assume that the patterns and laws of the universe are not capricious, then the distinguishing feature of natural systems is that they cannot be other than they are. Designed systems on the other hand, because they have been devised and possibly fabricated by human beings, could be. A human being is part of a natural system, but he or she may create and use designed systems, possibly from elements of another natural system, and indeed may do this whilst belonging to a human activity system. A human activity system can be thought of as a system in which a collection of human beings interact with each other and perform certain activities in an organized and purposeful way, as perceived by some human's point of view.

It is not necessary for members of a human activity system to know that they belong to it. Because the systems have to be perceived by an individual (who perceives things in different ways to others) a human activity system can obviously be other than it is.

We need to be careful how we classify so-called 'social' systems, which put in simple terms, are those groups of people to which we knowingly belong, the membership of which carries with it certain responsibilities and obligations, and from which we have certain expectations. Examples of these social systems are an ethnic group, our family, the Boy Scouts, a trade union or a commercial enterprise. Since it is possible to identify for any of these groups, a set of *human activities* which are characteristic to that particular group, they might be thought of as human activity systems. But the interpersonal relationships and emotional attachments which could be thought of as characteristic of *natural* groupings, our gregarious tendencies, although mostly prevalent in tribal and family groupings, can and do occur in many of the other social systems as well, so should they be thought of as natural systems?

Checkland (1981, pp. 120–1) says that a distinction which he attributes to the sociologist Tonnies more than adequately solves this dilemma. Under this classification scheme, a social system is thought to be a natural system if we *naturally* belong to it and do so with our *whole* selves. If as well as this, we *choose* to be a member of some other social system (for a while) in order to achieve some specific goal, but assign only a part of ourselves to membership of that social system, then it is best thought of as a human activity system. For instance I am, as a whole person, naturally part of the community I live in (a natural system), however, I donate *some* of my time and mental effort to the organization I work for (a human activity system) and I do this for a reason. (And it's not the money!)

The significance of this distinction is that as individuals we can and usually do belong to more than one social system, some of these will be natural systems and others will be human activity systems. We will thus have 'allegiances' to more than one social system, and the nature and strength of these allegiances will be different also. We are often 'bound' to natural social systems by very strong emotional ties, whereas with human activity systems the attraction may be only one of extrinsic rewards, which are possibly available elsewhere. Even if our membership of a human activity system is because of some intrinsic motivation, we have chosen it for some reason and the basis of this decision could change, for example our needs and objectives may alter, or we may perceive that the organization is no longer fulfilling our psychological contract (see Chapter 5). If forced to choose, would not many people place the welfare of their family ahead of that of the organization they work for or even their country? This potential conflict of goals, loyalties and responsibilities should never be forgotten, in fact it should be deliberately considered (with a view to ensuring some degree of compatibility amongst them), in any systems thinking that we do. We are, after all, using this (systemic) approach so as not to overlook interconnectednesses like this: we are attempting to get as complete a picture of things as possible.

Our aim here is to use systems concepts to help us deal with 'people' problems, situations which are characterized by human beings trying to take purposeful action, so our main concern would seem to be with human activity systems. These systems may include both natural and designed subsystems, and may also themselves be included within other natural or designed systems, and perhaps even transcendental systems!

The significance and fragility of human activity systems are illustrated by the following quotes:

> Social structures (organizations) are essentially contrived systems. They are made of men and are imperfect systems. They can come apart at the seams overnight, but they can also outlast the biological organisms which originally created them. The cement that holds them together is essentially psychological rather than biological. Social systems are anchored in the attitudes, perceptions, beliefs, motivations, habits, and expectations of human beings. (Katz and Kahn, 1966)

> Nearly all systems which include human beings are unstable and their instability is nearly always the unwilled result of man's actions, monstrously multiplied in power by technology but not correspondingly informed by increased understanding. . . . The extent to which we can redesign any part of it without disastrous impact on any other parts is very limited and we do not know and probably cannot fully know its limitations. (Vickers, 1981, p. 19)

11.4   The characteristics of a system

As we have seen, a system is a purposeful collection of interrelated elements, the whole of which can be distinguished from those things which are not part of the system, that is, its **environment** by its properties and the interconnectedness of its components. Therefore there must be a **boundary** between the system and the environment in which it exists.

In the first instance, we can define **closed systems** as those which are totally self-contained and do not interact in any way with the environment that they are in. A particular feature of closed systems is that they tend towards a state of disorder, chaos and total breakdown (or more technically, static equilibrium and entropy).

Entropy is a term taken from the study of thermodynamics, and in the study of systems is used to mean the tendency of a system to move towards a chaotic or random state, where it is unable to fulfil its function properly (there no longer exists a potential for energy transformation or work to take place). One example of entropy is the phenomenon that if you shut a human being up so that he or she can have little or no interaction with their environment – anything from 'solitary confinement' to the extent of suspending a person in salt water of the right density to simulate weightlessness, and which is warmed to body heat, and all this is done in a lightproof soundproof container, that human being will eventually go stark raving mad! Usually entropy is associated with mechanistic systems, for example, an automatic drilling machine which senses the arrival of a new part on a nearby conveyor belt, grabs hold of it, orientates it and then promptly drills x number of holes in it. If left to its own devices however, with no interaction (maintenance) from outside, it will cease to perform its drilling operations accurately and eventually break down completely, as wear develops on its drill bits and elsewhere.

The ubiquitous digital watch *could* be thought of as an example of a **dynamic** closed system. Assuming that it comes supplied with a new battery, it will continue to display the correct time (within an accuracy of a few seconds per month) for a couple of years or more without any interaction with its surroundings (providing the watch is not going to be subjected to a harmful environment which it was never designed to withstand). Slowly the energy being provided by the battery will diminish, and upon reaching a certain minimum threshold, the timekeeping accuracy will deteriorate, or as is more usual, the display will disappear rendering the system of no further use without a battery transplant.

It is interesting to note though that this type of closed system has an internal regulatory or **control mechanism**. The quartz crystal controls the electronic oscillations and hence the timekeeping, in the same way as the escapement mechanism controlled the release of the clockwork 'power source' and the movement of the cogs in an old-style analogue watch. Our drilling machine would have a control mechanism also, probably a program stored in a microprocessor. There are other things which can be thought of as **static** closed systems, such as a suspension bridge, which do not have such a control mechanism.

All of these systems have a reason for their existence though. The digital watch, the drilling machine and the suspension bridge can be thought of as designed physical systems; they were designed by human beings for a **purpose**.

This discussion has introduced certain features of a system such as the boundary with its environment, entropy, its purposefulness and its possible possession of a control mechanism. To identify automatic drilling machines, watches and suspension bridges as *merely* closed systems however, is an oversimplification. The distinction between open and closed systems is neither as precise nor as useful as this introduction may suggest.

An **open system**, while having all the characteristics mentioned above, is a system that *does interact* with its environment. There will be continual exchanges of material, information and/or energy taking place between an open system and its environment. We cannot really accept that replacing the battery in a digital watch is an example of energy being exchanged between the environment and the system because the current thinking is that in order to be an open system, a system must take an *active* part in these exchanges. A solar-powered digital watch would stand a better chance of being considered as an open system. It is true that the solar-powered watch does not go out hunting for energy sources, but it does have an internal **subsystem**, the solar panel and its associated circuitry, which (actively) 'absorbs' light energy and converts it into electrical energy whenever it has the opportunity to do so.

What we can say about both the drilling machine and our solar-powered digital watch is that although they take something in from their environment (undrilled parts, solar energy) and give something back to it as well (drilled parts, information about the time), neither of them has any way of detecting the effect that these outputs are having on their environment. Open systems do. If we took our solar-powered digital watch and added to it some electronics that could pick up radio waves containing time signals such that it could then automatically adjust its timekeeping from these signals, we might be getting even nearer to an open system.

Should a domestic gas-fired central heating installation be thought of as an open or closed system? It takes in energy in the form of gas from the environment. It converts this into hot water, which it transports (via pipes) to radiators which in turn export heat energy back to the environment. The installation also has sensors which monitor the temperature of the environment and its own water temperature and communicates this information (provides some **feedback**) to the control mechanism which determines the behaviour of the installation, that is, it provides information that allows the control mechanism to *decide* whether to switch the water heating mechanism on or off. It seems to remain in a fairly stable state, maintaining its environment at a constant temperature. But if a central heating boiler is left to its own devices (i.e. we do not intervene in its normal operations by having it regularly maintained), it too will eventually break down. Does this condemn it to being a closed system?

Open systems are thought of as having a dynamic but reasonably stable relationship with their environment; the interchange of material, information and energy is such that the system *itself* manages to allay the onslaught of entropy. If our domestic central heating required no maintenance, or was somehow self-maintaining, it would definitely be an open system. Human activity systems are open systems. There does appear to be, however, a desire amongst systems thinkers to subdivide open systems like these into two further categories.

Some open systems simply respond to stimuli via some sort of feedback loop. These are the ones that react to environmental conditions, in a seemingly perpetual self-correcting fashion, just barely (if the feedback mechanism is effective) postponing the inexorable decline into entropy's chaotic state. There are also thought to be other open systems which 'make the first move', that is, their interactions with the environment are not just responses to stimuli. These systems are proactive rather than reactive. Their exchange of materials, information and energy with the environment is such that not only do they hold back the devastating effect of increased entropy, but they can also improve their position by overcoming the effects of entropy (that is, they gain negative entropy). This suggests that they are potentially able to achieve a degree of 'immortality', or **continuity** anyway. The 'form' of these systems is more persistent than their constituent elements, which would need to have been 'replaced' many times over in order to achieve the systems' relative longevity. These open systems also have the potential to fall apart at any time very quickly. It is a very delicate balance, for as Sir Geoffrey Vickers warns us (1983, p. 13) 'no open system lasts for ever. Its stability can never be taken for granted', as it 'fluctuates' during its regulatory process, it can easily go beyond a point of no return 'and dissolve or change into something else'.

The main problem with the discussion so far is that things which are often thought of as closed systems are almost invariably components or subsystems of larger *open* systems, and so it is unrealistic to think of them as totally isolated entities. If the pricing and design of our battery-operated digital watch is such that we would replace the battery rather than throw it away and buy a new watch, then it can be thought of as part of a (time knowing) system that does interact with its environment, a system that also contains a human being who buys and fits a new battery when one is required. Even if we could not replace the battery, it could still be thought of as a part of an (open) profit-making system by someone. It could be said therefore that closed systems are nothing more than a philosophical abstraction.

The early, and unsuccessful, attempts at modelling organizations with closed systems highlight the danger of placing too much emphasis on the existence of closed systems, as it encourages the reductionist thinking we are trying to get away from. It is, however, open systems that are of special interest to us here, because we now believe that social systems, and organizations in particular, are best regarded as open systems. There are undoubtedly many that apparently behave like the first category of open system mentioned above, but surely to be described as successful, organizations should be such that they are perceived as the second category of open system.

11.5   Conclusions

Studying the behaviour of things we regard as systems is not without difficulty. First we have to overcome the cultural norm summed up by the old adage that tends to govern our thinking: 'If its working fine, leave it alone!' This advice would be all right if we could guarantee that systems always drift slowly and gracefully into a state of entropy. This is seldom the case.

┌───┐

Formal System Model (from Checkland, 1981, ───── *Frame 11.4* ─────
pp. 173–4)

The Formal System has:

- an ongoing purpose/mission   which might be unattainable in
                                      a soft systems situation

- a measure of performance
- contains a decision-taking   which permits regulatory action
  process
- components which are
  themselves systems
- components which interact   or show a degree of connectivity
                                      (which may be physical, flows of
                                      energy, materials, information,
                                      or influence) such that effects/
                                      actions can be transmitted
                                      through the system
- exists in a wider system   with which it interacts
  (environment)
- a boundary   an area within which decision
                                      taking has real power to cause
                                      action
- resources   physical, human and/or abstract
                                      which are at the disposal of the
                                      decision taking process

- some guarantee of continuity
  or long-term stability

└───┘

Another problem is that it is difficult to predict all the possible behaviours of a system until we have seen it fail. Unfortunately we often
have to wait for a system to fail before all its possible behaviours are revealed. When that happens there are many vested interests which
ensure that full records of what happened are difficult to trace. In addition, system malfunctioning often occurs suddenly and catastrophically;
one cannot expect people to start making detailed observations in the
middle of a crisis.

We have now introduced all the features that an open system, such
as one of the human activity systems that we are about to encounter,
should have. The so-called Formal System Model described in Frame
11.4 below can be thought of as a summary of these features. In the next
chapter we will be constructing models of various systems and will use
the FSM as a checklist to ensure that our model contains all the elements
that it, and the system it represents, should have.

12 Soft Systems thinking

The Soft Systems Methodology (SSM) was developed as a problem solving strategy for those faced with resolving highly complex and interrelated problem situations, where it is best to attempt to view the situation as a whole as opposed to restructuring it. Success with SSM depends more on our prior knowledge (systems concepts and systems thinking) and our experience than is the case with any of the other problem solving strategies described in this book. These factors suggest that SSM is more likely to be used by an 'external' consultant or team of consultants, than by someone within a group or organization. However Peter Checkland has recently demonstrated that SSM is equally useful to a manager going about normal day-to-day work as it is for a special high-lighted study (Checkland and Scholes, 1990).

Because SSM may be used by us as external consultants, it is important to remember two points pertinent to such a situation. Firstly, we should be aware that when we make an intervention into a real world problem situation, our presence *will* have an effect. Secondly, as 'outsiders' we should 'give' our problem solving expertise to the participants in the problem situation, by explaining the methodology as it is being employed, encouraging them to use and ensuring that they are in a position to continue to use it after we have left. Ideally, the problem owners should play an active part in the process while we are there!

12.1 An overview of SSM

The first stage in a Soft Systems investigation involves the careful observation of the problem situation with all its intricate details, and the recording of all that is perceived. This involves collecting qualitative data, such as attitudes and opinions concerning the problem situation, including reactions to our intervention in matters (as external consul-

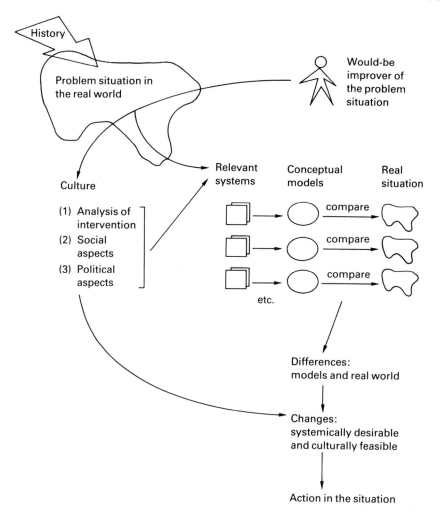

Figure 12.1 *An outline of Soft Systems Methodology.*

tants) as well as quantitative data. Following this, the essence of these observations is encapsulated in brief descriptions of human activity systems which we hope may later provide relevant insights into the problem situation. Models of these systems that are consistent with the different viewpoints expressed within the descriptions are built. In this way we try to capture as much as possible of the 'richness' of the real situation. Finally a comparison is made of the models with the observations of the real world situation; which is used in a discussion with the problem-owners to suggest systemically desirable and culturally feasible changes that it is hoped will lead to improvements in the problem situation. An overview of SSM is given in Figure 12.1.

The steps in the process which apparently form a logical progression (see Figure 12.2) may need to be refined for a given situation, and invariably form part of an iterative process.

12.2   Social and political dimensions

Concurrent with all this we should also explore the social and political dimensions of the problem situation. We need to remember always that 'every human problem situation is the product of a history, one which will dictate perceptions, judgements and standards' (Checkland, 1987b). These factors will have a considerable bearing on what is culturally feasible.

As soon as we intervene in problem situation we will become involved in its politics. Not only will the problem situation have political aspects, our intervention itself could and should be seen as a political act. In this sense, politics means the process by which interested parties reach some sort of mutual accommodation or compromise, including all the manoeuvring and intrigue that this entails. The concessions invariably made during this process will be overt or covert changes in the disposition of power. Attempting to unravel the politics of the situation should be one of the first things we do during the initial data gathering stage, but since it is unlikely to remain static, we should reassess the politics of the situation repeatedly as the investigation proceeds.

To appreciate the political dimensions of the problem situation fully, Checkland (1986) advises that we should identify the people within the problem situation who (could) occupy the roles of:

- client – the people who commissioned us and whom it is assumed can implement any changes which we may suggest;
- would-be problem solver – those people who will be trying to bring about some improvement to the problem situation;
- problem-owner – anyone who is affected for better or worse by the current problem situation.

We should do this by listing the roles and then assigning actual persons to them, rather than the other way around, thus helping to ensure that we realize that a particular person could and usually does occupy more than one of these roles. A person occupying the role of client need not also be considered as a problem-owner (which is a little different from the situation with other problem solving strategies, such as Synectics) however, perhaps they should be.

Peter Checkland (1981) defines a problem-owner as a person 'who has a feeling of unease about a situation, either a sense of mismatch between "what is" and "what might be" or a vague feeling that things could be better and who wishes something were done about it. The problem-owner may not be able to define what he would regard as a "solution",

┌─*Model of a Social System* ──────────────────────── *Frame 12.1* ──┐

Because a problem situation of the type we are considering can be viewed as a 'social system' it is appropriate to determine its social aspects using a model which can be thought of as a continually changing interaction of three elements – roles, norms and values; each continually defines and is defined by the other two. A role is a social position recognized by people in the problem situation which is characterized by expected behaviours or norms. Actual performance in a role (which changes the role-occupant just as his or her way of occupying the role will change perception of that role) will be judged according to local standards or values, beliefs about what is humanly 'good' or 'bad' performance (Checkland, 1986).

and may not be able to articulate the feeling of unease in any precise way.' It is also possible for someone involved in the problem situation not to recognize their own problem ownership. This should not prevent us from assigning them that role, because we should attempt to view the problem situation from as many standpoints as we feel appropriate.

When trying to identify would-be problem solvers, we as the external consultant should remember that we are (and should be seen as) problem solving facilitators rather than problem solvers. The only people likely to be able to resolve the problem will be those that have the power to implement any of our suggestions which are accepted.

Within any group there are key roles determining the effective operation of the group. We must ascertain what these significant roles are within our problem situation, who holds them, what behaviour is expected from them and whether they are considered to be fulfilling these roles well or badly.

Assuming that power is expressed through the possession of one or more usually abstract 'commodities', we should determine what these are in the organization we are dealing with. Listed below are some typical examples:

- size of departmental budget;
- chairmanship of certain committees;
- indispensability;
- personal charisma;
- intellectual expertise;
- external reputation;
- being under 40 years of age;
- rank;
- years of service;
- being someone who plays squash with the MD.

Although these criteria are highly variable, subjective and possibly contradictory, they do represent examples of how we go about attributing power to others in organizations. We need to identify also how these sources of power can be obtained, exercised, protected, preserved, passed on and relinquished or lost. Knowing the bases of power can indicate how situations have come about, forewarn us of difficulties we may encounter collecting the information we need and help us anticipate where resistance to or support for any changes we may later suggest is likely to occur.

Political issues are by nature never explicit, and can be very elusive, which often predisposes people to ignore them. Checkland (1986) strongly urges us to try to determine them, recommending that a good approach is to assume good faith on the part of our fellow human beings, as this often yields surprising dividends of goodwill. Having gained this goodwill we need to be careful not to say or do anything that might jeopardize it.

12.3   The SSM process

SSM was intended to be a flexible and evolving problem solving strategy. What follows are guidelines that can be adapted or modified for a particular problem situation. A schematic outline of the process is given in Figure 12.2, but it is not always necessary to start at stage 1. Work on several stages can be carried out concurrently, and it is likely that we will need to return to earlier stages and repeat various steps again. Note the clear distinction in the figure between the 'real world' activities and the abstract 'systems thinking'.

The fictitious case used here to illustrate this process is obviously artificial as it includes only a finite set of observations. In real life this would not be the case, and the analyst can at any time take steps to attempt to fill any gaps detected in the information so far obtained.

12.3.1   The problem situation unstructured

The description of the first stage as 'the problem situation unstructured' reinforces the idea that we should be entering the situation with a completely open mind. It is probably not obvious, though we may be told otherwise, what the problem actually is. We should not permit ourselves to jump to conclusions about it being a certain well-defined problem. This would tend to indicate that we know what the solution should be; it is not our place to decide what is an acceptable solution.

If the problem situation is so difficult to sort out that we have had to be brought in, then it is likely to be several interrelated problems. The people involved in the problem situation will have different views of it as there may be many valid opinions on what the problem is. It may

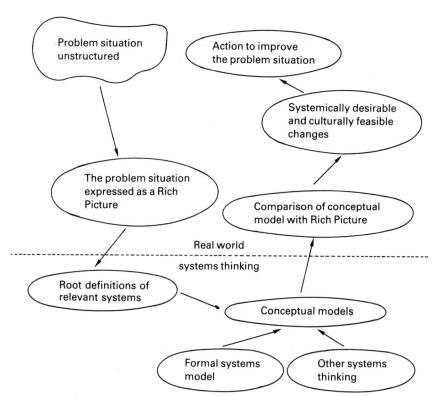

Figure 12.2 *The stages of SSM.*

even be that it is these differing perceptions of the problem situation that is preventing them from finding a way to resolve it. Frame 12.2 describes the situation of Woodson Loudspeakers, an organization with severe problems. We shall assume that we have just begun our first encounter with the 'mess' which constitutes the problem situation and we have spoken to the client, who has told us what the problem is *as they see it*. We have noted this for future reference and then immediately 'forgotten' it until after we have gathered all our data. We have also sorted out all the administrative details that are necessary to ensure the smooth running of the who, what, when, why and how of our information gathering, and we have made a start on collecting our data. One of the first things we have done is to start forming some impressions about the political aspects of the problem situation. We have determined which people occupy the roles of client, would-be problem solver and problem-owner, and also the whereabouts of the most 'sensitive areas': this has to be ascertained before the bulk of the data is obtained (Frame 12.3).

Both 'hard' and 'soft' data are needed in order to get a complete picture of the problem situation. Hard information consists of factual data, such as:

—— *Frame 12.2   Illustrative example: Woodsons Loudspeakers* ——

Woodsons Ltd is a small company producing and marketing loud-speaker enclosures for the Hi-fi market. Originally, it was a family business which operated out of a small factory in the West Midlands. Although Woodsons' design and build the enclosures themselves, they buy in speaker chasis units from LSI Ltd.

LSI is another family business. It was located on the same industrial estate, and in many ways the two companies had an ideal working arrangement. However, as the years have gone past, LSI has diversified into a variety of 'transducer' products and has become very successful supplying large electronic equipment manufacturers. LSI still supply the relatively small requirements of Woodsons, but do this more as a favour than as a viable trading proposition. Because of this and because LSI relocated to the Thames Valley, Woodsons now have to wait for 'a lorry to be coming their way' when they need to replenish their stocks of speaker units.

Woodsons was purchased in 1973 by a young entrepreneur, Rob Boston, when the company's fortunes were very low and it was on the verge of bankruptcy. Fierce competition from the Far East had almost eliminated the demand for UK mass produced Hifi equipment. Although he still owns the company and is a member of its board, Rick Boston has long since moved on to other things. The company is now managed by Peter Frood.

Boston was responsible for the drastic cuts and reorganisation that took place in the mid 1970s. One of the things which ensured that Woodson survived and are still trading today, is their dynamic sales team (hand-picked by Boston). At present Woodsons' main customers are small independent Hifi retailers. Woodsons' Sales and Marketing team have managed to increase orders every year, averaging a 4% annual growth.

The Sales and Marketing section consists of the sales manager, five salespersons and a marketing assistant. Each member of the sales team is responsible for looking after the requirements of their own group of customers; they report to the sales manager monthly. They are also responsible for keeping their own customer records and two of them have home computers that they use to assist with this process.

Each salesperson passes the orders that they make to the marketing assistant, one of whose responsibilities is to pass these orders on to the Production section. There have now been no less than seven different marketing assistants in the last year – most have left after approximately a month. Janet has been with the company for almost seven months now, and has survived by ensuring that any abuse she receives when handing the sales team's orders to the Production section is suitably deflected towards those she believes are responsible for invoking the abuse.

The other crucial factor in Woodsons' survival was John Smith. He was hired in 1974 as manager of the 'revamped' Research and Development team, and it was he who came up with an innovative design for a high quality compact loudspeaker system; a new product that saved Woodsons. Smith is now considered to be a bit of a maverick by his colleagues in other sections, due to his habit of forever chasing new concepts and ideas (some of which have gone down in the history of the company as 'Smith's follies'), instead of applying his team's expertise to developing and improving Woodsons' existing products. The R & D team consists of Smith, another designer and a highly skilled cabinet maker with a good working knowledge of acoustics.

Although morale has always been high amongst the sales team (this probably being due to the charisma and leadership of the sales manager, Sue Waterford), considerable frustration has been manifest in the last year at various meetings within the company. Nick Wright, one of the senior salesman, summed it up by saying 'We are really getting fed up with the fact that after all our efforts to cultivate new customers and orders, this effort and our reputation are being ripped apart by frequent complaints from our customers about failures to deliver goods on time and receiving only part-orders'.

The production manager, Tim Shaw, and his staff of 17, consider themselves to be efficient and overworked, and morale certainly cannot be said to be good in this section. In 1973 the whole section was pared down to the bare minimum as part of a cost saving scheme; the number of production personnel has not changed dramatically since then. Production planning is not helped by having a succession of 'high priority' orders arriving almost continuously from certain members of the sales team, who in the opinion of Tim Shaw 'are making irresponsible promises of delivery to their customers without first checking with me about the current production schedule, and are consequently placing impossible demands on my section'.

Another aspect of the company's operation that is giving concern is the low quality of the packaging and distribution. This is done by an outside contractor, Crow Packaging. Crow Packaging are also responsible for putting together the orders prior to distribution by road carriers.

Woodson has a small network of five IBM microcomputers that were purchased in 1984, as part of Frood's scheme to modernize the management of Woodson. Two of these machines reside in the General Office and are used mainly for the company accounts and payroll. The managing director himself has one in his office (or more correctly in his secretary's office); this machine, like the other machines located outside the General Office, is used mostly for word-processing, much of which is normal everyday correspondence.

There is a rumour that Rob Boston is contemplating selling off

Woodsons if things do not improve in the next six months. Woodsons is the least profitable of all the companies in his group. You have been hired by Peter Frood to perform an analysis of Woodsons' operations and to suggest improvements that might be made.

Frame 12.3   Woodsons Ltd: essential information and early impressions

Client: We have been employed by Peter Frood the managing director, so he is the client.

Problem solvers: Peter Frood is obviously in the best position to implement any changes we might suggest, but he will need the support, commitment and goodwill of his three managers.

Problem-owners: All the employees of Woodsons from the MD downwards have a stake in all this. And of course so does Rob Boston, though I'm not sure whether we can get his viewpoint in any more detail than that provided by the rumours. We might also consider LSI, Crow Packaging, and even Woodsons' customers as problem-owners. This would certainly give us a good mix of viewpoints.

It is a little difficult to say much about the political aspects of Woodsons' problem from such a brief account. A couple of potential power 'commodities' might well be 'being hand-picked by Rob Boston' (Sue Waterford and the five salesperons) back in the crisis years and the innovative and technical expertise of John Smith (it has brought him through several mistakes without too much damage).

Over the years it would appear that to be seen as dynamic and successful (by all but Tim Shaw and his staff) one needs to produce growth of 4 per cent p.a. Perhaps it is time that this norm is re-evaluated. Being hand-picked by Rob Boston and meeting their self-imposed targets seems to imbue in the sales team the feeling that they have (or at least should have) the authority to lead the organization. However, there is some dispute (from Tim Shaw) as to whether they should hold this position. Also, the behaviour of the person occupying the role of 'ideas man' (John Smith) is evidently not that which is expected by the rest of the organization.

- the divisions or departments within the organization;
- noteworthy individuals;
- the organizational structure;
- products;
- reporting channels;

- data flows;
- any quantitative data.

Soft information includes such things as:

- hunches, guesses, intuitions;
- perceptions of the people involved with(in) the problem situation;
- judgements about the helpfulness, skills, competence, efficiency, perceived status, attitudes, motivational needs of individuals;
- rumours about friendships and hostilities.

Soft information is highly subjective data, things that people often have qualms about saying, let alone recording. (There will always be exceptions to this, especially people with political, personal or organizational axes to grind.) Normally there is a natural anxiety about offering information that might offend, the meaning of which might be perceived incorrectly, the truth of which is uncertain and/or which might be relayed to the 'wrong' person. This type of information is vital and must be determined. Success with this will depend very much on the personality of the person collecting the information and their reputation for fairness, confidentiality and for being non-judgemental.

12.3.2   Rich Pictures, the Primary Tasks and the Issues of Concern

Once the necessary data have been gathered, the situation within which the problem is found is represented by a cartoon-style diagram called a Rich Picture. We must assemble this picture without imposing any particular structure on it. This is difficult, because we may have already seen some possible promising directions and we are keen to get started on the next steps.

We use a pictorial representation as opposed to a written description because:

- A picture can show far more information in the same space.
- It shows patterns, arrangements, connections and relationships far better.
- We are less likely to overlook vital links and interactions which may have given rise to unexpected or unintentional consequences.
- It permits us to see the whole of the problem situation in all its complexity, and gives us a 'feel' of its overall shape.
- It provides a representation of the problem situation that can be readily shared with others.

A Rich Picture does not have to be a work of art as long as it makes sense to us, its creator. We use vivid symbols wherever possible to represent aspects of the problem situation. For example, a big weight resting on the head of a pin man would indicate that someone in the

Figure 12.3 *Some symbols for a Rich Picture.*

Some Useful Symbols

people

under pressure
1 ton

unrealistic views/actions

serious disagreement, antagonism

'no go' area

'brick wall'

close relationships

Act of God.

under a 'black cloud'

volatile situation

friendship

'rising stars'

?
uncertain objectives

!
source of wonderment, concern

ideas

dangerous practice, 'piracy'

forbidden, taboo practice

peaceful situation

falling 'stars'

There will be other appropriate symbols unique to a given problem situation, we can also used symbols from other fields e.g. computing ⌐ = document, report.

organization is under considerable pressure. A set of useful symbols can be found in Figure 12.3. When we are sharing our thoughts or explaining our possible systemically desirable and culturally feasible changes later, we may wish to refer back to something 'seen' in the Rich Picture. There is therefore a case for not making it too idiosyncratic.

However, the fact that it may be seen by others should not be the main criterion in deciding how to construct it. The 'Guidelines for preparing Rich Pictures' given in Frame 12.4 indicate that we should include our subjective (soft) data as well as the factual data, even though they may be contentious. The differing perceptions of people within the problem situation can be shown using 'balloons' coming from the effigies.

We could construct two Rich Pictures, one complete and one omitting the subjective comments, the latter being intended for public consumption, but this presents us with an ethical dilemma. Remember, though, there is nothing to be gained by disclosing contentious information which is of no importance to the solving of the problem. However if a contentious piece of information is significant but has been given in confidence , we must get clearance from the originator before disclosing it. We should never attempt to disguise or give anonymity to a piece of data in order to 'publicize' it. The originator is almost certain to hear a garbled version of what was actually said, and even though that person may remain undetected as its author, our reputation for confidentiality will be compromised. Rich Pictures often need tidying up before public presentation and so could be judiciously 'simplified', though we should make it clear they are a summary of our findings and that if further details are required they will be given, if available.

Produce a Rich Picture for the Woodsons case study. For this you will need a sheet of paper, preferably larger than A3 as this size has been found inadequate for even this relatively small amount of information. Figure 12.4 shows the Rich Picture that I drew for the Woodsons example. This must not be considered an example of the 'correct' way to draw it, let alone a 'correct' answer. It has been slightly tidied up to give a glimpse of my thinking whilst compiling it. Your picture will of course be different, but should contain the same amount of detail. Do this by hand. Presently available computer drawing packages, even if you are experienced in using them and you have already created a set of standard symbols, are too time consuming to be cost-effective.

How do we know when we have finished? In practice, the picture will never be completely finished as representing all the information you have gathered into a Rich Picture is not a finite activity. We will need to add to our picture as our investigations continue and we come across additional information. This makes it difficult to determine when it is complete enough to allow us to move on to the next phase. The best advice is try it and see. Later, when formulating your Root Definitions or comparing our Rich Picture with our Conceptual Model (see below), inadequacies resulting from a lack of information will become apparent. We will then need to find out this information and add it to the Rich Picture. Only experience can be our guide.

When we feel it is time to move on, we should take some time to reflect upon the picture. The transition to this next stage will be easier if

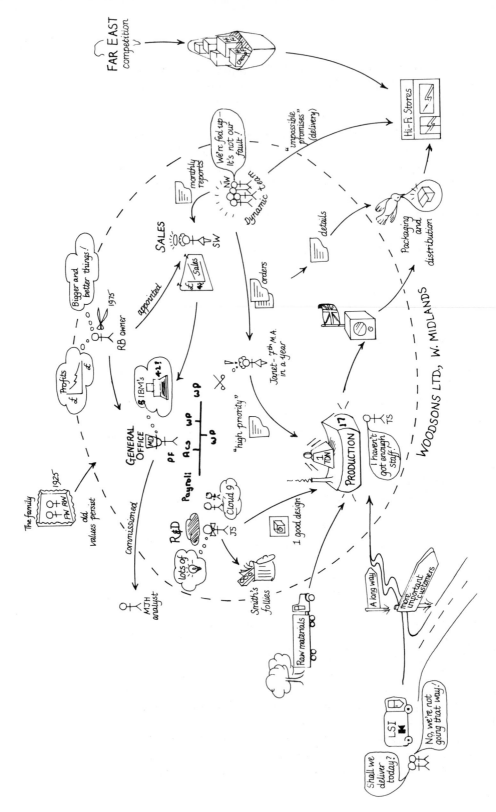

Figure 12.4 *Rich Picture for Woodsons example.*

we take a break between the building process we have just finished and reviewing our picture to try to discover what it all means.

As we review our Rich Picture we should be looking for new and insightful ways of looking at the problem situation. We would like to find a new angle, perspective or a totally different way of viewing the problem situation. This task is often helped by first trying to determine:

- the tasks that the organization was originally created to perform,
- the activities they must engage in now in order to 'survive' the problem situation.

. . . these are the organizations' *Primary Tasks*, and also . . .

- the things which are or should be the organization's primary *Issues of Concern*.

Frame 12.5 identifies the Primary Tasks and Issues of Concern for Woodsons Ltd; your interpretation of the situation might be different.

12.3.3   Root Definitions of relevant systems

We are now approaching the crucial stage of SSM, deciding on our Root Definitions. A Root Definition is a concise verbal description of the system we intend to model and which, when compared with the real world problem situation, will, we hope inspire ideas for changes that may resolve the problem. It is a major step to move from our Rich Picture to here, so how do we summarize the essence of the problem situation from all the detail in the picture?

We have already taken some tentative steps in this direction by listing the organization's primary tasks and its issues of concern. Now we need to think of some systems which are likely to be relevant ways of viewing the problem situation, and write down brief (often 'one-line') descriptions of them. How to know that they are going to be relevant? Don't worry about this. We can only be certain that a particular system was not relevant at the end of our efforts, if the changes we suggest are rejected. It is usual and a wise precaution to proceed through the next steps developing at least one possibly relevant system.

The problem situation seen through our Rich Picture should give some clues as to which system(s) we should employ to make some sense out of it. There is presumably a mission or purpose somewhere, and if this is worthwhile there should be a human activity system that will assist with our appreciation of the problem situation. A useful strategy for generating our relevant systems is to do some Brainstorming, as we would particularly like some unusual ones.

Let us suppose that the situation we are studying is a rugby football match, how might we view the purpose of this phenomenon? An obvious one would be to think of a rugby match as merely a recreational

──────── *Frame 12.4   Guidelines for preparing a Rich Picture* ────────

- Look for things in the problem situation that tend to change slowly with time and which are relatively stable – the Structure – such as the sales and production sections, loudspeakers, etc. Look for things that are continuously changing, such as the various activities taking place within the structure – the Process – for example, the R & D activity, which go on within the structure. And see how these elements of structure and process interact with each other; are there any mismatches or conflicts in the way they relate – the Climate.*

- Try not to think and certainly do not represent the parts of the situation as systems, because that would imply that they have all the properties of a system, including things such as control mechanisms and efficient communications channels providing feedback. For instance, in Woodsons the marketing assistant could be seen as the 'interface between a marketing system and a production system'. Once identified as such, these 'systems' may become 'untouchable' entities.

- Ensure that you have shown both 'hard' and 'soft' information. If we have a lot of quantitative data it is usually easier to depict this by placing on our Rich Picture an appropriate symbol annotated by an equally suitable cryptic comment, and keep the bulk of the data on a separate sheet.

- Determine which are considered to be the important, meaningful or useful social roles within the situation and note the behaviour (in a very general sense) that is expected from the people who fill these roles. In other words, what are the cultural norms of the organization? Be very careful not to make your own value judgements about what kind of behaviour is good, bad or acceptable.

- Since each of us has a set of attitudes, opinions, values and beliefs which colour our perceptions, we should not forget to include ourselves in the Rich Picture along with the sponsor.

───────────

*An example of 'climate' in the Woodsons situation is that whilst many other things may have changed in recent years, such as the growth in sales, the size of the production section has not, hence there is a mismatch between Process (sales) and Structure (the staffing of the production section).

system or a revenue generating system, but how about, a thirst producing system, a system for preserving 'amateur status' in sport, a system for the 'safe' release of pent-up communal rivalries, a system for attracting potential male voice choir members, a system for permitting intimate

---

Woodsons Ltd: Primary Tasks and Issues of Concern — Frame 12.5

Created to perform
Produce & market hi-fi speakers
Make a profit
Improve the design of
    loudspeaker systems
Provide employment?

Must do to survive
Be competitive
Improve customer relations
Improve business operations,
    planning/scheduling,
    administration
Enlarge production team
Market Research?
Maintain a quality image?

Issues of Concern
Possible sale of the company
Packaging and distribution
Maintaining an adequate supply of speaker units
Communications between sales and production
Morale (particularly of the production team)
'Misguided' R & D effort
Under-used computing facilities?

Those items marked with a (?) seem at first sight not to be as important or relevant as the other items, but have been included so that they will not be overlooked, just in case we should change our minds later.

---

contact between adult human males within a society that generally disapproves of overt displays of such behaviour, a product testing system for washing powder manufacturers, a system for utilizing mis-shapen footballs?

When searching for relevant systems, we should not attempt to evaluate their potential usefulness, as this will reduce the likelihood of us coming up with new and insightful ways of seeing the problem situation. Frame 12.6 lists some relevant systems for the Woodsons case study.

When trying to generate names for new products we said that the merit of a good one will usually be obvious. The same is true of relevant systems: we tend to recognize a really insightful system as soon as we have thought of it, because it provides us with an unexpected perspective on the problem situation. Remember, these systems are not intended to solve a given problem, nor are they ones that anybody is ever likely to implement.

We now try to form a synthesis of the most appropriate of our relevant systems, a distillation which is manifested as a precise verbal description of the essence of the main processes implicit in them. We are not trying to state the crux of the problem, but the spirit of the way things were intended or are now wanted to be. The word 'mission' seems to

Frame 12.6   Woodsons Ltd: Relevant Systems

A commercial system for manufacturing and selling Hi-fi loudspeakers.

A system for designing and testing Hi-fi loudspeakers.

A system for encouraging/helping the survival of the UK Hi-fi business.

A system for supplying independent Hi-fi retailers with good quality loudspeaker systems.

A system for providing business for external manufacturers, packers/ distributors and retailers.

A system for promoting the European 'sound' of loudspeakers.

A system designed to enhance the quality/esoteric image of UK Hi-fi, particularly its excellence in loudspeaker design.

A system for improving the design of loudspeaker systems.

A system for providing employment for acoustic designers and cabinet makers.

A system designed to challenge/arrest/regain the inroads being made by far-Eastern Hi-fi manufacturers in the UK. A system for providing humans with the ability to make more noise.

A system for providing an effective investment for the owner.

A system for testing the potential of 'gifted' staff by subjecting them to a situation which causes confusion and frustration.

summarize nicely what we are trying to do here. We have gathered together a number of relevant systems each of which highlights some aspect of the main function that we perceive the organization to be performing, and are now trying to mould these into a mission statement – our Root Definition. There will be conflict between providing a full description in our Root Definition and our overall aim to be concise. We should also ensure that the level of detail is consistent throughout the definition. However, we need to get something down on paper fairly quickly so that we can discuss our thoughts with the problem-owners.

In choosing which relevant systems to incorporate into our Root Definition, we need to make a conscious decision as to the direction in which we think we are heading. If we select relevant systems which have come from our Primary Tasks, we are likely to get a fairly conservative Root Definition that effectively describes the mission of the organization. This is appropriate if we believe that we are dealing with a problem perceived to be one of organizational design or information system provision and where the mission itself is not contentious. A Root Definition derived from issues of concern is a more radical proposition as it may challenge fundamental attitudes or major policy decisions. An insightful relevant system is more critical, if not essential, for dealing with a problem situation (Checkland and Wilson, 1980).

Woodsons Ltd: Root Definition ————————— *Frame 12.7* ——

A (privately owned) limited liability commercial system which designs and builds Hi-fi loudspeaker enclosures (and whose production capacity is led by market forces), from materials (in particular, speaker chassis units) obtained from external sources, and who sell and distribute these enclosures primarily to independent Hi-fi retailers; whilst maintaining the excellent reputation of British designed loudspeaker enclosures.

We should develop more than one Root Definition through the remaining stages of the SSM process. This is a wise precaution since it would be embarrassing to have our one and only set of desirable and feasible changes rejected by the client. (We should not in any case allow ourselves to get so detached from the perceptions and likely responses of the people involved that our suggested changes will meet this fate. Right now we should be sharing our thoughts on relevant systems with the problem-owners; we also could have involved as many problem-owners as possible when trying to Brainstorm our relevant systems.) Trying out alternatives does not require much extra work: the bulk of our effort has already been made. It may be appropriate in certain circumstances to take a primary task *and* an issue-based Root Definition through to a conclusion. Woodsons is possibly such a situation; they are in such a mess that it is debatable as to which direction we should take. Should we concentrate on improving their internal communications, or would the company benefit from a strategic policy rethink?

Woodsons is a manufacturing company. There are often problems in a manufacturing setting in getting agreement on what should constitute the Root Definition (Rhodes, 1985). Everybody usually agrees what transformation is taking place, but this may be constrained by the desire to 'satisfy' the market effectively, or by the need to use production resources efficiently. Is it possible to balance the needs of these two constraints? Those holding prime positions within an organization, such as managing director, works directors, sales director, chief accountant, will have an opinion on how this should be. Unless agreement is achieved at the outset, attempts to produce conceptual models and arrive at feasible and desirable changes could turn out to be to no avail.

At Woodsons no official policy had ever been made concerning this. There did not seem to be a need until recently. In practical terms the company has been led by the sales team and market forces, but there had been no problem until now. We shall assume that there is tacit approval (with certain reservations) for this state of affairs to continue.

Root Definitions need to be worded with care and precision without inhibiting imagination, because a systems model has to be built logically from them. Smyth and Checkland (1976) believe that the following elements should be found explicitly in a well-formed Root Definition, all except the transformation process may be deliberately omitted but only for a very good reason.

Transformation process – 'the means by which the defined inputs to our system are transformed into its defined outputs'.

Ownership of system – some agency that has 'prime concern' for the system and which has the ultimate 'power to cause the system to cease to exist'.

Actors – the people (expressed in terms of roles) who 'carry out or cause to be carried out the main activities of the system, especially its main transformation'.

Customers – the people within or outside the system who will be the beneficiaries or victims of the effects of the system's activities.

Environmental constraints – features of the system's environment (including any wider systems of which our system is a component) which have to be taken as given.

Worldview (Weltanschaung) – the standpoint from which we have chosen to view the system. Because of its nature this element is not usually explicitly stated in the Root Direction.

Try to form Root Definitions for the Woodsons case study. The one I have chosen to work with is shown in Frame 12.7. Your Root Definitions may be different from mine, though it is likely that you will have constructed one that is similar. I have assumed that Woodsons' mission was not a matter of controversy, and decided to build a model based on a Primary Task-based Root Definition.

The problem situation at Woodsons appears to be due mainly to a lack of communication. Since the crisis in the early 1970s, they had been doing well, until recently. They had staved off Japanese competition in their sector of the hi-fi market, and even producing a steady growth in sales! A further consideration in my choice of a relatively conservative rather than an insightful Root Definition was for it to lead to a model whose logic will be most universally understood, in order to demonstrate as simply as possible the steps involved in SSM.

In a real situation, amongst other ideas, I would have pursued a Root Definition that would focus attention on the R & D activity taking place at Woodsons, and which could be derived from the relevant systems:

- A system for improving the design of loudspeaker systems.
- A system designed to enhance the quality/esoteric image of UK hi-fi, particularly its excellence in loudspeaker design.

Another possibility could have been a Root Definition leading to a model highlighting changes needed to enable the realization of the aim implied within the relevant system:

- A system for providing an effective investment for the owner.

Woodsons Ltd: Checking the Root Definition ——————— **Frame 12.8** ——

Possible contenders for:

Customers:	the independent Hi-fi retailers.
Actors:	the company's employees.
Transformation:	the design, manufacture and marketing of loud-speaker enclosures to meet market demand.
Worldview:	commercial enterprise.
Owners:	the owner of the company.
Environment:	the speaker chassis suppliers, competitors, Hi-fi retailers.

Next, we should verify its 'completeness' by checking it against the list of the essential elements of a Root Definition on page 243 (Frame 12.8).

12.3.4   Building the conceptual model

The next stage in SSM is to construct a 'conceptual' model of the systems described with the Root Definitions. Here the precise nature of this verbal description is all important, for we now have to build our model logically from that description. Root Definitions are descriptions of human activity systems, and so activities are the entities which form the components of our model. The Root Definition determines which activities are incorporated into the model. We call it a conceptual model to stress the fact that the system modelled is an abstract thing that exists only in our minds and because an implementation of it may never exist in the real world. We represent our model diagrammatically because that is the best form in which to compare it with our Rich Picture. Essentially it is a number of shapes representing the activities taking place within our system, linked by arrows denoting the logical dependency of one activity upon another. How then do we actually put this model together?

The first stage in our model building is to look at our Root Definition and list all the (transitive) verbs, describing things we 'do', or human activities. We try if we can to put them down in some sort of logically coherent order. Scanning the Root Definition for the Woodsons case study we come across the following verbs pertaining to the system:

- design
- build
- obtained
- sell
- distribute
- maintaining

These describe the main activities necessary for our system to perform as desired. Next we examine this list (and the Root Definition) for any other activities implied by them, but not explicitly mentioned in the Root Definition. For example, the activity 'obtain materials' implies 'maintaining relationships with potential suppliers'. Another implied activity is that, in any commercial system, there must be some fundamental business activities (book-keeping, paying employees, etc.) taking place somewhere. For the moment I shall group all these together under 'administrate'. We should be aiming for somewhere between five and ten main activities altogether.

Having identified the main activities taking place within our system, we now need to decide whether any of these activities should be broken down into a number of smaller activities. For example, the activity 'build loudspeakers' comprises a number of other activities such as 'draw up a production schedule', 'manufacture the speaker cabinets', 'assemble speaker systems', 'perform quality control checks'. We should be looking out for similar activities apparently occurring in several places, as this may reveal that certain activities should be grouped together in a subsystem. A list of main and secondary activities to be included in the conceptual model for the Woodsons case study is given in Frame 12.9. As our Root Definition gives specific emphasis to maintaining a quality image, it is not surprising that the activity 'perform quality control checks' appears twice in this list, as does the activity 'design improvements/new products'. Our system ought to have a 'quality' subsystem somewhere.

During our model building we must guard against allowing activities (even subsystems of activities) known to take place in the real world problem situation to creep into our conceptual model. Only activities which can be logically deduced as taking place from what has been described in the Root Definition should be included. Remember, we are building an *abstract* alternative view of the problem situation to compare against the reality. We should also be concentrating on what is going on, what activities are taking place, for example, 'maintain accounts', while totally ignoring how this could be accomplished, as this is irrelevant at this point.

Difficulties encountered constructing our conceptual model may indicate that some detail in our Root Definition is missing or inappropriate. Going back and forth between the two, making refinements to them should be considered as a normal part of the process of model building. However, we must resist the temptation to simplify the Root Definition solely to alleviate these difficulties.

Once we have a list of the minimum necessary activities to accomplish the mission set out by the Root Definition, we need to decide whether any activity in this list is logically dependent on another activity so that we can complete our diagram or conceptual model. There are two problems with this step. First, one person may see a logical dependency

Major activities

Obtain materials
- Order speaker chassis units, raw materials, etc. and check deliveries.
- Control stock.

Design enclosures
- Design improvements/new products.
- Build and test prototypes.

Build loudspeakers
- Draw up production schedules.
- Manufacture speaker cabinets.
- Assemble speaker systems.
- Perform quality (control) checks and monitor work-in-progress and production costs.

Sell loudspeakers
- Select, design and implement advertising.
- Decide pricing policy, trade discounts.
- Obtain (provisional) orders.
- Confirm orders and agree delivery dates.
- Keep/update end-user records and provide customer service.
- Conduct/analyse market research.
- Control credit.

Distribute loudspeakers
- Package loudspeakers.
- Despatch loudspeakers.

Maintain quality
- Perform quality control checks.
- Analyse existing products (including those of competitors) and perform repairs.
- Design improvements/new products.

Administrate
- Maintain accounts, payroll, etc.
- Prepare short- and long-term plans, budgets and decide policy.
- Compare actual performance with plans.
- Invoice customers.

between two activities where another may not, especially if one of them is not sure what logical dependency is. Secondly, the ease with which the conceptual model can be logically deduced from the Root Definition is likely to be related to a person's experience.

Checkland has suggested the use of a Dependency Matrix such as the one shown in Figure 12.5. This is essentially a table which has a list of activities as both row and column headings. By asking the question 'Does Activity A logically depend on Activity B?' repeatedly we are able to fill in the upper right portion of the table with a tick denoting where logical dependency exists. This leaves the bottom left of the table unused.

It is suggested we should use this part of the table to indicate logical dependency in the sense of feedback, where one activity benefits (learns or changes) on the basis of what (usually information) it receives from the other activity.

This technique will help us systematically to ensure that we have the right arrows in the right place on our diagram, but it does not help us to determine logical dependency, and becomes somewhat cumbersome with a large model anyway. Ian Woodburn (1985) suggests another way of determining logical dependency using the mnemonic DIME:

D   Dependency
I   Information
M   Material
E   Energy

For there to be Dependency there must be a significant amount of Information, Materials or Energy given out by Activity X which is also a significant input to Activity Y. If there is then Y logically depends on X. The choice of what constitutes a significant amount is determined by the analyst and depends on the level of detail at which his or her analysis is conducted.

Woodburn also suggests that, since we have asked about these significant amounts of information, materials and energy and have named them (for example, production schedules, speaker chassis) they can be included in the conceptual model. This has the potential for making the conceptual model more informative and also easier to comprehend. However it has been argued that this can result in a model too complicated to be useful when making our comparison with the real world via our Rich Picture. Our initial overview, a basic model (see Figure 12.6), should depict only major dependencies, not each individual flow of materials, energy, information and influence, etc. Parts of this model can be elaborated in separate diagrams if this is desirable and flow versions prepared from these.

When we feel our conceptual model is 'complete' it is possible to check it out. We should also verify that our model contains all the com-

Depend on:	Design enclosures	Obtain materials	Build loudspeakers	Sell loudspeaker
Design enclosures		√	√	
Obtain materials				
Build loudspeakers				√
Sell loudspeakers		√		

Activities:

Figure 12.5 *Woodsons Ltd: a dependency matrix.*

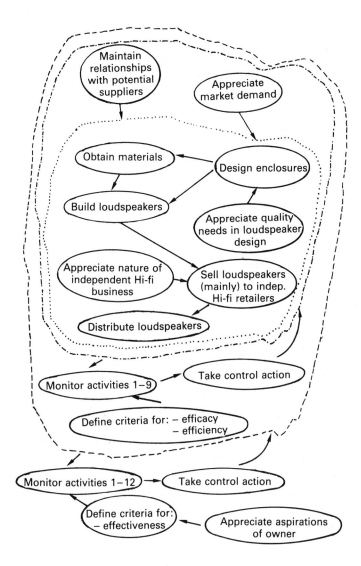

Figure 12.6 *Conceptual model for Woodsons.*

Efficacy: business demonstrably in operation.
Efficiency: returns from the business/cost of resources used in running it.
Effectiveness: owner's aspirations being met while maintaining the reputation of British designed louspeaker enclosures.

ponents it should have by comparing it with the Formal Systems Model (Chapter 11). This is supposed to contain all the elements and properties that an open system such as our human activity system should have. The Formal Systems Model suggests that we should ask of our model questions such as:

- Are the system boundaries clearly defined?
- Are there the means to measure the system's performance somewhere

in the model? What is considered to be 'good' and 'bad' performance?
- Where in the model is the decision-making process located?
- What subsystems are there in the model? Are there effective inter-connections between them and the rest of the system?
- Although we cannot guarantee the validity of our model by this means we can at least ensure that they are not so sloppily constructed as to be useless.

12.3.5   Comparison of Rich Picture and Conceptual Model

Once we have checked out our model, we should not spend too much time adding finishing touches to it before actually using it. We can always refine it later if necessary after initiating the comparisons. We now compare the real world problem situation as depicted by our Rich Picture with our model. We hope this will inspire ideas for systemically desirable (consistent with our system model) and culturally feasible changes, which will improve the problem situation. Culturally feasible changes are those possible given the history of the situation and its present characteristics (e.g. prevailing cultural norms and power structures), coupled with individually shared experiences and prejudices. Determining what is culturally feasible should be done with the concerned participants in the problem situation. It may be difficult to meet both systems and cultural criteria, but if something is not culturally acceptable the chances of it ever being implemented are remote.

Checkland (1981) has found that different kinds of study require different methods of comparison and suggests four ways in which we can perform this comparison.

(1)   Where the conceptual model and reality are very different, we should not try to convince the problem-owners that according to our model they have been doing things wrongly in the past. A wiser course of action is to produce a checklist of questions that you can ask of the real world problem situation. For example, for each activity in the model:

Does this happen in the real world?
If not, why not?
If so, who does it and why?
    Have the people doing this been considered to be successful?
    If not, why not?
    Why is the activity done this way?
      Has the activity been considered to be successful?
      If not, why not?
    Which activities (in the real world) are dependent on it
    Why is this?
      Is this the same as in the model?
      If not, why not?

Woodsons Ltd: comparisons between Rich Picture ———— *Frame 12.10* ————
and conceptual model

No systematically planned/conducted advertising
No apparent policy re. production capacity determining sales or vice
   versa
No feedback from production to sales
Insufficient customer information
No apparent market research
Complaints
Misguided R & D
Erratic suppliers
LSI favour
Computer use
Production pressure
No pricing policy
No effective planning of R & D
No effective communication and reporting channels
No stock control system

Which activities (in the real world) provide feedback to it?
Positive or negative?
   Is this the same as in the model?
If not, why not?
Does it provide information for control/decision making use?
If not, should it?
What links (if any) does it have with the (real world) environment?
   Is this the same as in the model?
   If not, why not?

(2)   We could take an incident in the problem situation and 'replay'
it through our model, comparing what has happened historically with
what might have happened if our conceptual model were to be implemented in the real world.

(3)   If we suspect that major strategic changes may be required, typically where we have begun to question the utility of an activity, it is
probably best to use the comparisons to provide questions of a very
general nature, such as asking what is different between the model and
reality and why this is so.

(4)   In well-structured problem situations, we could construct an
activity model of the actual problem by redrawing our Rich Picture to
show just the activities actually taking place and how they are interlinked. Doing this carefully, ensuring that activities that are common
to both the real world and the conceptual model are drawn in similar

positions on the two diagrams, allows us physically to overlay the real world situation with our conceptual model, vividly showing the differences between the two.

Comparisons of 'what is' with 'what perhaps should be' are fine as long as there is a something already existing to compare with! When you are designing a new system we can only compare it with 'some defined expectation', a theoretical ideal. Such an analysis is likely only to show up basic omissions in the design.

With Woodsons I have opted for the third route, as there appear to be major changes necessary within that organization. In Frame 12.10 I have listed activities that were evident in one diagram and missing from the other.

Although we have been working with the problem-owners throughout, their reactions to our comparisons may reveal inadequacies in our initial analysis or in the formulation of our Root Definition. We may have to do some back-tracking to the earlier stages of the process to fill in these deficiencies.

12.3.6 Systemically desirable and culturally feasible changes

The purpose of these comparisons is primarily to initiate a debate with the people concerned with the problem situation, and therefore some form of agenda needs to be prepared. The comments and suggestions comprising this agenda should be couched in terms of 'what' rather than 'how'. This has the benefit that, if acceptable, it leaves the problem-owners to determine the best methods in their particular circumstances rather than forcing a specific solution on them. For example, 'We feel that the sales team should receive regular updates of the production schedule including advice on work in progress' indicates what we feel may be missing from Woodsons' present operations. However, 'We suggest that a ZY42000 computer system should be installed to facilitate production scheduling and that a terminal giving access to this machine should be placed in the sales office' is just one, and possibly not the most appropriate, way of describing how the former change may be implemented.

Reflect on the differences that have been noted between the Rich Picture and the conceptual model for Woodsons, and try to generate a set of suggested changes that can be incorporated into the agenda for our debate (my ideas are in Frame 12.11).

12.3.7 Implementation of the changes

We may have suggested changes of a number of different types, such as:

- changes in structure, organizational groupings, departments, reporting structures, lines of command/functional responsibility/communications, physical layout;

┌─ *Woodsons Ltd: Systemically desirable and* ─────── *Frame 12.11* ──────
│ *culturally feasible changes*
│
│ • Internal communications should be improved: production ↔ sales;
│   distribution of regular production schedules, advice on work in
│   progress, sales → market research → R & D.
│ • Consider the expansion of the production department's workforce.
│ • Adopt an agreed R & D policy, perhaps a small team engaged in
│   relatively esoteric research while the rest are developing existing
│   products.
│ • Institute a stock control system with particular emphasis initially
│   on second-sourcing loudspeaker chassis units.
│ • Consider ways of encouraging teamwork across divisions.
│ • Investigate whether better use can be made of the IBMs, e.g.
│   production scheduling, customer data base etc.
│ • Reappraise and/or re-establish an advertising policy.
│ • Perhaps initiate an independent analysis of Woodsons' market
│   and/or financial position.
└──

  • changes in procedures, changing the way that some activities are
    done, such as changing the processes by which informing and re-
    porting takes place within the structures of the organization;
  • changes in policy, repositioning the company, modifying goals and
    strategies.

These types of change are relatively simple to specify and not too difficult to carry out, especially if the persons desiring the change have the
necessary authority or influence. However, although these changes may
be easy to bring about, they may still have unexpected consequences.
The use of Rich Pictures in the early stages of the process should have
minimized the possibility of overlooking any important interactions or
interconnections that might cause such problems. A further precaution
the problem-owners could take would be to carry out something similar
to Kepner–Tregoe's Potential Problem Analysis (see Chapter 10) before
actually embarking on implementation.

   Although given the authority and resources it may be easy nominally
to effect some changes, commitment is necessary to carry them through
effectively. We have seen that people are often antipathetic to change
and need to be 'sold' its benefits. If all the problem-owners have had
the opportunity to play a part in resolving the problem situation, then
changes such as those above should be achievable. But, SSM does tend
to assume that these participants are rational beings and responsive
to fair and reasoned arguments backed by irrefutable and impartial
evidence. There is, however, another type of change we may feel is
necessary.

— *Frame 12.12*   *SSM: background information* —

The Soft Systems Methodology (SSM) was devised by Professor Peter Checkland and has been developed by him and others at the University of Lancaster's Department of Systems since 1969. SSM was conceived as a strategy for dealing with the 'soft', ill-defined, complex problems of the real world, by considering these problem situations as 'human activity systems'. In other words, SSM was specifically intended to be a way of dealing with what we have called elsewhere 'people' problems.

SSM evolved out of an attempt to overcome the apparent deficiencies of the traditional methods of systems analysis which, although primarily intended as a means of tackling 'hard' engineering (machine) type problems, were then being increasingly used (without too much success) on problem situations involving people (and sadly, still are).

Briefly, the shortcomings of these methods which SSM has sought to replace are that they have tended to assume that the problem could be simply stated, and have then concentrated on what was being done and have sought to improve this (often, some people would say, by just patching it up), without considering why it was being done or indeed whether it should have been done at all.

The product of SSM is a list of possible changes which should improve the problem situation, and which are both systemically desirable and culturally feasible. Traditional methods of systems analysis seldom considered the latter.

● changes in attitude both at an individual level and universally throughout an organization, as in attempting to change people's expectations concerning the behaviour associated with certain roles.

Realizing changes of this type is a difficult task to accomplish. The extent of this difficulty will depend on the type or content of the organizational culture in which the change is to take place and its strength, and whether the attitudes at the centre of interest are those of individuals or are widely shared by many within the organization. Checkland advises (1981) that if a deliberate attempt is made to change attitudes, continuous monitoring of the effects are essential, because of the unpredictability of such an operation.

Many people believe that it is anything from foolish to downright impossible, even rather sinister, to try deliberately to change people's attitudes. They say that such things happen only as the result of personal and collective experience. However, that is not to say that people's attitudes, expectations and influence are not suitable material for our debate with the problem-owners. If there is to be any change in attitudes as a result of an SSM (or any other kind) of intervention, it will probably come about as a by-product of the participants having been involved in the experience of sharing their perceptions of the problem situation.

12.4 Postscript

Suppose we give our report to Woodsons and they say that our suggestions are impractical, or decide simply to do nothing. What should we do? The answer is *nothing*. We have to accept this state of affairs. The first of these possibilities should not occur if we have considered enough possibilities along the route and have checked periodically to make sure we were remaining within the bounds of cultural feasibility. If they decide to do nothing, even though we have put in a lot of work, we must simply accept their point of view, as sometimes doing nothing may seem to the problem-owners to be the best policy.

12.5 Timing

The initial stages, the determination of the politics of the situation and the gathering of hard and soft data required for the production of the Rich Picture, take the bulk of the time involved in the process, perhaps weeks or months. Devising the Root definitions and the construction of the conceptual models may only take hours or days in a project lasting several months. This is why it is recommended to construct and try out several models; apart from being desirable, it is also practically feasible. The amount of time required by the later stages, starting with the comparison of the models with the problem situation (via the Rich Picture) and culminating with the debate over what constitutes systemically desirable and culturally feasible changes, is a little less easy to predict, depending as it does on the complexity and sensitivity of the circumstances 'discovered' during the intervention. It will typically take days or weeks – considerably longer if we include in this estimate the time taken to implement and monitor the changes agreed.

C H A P T E R

13

Really complicated problems

13.1 Comparison of the Soft Systems and Synectics approaches

These two methods have many similarities, particularly at the ideological level. For example, they provide more 'front end' stages with no prejudgements than some other methodologies, which attempt to ensure we are solving the right problem. There are also some differences. The aim of this short section is to summarize and extend the comparisons made earlier, concentrating particularly on the differences. This should enable you to decide whether these are significant enough to preclude the use of one or another technique under certain circumstances, but perhaps more importantly this section shows how a synthesis of the two methodologies can be usefully achieved.

The most apparent difference is right at the very beginning. With the Soft Systems Methodology (SSM), a lot of data is gathered initially, in an attempt to take into consideration the whole picture. From this we try to develop insightful perspectives on the problem situation. Synectics, on the other hand, values the 'ignorance' of many of the problem solving resources (group members) for its potential in providing us with a fresh view of the problem situation, maintaining that there is no need for the majority of the group to understand the problem in order to assist with its resolution. The subsequent 'scatter gun' approach of Goal Wishing then amplifies the brief description of the problem given by the problem-owner into many other views of the problem situation, both possible and wildly speculative.

Whether we prefer a fairly 'systematic' means of getting many perspectives on the problem situation (with SSM) or the more 'random' approach of Synectics, we should be aware of (i) the greater difficulty of later getting away from the problem having once gathered large quantities of data, and (ii) that Goal Wishing is more likely to send us down the route towards innovative solutions.

I have said that when we have a problem situation of such complexity that the number of problem-owners is well into double figures, the employment of the Synectics process may require a restructuring of the problem situation and the involvement of several groups of problem solvers, which could possibly incur some administrative difficulties. And since it could be argued anyway that collecting a lot of data in these circumstances is often necessary, SSM may seem to be a more appropriate way to proceed. This latter point should not be taken as a criterion for choosing between methodologies, because Synectics is not opposed to gathering and using data, it simply does not place the same importance on this initially. Not unrelated to this is the time factor. A Synectics session may take only a few hours, while an SSM intervention may take weeks or months. The data collection aspect of SSM is obviously a time-consuming activity, but the time required is also a function of the complexity of the problem situation. If we tackled situations as complex as SSM often does using only Synectics, we would need to have many problem solving sessions, interspersed with planning meetings and plenary discussions, all of which would take considerably more than a few hours.

Both strategies require the use of skilled practitioners, but in rather different ways. The Synectics approach requires a trained and highly skilled process leader, whereas someone conducting an SSM investigation (although possibly needing some process leading skills during discussions with the problem-owners) needs to have knowledge and experience of systems theory, because in an SSM study it is the consultants who effectively 'do the problem solving' in so much as it is they who *carry out* the process. This really is the fundamental difference between the two methodologies, although both emphasize close liaison with the problem-owners and it is they who ultimately determine what constitutes a solution. With the Synectics approach the consultant/ facilitator solely guides the process – it is the problem-owner who does the problem solving. SSM's involvement in the problem content has another implication; Checkland speaks of our obligation to 'donate the technique' when the intervention is completed; this is admirable, but not quite so easy as it is with Synectics.

Returning to the actual stages in the process, both systems attempt to ensure that whoever commissions the problem solving is checked out as to whether they have the motivation to reach a conclusion. With Synectics the client is necessarily a problem-owner; this need not be so with an SSM study, and anyway it will probably be impractical with SSM to ascertain the motivation of all the problem-owners.

Both approaches embark, after the 'initial analysis', on amassing ways of viewing the problem situation (Relevant Systems v. Goal Wishing). It is likely to be more difficult for a lone SSM problem solver to produce as many different perspectives as a group performing Goal Wishing. This is why it is recommended (Chapter 12) that the Relevant Systems are obtained at least partially from a Brainstorming session (or Synectics' Goal Wishing) with the problem-owners.

A significant difference is encountered in the idea generation phase. When there is a need to get right away from the problem, bring in new material and start to put together some thoughts which will, we hope, lead to the resolution of the problem, SSM calls upon abstract systems thinking. Synectics on the other hand uses Excursions. The former is a very logical development of a systems model from a beginning idea (Root Definition); the latter is a somewhat irrational process. Excursions are likely to be more effective at getting this distance, because many unskilled SSM practitioners will experience difficulty in leaving the problem behind after they reach a Root Definition. With the absurdities of some types of Excursion it is virtually impossible not to forget the problem! If the problem situation is such that eventually (once the problem has been identified and suitable changes have been suggested) a 'hard' systems analysis and design process (for example, SSADM) will need to be initiated (e.g. in a highly technological environment), the building of the conceptual model in SSM will have been an extremely useful starting point.

The finale of SSM is the discussion with the problem-owners of the changes suggested by the comparison of the conceptual model(s) with the real world situation. Even if the SSM facilitator has kept in close touch with the problem-owners throughout the intervention, this meeting has the potential for a conflict of views over these 'systemically desirable and culturally feasible' changes. Such a meeting is likely to achieve more consensus if some Synectics' principles are incorporated.

Participation in a Synectics problem solving session nearly always improves communications between group members and builds team spirit. If this does happen, then this will assist the implementation of the possible solution later. The SSM process, because of its *modus operandi*, is not likely to have the same effect, except perhaps in a minor way because the problem-owners have been party to an indirect exchange of viewpoints.

Synectics is committed to openness because of its positive secondary effects on team building. A frank interchange of differing views is not so likely to happen with SSM. Although in an SSM intervention we need to collect the soft attitudes, opinions, prejudices, likes and dislikes, etc. of the people involved, they are not necessarily (in fact rarely) passed on by the facilitator to other interested parties. Synectics seems to be prepared to lose the occasional battle that might result from this openness, perhaps knowing that eventually even confirmed autocrats have to acknowledge that other people have a right to express an idea or a contrary viewpoint without risking crucifixion. The SSM approach is a little more cautious. This does not imply that the SSM practitioner can be less skilled in open-mindedness, inspiring trust and confidence in others and the other human relations attributes required by a Synectics process leader. These qualities are still needed for gathering information from problem-owners. It is just that the SSM process usually tries to avoid the potential conflicts that complete frankness between problem-owners might give rise to.

There is a potential difficulty with Synectics of getting all the appropriate people involved. The bosses, whose presence may be essential, may be reluctant to give up their time for a problem solving session. If they can be encouraged to participate, then the process leader is going to have to work harder generating the desired atmosphere for creativity where, temporarily, everyone is equal, everyone's contributions have the same merit and openness prevails. Technically it is easier to collect the 'soft' information in a personal interview, as one might in an SSM investigation; it would certainly be less time-consuming for those questioned. But we still need approval from an authority figure to guarantee that an SSM intervention can be carried out effectively. Finally, because the problem-owners actually take part in the problem solving process with Synectics, there is less danger that at the end of the day the problem solving facilitator will be completely off-track in respect of the solutions obtained by the process.

13.2   A complicated problem

I have tried to show that Synectics and the Soft Systems approach are probably two of the best problem solving strategies currently available for dealing with the complex and interwoven people problems we come across every day. Having shown their similarities and contrasted the differences in their approaches, it is appropriate now to demonstrate how this might affect our choice of methodology by posing what I hope is the most complicated scenario so far, and then considering which of the strategies mentioned in this book might be used in this situation, and how. It is *not* my intention that you should attempt to try actually to resolve this problem situation *now*; you should simply read through the story in Frame 13.1 and start thinking about how you might tackle it.

What should we suggest to Michael Pantoni? One place to start could be to invite Pantoni, his six line managers and some six or so other people from within the department to a Brainstorming session on 'How to improve the "internal" operations of SLG'. I was once involved in a Synectics-style problem solving session for a charitable organization concerned about the low profile and confusing image they were portraying to the general public. They were seeking ways of improving this situation in the hope of gaining more funds and resources for their

────── *Frame 13.1* *Illustrative example: Business Equipment* ──────
International

Our story is set in the marketing division of Business Equipment International PLC(BEI) who are part of a multinational organization manufacturing and selling office equipment. Their product range is quite diverse and includes equipment such as computers, photo-copiers, fax machines, etc. They also develop the software required by some of the machines they sell. All product development takes place through the coordinated operations of the marketing divisions of the ten national companies. Except, of course, for some fairly esoteric research work going on at BEI's separate and very prestigious Advanced Designs Laboratory (ADL) on the West Coast of North America. Most of the innovative ideas that come out of ADL eventually end up filtering into the company's product range, via periodic research reports sent out to the marketing divisions throughout the world.

Within the marketing division there are a number of fairly autonomous departments, each one mainly handling its own particular function. These departments are New Products (NPD), Existing Products Enhancement (EPE), Customer Services (CS) and Software and Logistics (SLG). SLG is responsible for the development of the software required by the computer products sold by the company in the UK. Its chief product is an 'integrated office' suite of programs that incorporate a fairly full management information system. It is also very much into computerized project management. It is possibly for these reasons that SLG is also responsible for coordinating the development projects of the other three departments.

The morale of SLG is generally good, comprising a small, friendly and cohesive group of people; however, initial investigations suggest that the six line managers within the group have considerably different perceptions of their own roles within SLG, and that of their fellow managers. So despite the group's apparently satisfactory 'team spirit', their overall effectiveness could, in the opinion of the group (departmental) manager, be improved.

SLG's operations are further complicated by the apparent lack of cooperation between the other departments within the marketing division and themselves. From SLG's viewpoint, its role within the division should be to monitor the progress of the other departments' projects so as to ensure the overall efficiency of the division, and to provide access to, and coordinate the usage of, the additional resources required from time to time by the other departments.

For example, by monitoring a project being conducted by say EPE, the purpose of which is to determine the most cost-effective upgrade that can be offered to customers having computer equipment more than two years old, SLG would be aware that what EPE desperately needs at this time is some input from a programmer with experience of the latest developments in systems software. If they also knew (as they should) that Joe in NPD has this expertise, and is kicking his heels (on his latest project) whilst waiting for some test results to come from the States, they could put the two parties in touch.

Currently hanging over the head of the whole of the UK operation is the threat of rationalization. There is a perceived need to increase its productivity whilst decreasing costs, thus improving profitability. This may be the reason why the other three departments view any enquiry from SLG with a certain amount of suspicion, and respond to such requests usually somewhat belatedly and always with in-complete information. Out of sheer necessity, however, the other three departments are continuing to maintain (and are often im-proving) links amongst themselves. The SLG manager has been heard to defend his group's lack of brilliant performance with com-ments such as, 'They're just not talking to us anymore!', 'They keep leaving us out of important discussions and decisions.' Obviously, this attitude is not helping SLG perform its coordinating role!

We (in the role of a new, keen, junior and thus highly expendable manager) have been asked by Michael Pantoni, the SLG manager, to suggest how the department (or indeed, the division) should best deal with this mess. He wants our advice on suitable 'problem solving' methods that might help him to resolve the unsatisfactory situation that he perceives himself and his department to be in.

Michael Pantoni's initial thoughts are that SLG should tighten up its own internal operations before any attempt is made to resolve the wider issues.

work. This situation has certain similarities with the situation at BEI. In the early stages of the session with this charity, it became apparent that there were some very different perceptions of what the organization's 'mission' actually was, and that this might have been why they had so far been unable to decide on the best way to proceed in changing their image.

SLG's six line managers have different perceptions of their own and each other's expected contributions to the overall objectives of the de-partment. This may be why, despite relatively ideal working condi-tions, SLG is perceived (by its manager and others outside the depart-ment) as not being as productive as perhaps it should be.

The use of the early stages of the Synectics process (for example, Goal Wishing) are invariably effective with regard to 'opening up' the prob-lem. This is particularly so when you have a problem situation with several owners, as it provides a 'safe' environment for the airing of differing perceptions, attitudes, opinions and beliefs of the problem-owners. With the charity, by the time we had filled two walls with some 100 Springboards, the group members knew better what each other's opinions were, had realized that there was a greater degree of agreement amongst these than they thought, and were getting close to coming to an agreement on a common mission.

Since a friendly and unantagonistic attitude supposedly exists amongst both SLG generally and its senior management, an ideal place to start might well be a Synectics-style problem solving session with the line managers and their boss, Michael Pantoni, the purpose of which would be to reach a consensus on the roles of the six line managers in the context of the department's overall mission. We would work first with Michael Pantoni as the client or problem-owner, because he has ultimate responsibility for the department's activities. Then we would try to resolve the problem as seen by each of the individual line managers in turn (as with the Northcliffe Sands problem in Chapter 7).

Even if we were less ambitious and were satisfied at this stage with just a sharing of views, Synectics is likely to be more effective than 'straight' Brainstorming. On the other hand, if it seems reasonable to be more 'ambitious' and question the department's stated objectives as well, we would still have a highly suitable vehicle for this in Synectics. We might have been able to use SSM to equal effect on these same issues within SLG, however, since we apparently have the makings of 'team spirit' already, it would be a shame not to capitalize on this and get the active participation of the seven managers *together* simultaneously in the resolution of the problem situation.

The wider issues of the marketing division and SLG's place within it is a far more complicated situation, which involves considerably more interested parties (problem-owners), and possible 'outside' forces from the parent company in the United States.

It is conceivable that, once SLG has been seen to sort out its internal 'problems', our wider concerns may start to dissipate as Pantoni seems to hope. However, there seems to be a fundamental communications problem fermenting in the middle of all this, which I suspect will worsen in the time it takes SLG to demonstrate its 'new efficiency'. Furthermore, if the root cause of this is due to a fear of rationalization and the perception that SLG's data gathering may be a part of this, seeing a 'new, dynamic and together' SLG arising from the midst of things is just as likely to put the fear of God into the other three departments even more! Perhaps the marketing division's director (through Pantoni) should be advised to commission a Soft Systems study of the whole division's operations, preferably to be undertaken by an independent consultant. The distrust that appears to exist between the departments from our initial investigations seems to indicate that it would be difficult for someone within the division to gather the subjective, 'political' information that we need. This should not, however, preclude the possibility of conducting another multiple problem-owner Synectics-style session with the four departmental managers, the marketing division's director and one other person from the lower echelons of each department, to thrash out the communications problem. This could be done in addition to the SSM study, as a means of gathering perceptions of the situation, and people's 'best current thinking' on possible solutions. Or it could be our first (and cost-effective) attempt to resolve the wider concerns before someone has to decide whether to invest a considerable amount of time and money on a full SSM study.

If at the end of our problem solving we have a number of possible solutions, systemically desirable and culturally feasible changes, which we need to choose between, then it would be reasonable to employ Kepner and Tregoe's Decision Analysis to help us with this selection. Finally, when we have our chosen solution it would be wise to use something akin to Potential Problem Analysis to check out our ideas, before we start to expend effort, time and money on implementation of our chosen solution.

13.3   Steps towards a synthesis

From my suggestions on tackling the 'BEI' problem, it should be poss-ible to see how we might *augment* an SSM intervention with some elements of Synectics. First, we might use Goal Wishing with groups of problem-owners as a means of gathering much of the soft data that we require, for instance, their perceptions of the problem situation, what their individual concerns are, some 'beginning ideas' and perhaps also their 'best current thinking' on possible solutions. The idea behind 'best current thinking' is that it is generally accepted as not being perfect, and it is being offered as a basis for discussion. It will not be dissected and examined in minute detail and we will not be called upon to defend it.

Secondly, the generation of relevant systems (and even the distillation of these into Root Definitions) may be achieved by Goal Wishing with groups of problem-owners as well. We might actually find that some of the Springboards from the data collection sessions imply relevant systems that we should consider. Do not forget that a relevant system is just a (systemic) way of looking at the problem situation which we hope may turn out to be relevant later on (in the sense that the comparison of the Conceptual Models, built from them, with the real world situation will suggest useful changes). For example, person X may see SLG as a 'software development system', person Y as a 'project management system', or person Z, an 'intelligence gathering system' for the US parent company. Many of the Springboards obtained during Goal Wishing will express ways of looking at the problem situation. Remember that I have likened Cognitive Mapping to an 'extended and more systematic' form of Backward/Forward Planning and Goal Wishing and so that too finds a place here.

Finally, after SSM's comparison stage, when we get down to discussing with the problem-owners which of the changes suggested by our systems thinking are not only systemically desirable but also culturally feasible, we might choose to run this debate in the form of a Synectics 'Consensus' problem solving meeting. We might start things going by asking each of the problem-owners to give an Itemized Response to the suggested changes. This should give us an indication of the amount of agreement that exists over which of these would provide an acceptable resolution of the problem situation, and also highlight each problem-owner's outstanding concerns. Then we would try to resolve each problem-owner's concerns in turn and, we hope, ending up with a proposed course of action that is acceptable to everyone concerned.

Turning things around, how could aspects of SSM enhance the Synectics process? This is more difficult since the *modus operandi* of SSM (in the sense that the person conducting the SSM investigation becomes involved with the problem content) is antipathetic to the Synectics approach. However, I can see how conceptual model building from appropriate Springboards followed by comparison with reality (which parallels Synectics' 'Force Fit' procedure) could be modified and employed in a group setting so producing an alternative type of Excursion. Also, whilst Synectics already use some drawing exercises as 'ice-breakers' and excursions, it might be fun (and productive) to invite all the problem-owners to produce a cartoon (a sort of mini 'Rich Picture') of their view of the problem situation. These could then be displayed (possibly anonymously) and used as raw material for ideas; for example, we might ask people to choose a cartoon they like (other than the one they have drawn) and offer Springboards describing what they think the cartoon is depicting about the problem situation. This could be a means of gathering individual perceptions of the problem situation when people are anxious about providing this information verbally. Or could be used to 'exchange' perceptions between groups working on different parts of the problem situation.

You will remember that the usual Synectics group size is approximately six to eight people and that the Synectics 'Consensus' method for dealing with multiple problem ownership (see the Northcliffe Sands problem in Chapter 7), attempts to resolve the problem for all the problem-owners 'cyclically', dealing with only one problem-owner at a time. This might cause us some administrative difficulties with a large number of problem-owners. It would be nice if SSM's ability to cope in these circumstances could be imported into Synectics, but this is not really possible without wrecking some of the more important attributes

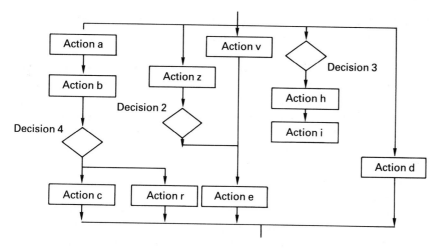

Figure 13.1 *Part of a
Decision Point Plan.*

of the Synectics approach, such as the group interactions. However, one of Synectics' more recent developments is a technique that can help us specifically to tackle problem situations complicated by having many problem-owners, as well as assisting in planning the implementation of change. It helps deal with the 'problem' of many problem-owners by providing a reasonable way of breaking down a complex situation into parts. **Decision Point Planning** (DPP) evolves from Synectics' definition of a problem as 'the gap between the present situation and a more desirable one'. This more desirable situation is often only vaguely perceived. Let us suppose that earlier discussion with the problem-owners has revealed a fair degree of consensus as to where they want to end up, but they are uncertain as to how to get there.

In group sessions (which can be larger than usual) we map out the things that the problem-owners feel ought to be done, their implications in the sense of what needs to be done before or after them, and all the decisions that they need to make *en route*, in order successfully to navigate the gap from where they know they are now, to where they think they want to be. The resulting diagram that charts this proposed odyssey, which often runs to several sheets of paper, looks vaguely similar to a flowchart except that only two symbols are used. A rectangular symbol is used to contain the actions that need to be carried out, whilst an annotated diamond shape as usual denotes the decisions to be taken. The arrows denote the logical dependency of one activity on another (Figure 13.1).

Once all problem-owners are content that all essential actions and decisions have been suitably recorded (the diagram may go through several versions before this is so), we then fill in the names of the people who have action responsibility for the various parts of the project and any decisions to be taken, along with those others who are directly involved to the extent that what may happen could impinge on their action responsibility. By this means, as we can identify each problem-owner with only some part(s) of the situation, and a fairly complicated problem can be safely broken down (restructured) without fear of missing important interconnections and interactions. We should then be able to break off into smaller problem solving groups in order to tackle any outstanding concerns that we still have with our part(s) of the project. When we have resolved all these issues the Decision Point Plan can serve as the basis of an implementation plan.

This extends the utility of Synectics into many complex problem situations, even those with many problem-owners, though it could still be argued that it falls short of the holistic approach to which SSM aspires. My main concern with SSM, however, is the small amount of involvement the problem-owners may have with the actual problem solving. Without involvement we cannot expect any commitment to the changes we obtain, which I feel is the more serious issue. Although we may be obliged by the client to operate in this way (as an external problem solving consultant, as opposed to a facilitator), it is not a desirable state of affairs. This is why if a synthesis of these two methods is to be achieved, it would have to come by injecting Synectics techniques into the basic SSM structure, the aim being to incorporate more problem-owner participation within SSM. SSM applied skilfully can get very close to tackling the *whole* of a complex problem situation, whereas Synectics can encourage more open communications and help build team spirit, and thus can often offer a (positive) *cultural change* along with a solution.

In time the distinction between the two systems may become even less clear-cut. In current work Checkland is attempting to show that SSM is not just a strategy for special highlighted major studies into complex situations, but is equally usable as a way in which a manager can go about his or her normal day-to-day managerial work. Likewise Synectics is not just a creative problem solving process, but a *continuously* developing body of knowledge, skills and techniques concerned with innovation, problem solving, communications and teamwork. It is also the name of the international group of companies responsible for the ongoing enhancement of the original Synectics concepts, DPP, a part of their current efforts to apply Synectics principles to project management, is but one example of this.

13.4   Comparative evaluation of the strategies

At the end of Chapter 2, I attempted to give a 'route map' suggesting where and in what circumstances a particular strategy may be most appropriately used. To take stock and review what has been said, I have

Table 13.1 *Evaluation of the strategies*

Strategy	Strengths	Concerns
Brainstorming	Produces a lot of ideas, very quickly Can produce innovative ideas/solutions Fun!	Cannot cope with ideas/solutions that need some development Usually requires restructuring of the problem situation
Synectics	Designed to produce innovative ideas/solutions Encourages looking at problem situations from many viewpoints Produces many useful ideas/solutions, in relatively little time Protects basically good ideas long enough to permit their development and provides the means for doing this Provides a 'safe' way of sharing different perceptions of the problem situation Facilitates the resolution of conflicts Improves communications Develops a team spirit Engenders a 'winning situations for everyone' attitude to work and life in general It makes you feel good!	Requires all interested parties to be in the group, which can be difficult with many problem-owners May require restructuring of the problem situation Really requires a trained facilitator
Kepner–Tregoe	Situational Appraisal (SA) provides sound advice for everyday planning Problem Analysis (PA) is an effective analytic way of dealing with purely 'machine'/diagnostic problems Decision Analysis (DA) is a useful aid to decision making, given a clear objective and the availability of suitable options, criteria, etc. Potential Problem Analysis (PPA) is a systematic way of approaching contingency planning, prior to the implementation of any idea/solution PA and DA provide a 'common language' that can be used retrospectively to explain/justify the process that has led to the solution/decision A logical/common-sense approach that is appealing to many	It assumes that we always have clear objectives and goals! Does not easily allow for multiple views of the problem situation PA's behaviourist 'inclinations' and 'hard' systems approach makes it inappropriate for most, if not all, 'people' problems PA invariably requires restructuring of the problem situation Does not require the use of creative thinking, though it would be foolish not to do some Due to our cultural disposition for the rational, it can be easily abused

Table 13.1 *Con't*

Strategy	Strengths	Concerns
Morphological Analysis	Attempts to cover 'all' possibilities The systematic 'search' for new ideas/solutions appeals to many who feel that they are not creative	Success depends on how appropriately and comprehensively the axes have been labelled, that is, how the problem is (re)structured Often requires additional creative thinking techniques actually to 'bring out' the ideas that will 'satisfy' the opportunities that MA has revealed The name is extremely pretentious and for some can be frightening!
Soft Systems	Designed to incorporate different perceptions of the problem situation and deal with many problem-owners Attempts to encompass the whole of the problem situation Attempts to identify the political climate explicitly Highlights the impact that investigator/problem solver has on the problem situation Can be employed by an individual on a multi owner/client problem situation	Does not require the use of creative thinking, though it would be foolish not to do some Too easy to misuse by slipping into traditional 'hard' systems thinking May take up a lot of time and resources Requires a grounding in systems thinking

attempted in Table 13.1 to perform a sort of Itemized Response on the main strategies described, listing their strengths along with my major concerns about their applicability.

This analysis is not definitive; good problem solving strategies are always being modified and improved by their creators and users. Synectics and SSM particularly are continuously evolving, and the reader is directed to the sayings, writings and doings of the originators for their 'best current thinking'.

13.5 The ideal problem solving system?

The features that we might expect of an ideal problem solving system are listed below. In true 'Kepner–Tregoe' fashion, these are categorized into things which I believe an ideal problem solving system must do and those which I would want it to do.

MUSTS

- Search out and assimilate both hard and soft data (especially, political and cultural aspects of problem situation).
- Provide the means for looking at the problem situation from many viewpoints.
- Provide ways of generating ideas, by 'getting away' from the problem situation.
- Actively involve the problem-owners, and accept input from them at various stages during the problem solving process.
- Provide the means of nurturing and developing ideas/possible solutions.
- Provide the problem-owners with a way of learning about the problem situation.
- Provide a conflict-resolving process.
- Provide the problem-owners with the means for evaluating possible solutions.
- Monitor its own performance and provide corrective feedback when appropriate.

WANTS

- Take a holistic view of the problem situation.
- Incorporate the perceptions of everyone with a 'stake' in the problem situation.
- Be flexible in its application.
- Encourage the participation/involvement of problem-owners in the problem solving/decision-making process, preferably in groups.
- Facilitate subsequent cultural changes.
- Possess the means to allow problem-owners to 'incubate'/'reflect' upon ideas.
- Check out the motivation of the problem-owners.

Many of these *wants* are essential, but you will remember that Kepner and Tregoe stipulate that *musts* have to be something that we can definitely say an option does or does not satisfy. Although highly desirable, it seems unreasonable to insist that a certain problem solving system takes into account the perceptions of *all* those that have a stake, takes in the *whole* problem situation, etc. It is more realistic to compare problem solving systems on the extent to which they achieve these wants.

13.6   Summary of good practice

I shall close this section with some advice on 'good practice', some Do's and Dont's to summarize all that has been said so far on problem solving and decision making. Each category is subdivided into general advice for solving a problem you own, and followed with advice specific to situations where you are helping others to solve their problem.

DO

... search out and assimilate both hard and soft data (especially, political and cultural aspects of the problem situation).
... try to take a holistic view of the problem situation.
... look at the problem situation from many viewpoints.
... incorporate the perceptions of everyone with a 'stake' in the problem situation.
... try to do some 'approximate/mistaken' thinking.
... try to generate ideas, by 'getting away' from the problem situation.
... give yourself a chance to reflect on your ideas.
... be flexible in the application of problem solving strategies.

... check out the motivation of the problem-owners.
... exchange ideas and information with the problem-owners at various stages during the problem solving process, and preferably ...
... actually involve the problem-owners in the problem solving/decision making process, preferably in groups.

DON'T

... evaluate ideas too early.
... jump to conclusions.
... take anything for granted.

... forget that in order to collect the data you will need to create a rapport with the problem-owners of openness, trust and empathy.
... ever think that you know better than the problem-owners.

Coping with change

14

Rapid change is commonplace. Complexity, disorganization and frustration are all natural aspects of our daily lives and normal features of organizational life. We would probably be surprised by their absence.

Buchanan and Huczynski (1985) *Organizational Behaviour*, p. 410

The basic premise underlying all that we have discussed so far has been that we need to develop and utilize a flexible yet systematic approach to problem solving and decision-making; one that can help us cope with and plan for the rapidly changing environment so that our business and other organizations can survive and maintain their competitiveness. Once we have a solution, or a decision on what course of action to take, however, it is inevitable, unless we decide to do nothing, that the implementation of our solution or decision will involve us centrally as an **agent of change**.

Further, in order to cope with the changes taking place around us, it is not merely sufficient that *we* are effective problem solvers; we ideally need everyone in the organization to be so as well. The use of any systematic problem solving and decision-making strategy will be much more difficult for an individual to apply alone, because that individual will require a supportive climate in which to operate effectively. This may involve anything from 'extra' time and support facilities, through improved and flexible access to information and people, up to and including quite drastic attitudinal change. In other words, we may want (or need) to change the organization so that the use of these methods becomes the norm.

Not only do we need to be able to cope with change, by alleviating undesirable effects and exploiting opportunities, but also we need to be able to initiate and manage change. Whether our intention is simply to spread the use of effective problem solving strategies or just to imple-

Frame 14.1 *Causes of Resistance to Change*

Fear of the unknown*
Lack of information*
Misinformation
Historical factors*
Threat to core skills and competence
Threat to status
Threat to power base
No perceived benefits*
Low trust organizational climates
Poor relationships (for example, the autocratic boss)*
Fear of failure*
Fear of looking stupid*
Reluctance to experiment (and take risks)*
Bound too closely by tradition and custom*
Reluctance to let go (to relax, speculate, reflect, etc.)*
Strong peer group norms (or the perceived need to conform)*

From Plant (1987, p. 18) (my additions in paretheses)

ment their results, we will come up against the prevailing organizational culture, and by its major manifestation, resistance.

14.1 Resistance to change

'Resistance to change is a natural phenomenon. It does not come from sheer cussedness, it needs to be recognized, understood and managed' (Plant, 1987, p. 29). We began to consider the difficulties of implementing change at the end of Chapter 12. Why do people consistently resist change? Some reasons, such as a low tolerance of ambiguity and uncertainty, were suggested in Chapter 4, in discussing how our creative thinking skills may have become inhibited. Roger Plant provides us with a useful list of the most frequent causes of resistance (see Frame 14.1; those discussed already are marked with an asterisk).

We will almost always have some vested interest in the way things are and we will usually resist anything we perceive as having a negative impact on our lives. We may simply identify too strongly with the part we have played in shaping current affairs, or we may perceive the effects of change as going beyond the confines of the organization or as posing a threat to an important part of our lives. As Buchanan and Huczynski neatly summarize (1985, pp. 419–20):

> Organizational changes may mean the loss of power, prestige, respect, approval, status and security. Change may also be personally

inconvenient for a variety of reasons. It may disturb relationships and arrangements that have taken much time and effort to establish. It may force an unwanted geographical move. It may alter social opportunities.

People attempting to implement changes often do not appreciate that *they* may have already had the chance to think through the consequences of the proposed changes, whereas the rest of us probably have not. It is a natural reaction to try to halt or slow things down until we have had a chance to do this. Even if these changes do not involve a dramatic reshaping of our lives, we still need time to satisfy ourselves of this. More serious is the possibility that the changes are being seen as having 'unpleasant' side-effects, because of incorrect interpretation of their consequences, or that the resistance is due to *the way* changes are being suggested or implemented.

In Chapter 12 we identified four types of possible change – changes in structure, procedure, policy and attitude – and we remarked that the last was extremely difficult to accomplish. We can also differentiate two main forms of resistance to any of these changes. The first, **'cognitive' resistance**, is connected with the possession or lack of knowledge, the second is due to **'behavioural'** (or emotional) **reactions**. The latter is the more difficult to deal with. However, it should not be assumed that only attitudinal changes can cause emotional reactions.

We may resist a change because we do not know or have not been told what is really going on (lack of information) or how this might affect us (fear of the unknown), because we have been fed wrong and 'disagreeable' information about the change being proposed or implemented (misinformation), or because of fear that we do not possess the appropriate knowledge, information, skills, managerial capacity, etc. to cope in the new situation. Modern business organizations attempt to minimize these uncertainties through good communications, counselling and training. However, such attempts to deal with cognitive resistance may simply mask it, because we may feel there is nothing we can legitimately complain about, due to the cultural unacceptability of saying that we feel threatened or inadequate. There could still be a host of subjective, interpersonal and political factors fuelling the resistance, which will continue covertly by methods limited only by the ingenuity and integrity of those involved. We *should not* assume that a source of resistance with such a cause is necessarily amenable to rational solution.

The emotional reactions that give rise to behavioural resistance are often precipitated by the perceptions individuals or groups have of a situation, and the assumptions they make on the basis of these. These perceptions and assumptions could be 'incorrect' or unfounded, and so could theoretically be allayed by providing the right information. However, if by then we no longer trust the initiators of the change, this will result in behavioural resistance that is difficult to assuage. The level of a person's resistance to change is inversely proportional to the amount of involvement in and information known about that change. Thus the importance of keeping people informed right from the start cannot be over-emphasized. 'Before fighting resistance, one should ask why these seemingly reasonable people are doing seemingly unreasonable things' (Sathe, 1985, p. 281).

Whatever the personal sources of the resistance, the likelihood is that they will be reinforced by our next area of concern, organizational culture.

14.2   What is culture?

The study of the effects of culture, and particularly of **organizational culture**, is relatively new and much work is still going on in this field. Culture is accepted as a very important aspect of organizational behaviour, and interest in cultural effects, both within an organization or group, or external to them, is a natural progression from viewing organizations as open systems. Full treatment of the topic of organizational culture requires a book in itself, thus what follows is necessarily a brief overview.

Due to its relative newness as an area worthy of research there are a variety of definitions of culture around, although the following are fairly typical:

> culture is the total pattern of human behaviour . . . embodied in thought, speech, action, and artifacts . . .' (Webster's Dictionary).

> organizational culture is the unique configuration of norms, values, beliefs, ways of behaving and so on that characterise the manner in which groups and individuals combine to get things done' (Eldridge and Crombie, 1974, p. 89).

It has been suggested that an organization's culture is a product of the environment it operates in, the technology it uses, its structure and internal functioning, its members' psychological contract with it manifested in their attitude to work, or even some combination of all these. Graves (1986) comments that these ways of looking at culture tend to see it as an objective phenomenon, whereas he sees it as totally subjective: the reason why a particular culture is commonly perceived by people is not because it is an objective reality, but because the *way* those people perceive it (their mental set) is the same. Graves cites as evidence for this view the fact that outsiders invariably view someone else's culture differently from those inside it. If culture is a common perception of the environment which gives rise to common behaviours (a sort of collective personality), the ideas that we as individuals are attracted to in an organization will be those that fit our personalities and through which we can fulfil our self-concepts and satisfy our needs. By the same token, organizations will likewise select us on the expectation that we will enhance their cultures.

If, as suggested, our psychological contracts are somehow interwoven with culture and if we perceive that some proposed change is likely to alter this organizational culture, it would not be unreasonable of us to be anxious or fearful that this will lead to an imminent worsening of our psychological contract. Such anxieties are highly likely to result in resistance to the change.

The basis of any culture is the set of often unstated assumptions commonly shared by the members of an organization or group, which determine the way they communicate with and behave towards others, and how such actions are justified. These assumptions include **beliefs** about the world they live in, how it functions, their place in it, etc., and **values** concerning ideals which are considered to be preferable, desirable or good and hence worth striving for. These values can be end-states, e.g. equality, self-fulfilment, freedom, or ways of conducting oneself, e.g. courage, honesty and friendship. Beliefs and values derive both from personal experience and from the opinions of others whom one trusts and identifies with. Many of these beliefs and values become internalized, that is they become so well assimilated that we think of them as our own to the extent that they govern what we say and do without our being aware of it. Beliefs and values often take time to become internalized, but once they do, they can become almost immutable and affect not only behaviour but attitudes as well Vijay Sathe (1985) says that people are typically stubborn or intolerant when their values are challenged. Values occupy too central a position in one's belief system and are too important an aspect of one's personality to permit them to be readily changed. Attempts that others make directly to confront and change a person's values are rarely effective and are likely to provoke emotional reactions or hostility.

Our beliefs and values do not necessarily have any rational basis, and it is even possible for us to be unaware of an unresolved inconsistency between them, because we have repressed it rather than faced up to the pain of recognizing it. Culture can be both an asset and a liability. As Sathe remarks, it 'eases and economizes communications, facilitates organizational decision making and control, and may generate higher levels of cooperation and commitment in the organization. The result is efficiency, in that these activities are accomplished with a lower expenditure of resources, such as time and money, than would otherwise be possible'.

Once formed, it can be very difficult for members of an organization to change its culture, and if the culture is no longer compatible with the needs of the organization and its members, it can become a millstone around the corporate neck. This may happen when an organization has

——— *Frame 14.2   Organizational norms* ———

Organizational and personal pride[†]
Performance: excellence[†] v. adequacy
Clarity of goals, tasks and rewards[*]
Leadership[*] v. supervision[†]
Collaboration and teamwork[†*] v. individualism
Open communication (honesty)[†*] v. guarded/secretive
Relationships[†]: warm, supportive and trusting[*] v. competitive
Training and development[†*]
Individual/group responsibility and autonomy[*]
Participation and involvement[*] v. autocratic
Conflicts/differences of opinion (permitted)[*]
Innovation and change[†*] v. conservatism and stability
Risk taking/challenges/learning from mistakes and failures[*]
Customer/consumer relations[†] (quality, helpfulness, etc.)
Profitability and cost effectiveness[†]

———————
[†] Allen and Pilnick's norms.
[*] Factors achieving heightened motivation.

to make a fairly major alteration to its objectives and/or operations in order to cope with some sea-change in its turbulent environment.

Culture is manifested by certain standards of expected behaviour, including the way we communicate with others and present ourselves to them. These norms reflect the underlying beliefs and values that are held to be important. For example, a belief in equality might be demonstrated by the exclusive use of first names as the usual mode of personal address, or a respect for the individual might be expressed by always being punctual for meetings. Norms are what the members of an organization *actually* say and do, as opposed to what people might have you believe that they say and do.

Research into culture and its effects (using Factor Analysis) suggests that we may usefully group norms together under general headings (sometimes confusingly called **climate** variables) such as those listed in Frame 14.2. This essentially comprises the ten norms (marked †) that have been identified (Allen and Pilnick, in Plant, 1987, p. 141–2) as having the most impact on the effective performance of organization. This list is slightly modified (to make it more complete) from other sources, particularly the Human Relations Institute's Normative Systems Indicator. There is a positive and negative aspect to each of these (the negative aspect often being simply the lack of the behaviour specified) and these norms are interrelated; for example, open and honest communication is unlikely in an organization that encourages a highly competitive attitude amongst and between its members.

The list in Frame 14.2 is not a particularly definitive set of norms, and there is a degree of overlap between some of the individual items, especially around the 'teamwork'/'relationships' area. However, it does demonstrate further how norms reflect the underlying beliefs and values of a culture – the belief that one should value the contributions of individuals could well be indicated by behaviours that positively support things like 'training and development', 'participation and involvement'. In some items (e.g. 'responsibility and autonomy', 'conflicts/differences of opinion') an underlying element of structure, informal v. formal – rules, regulations and hierarchies – can be detected. Also, some ten of the norms (marked *) are virtually the same as the factors that contribute towards achieving heightened motivation amongst followers mentioned in Chapter 5.

Organizational norms are important to us for a variety of reasons. For example, by observing these patterns of behaviour we can attempt to discern what an organization's culture is and ascertain how difficult it may be to make any changes. The extent to which we conform to norms is perceived as a measure of our fit with an organization, and thus on how effective we can be within that organization, whether as an agent of change or anything else. The content of an organization's culture depends on the values and beliefs its founders held and those which subsequent leaders and others brought with them when they joined and the relative importance that these people place upon these assumptions. These will have to be modified incrementally in the light of the experience of solving the organization's day-to-day problems, adapting to changes in its external environment and maintaining internal coherency.

The strength of culture, and the intensity of the related behaviour, depends on a culture's 'thickness' – how 'far-reaching' and all-encompassing the shared beliefs and values are (how many aspects of our lives they cover), the clarity and consistency of the ordering of these assumptions, and the extent to which they *are* commonly shared by members of the organization. The number of people in the organization and its geographical dispersion are also relevant factors. The stronger the culture the more resistant to change it is, and the amount of resistance actually encountered will be a function of both its strength and the extent of the change planned.

14.2.1 Deciphering organizational culture

Before we try to initiate change we ought to attempt to decipher the prevailing culture, so that we can anticipate likely reactions and prepare some ways for dealing with the organizational norms we are bound to come up against. Sathe (1985) offers the following advice on where we should start looking for clues:

> Both implicit and explicit forms of communication must be attended to when examining the manifestations of culture. The former include rituals, customs, ceremonies, stories, metaphors, special language, folklore, heroes, logos, decor, dress, and other symbolic forms of expression and communication. Examples of the latter are announcements, pronouncements, memos, and other explicit forms of expression and communication.

Sathe reminds us to reflect also on what is missing, i.e. what is not seen, said or done. This will help us uncover organizational taboos. He suggests that we need to discover as much as we can about the following by both direct observation and questioning:

- the background of the organization's founders and those that followed them;
- the organization's response to crises or other critical events;
- the people who are considered to be 'deviants', and how they are dealt with;
- the most important (unspoken) assumptions about work, human nature and human relationships shared by the organization's members;
- the organization's motto;
- the people within the organization who are respected and/or considered to be highly successful, its heroes;
- that which constitutes a serious punishment in the organization, and hence the mistakes that are not forgiven;
- the company folklore, rituals, symbols and ceremonies;
- the main rules that everyone has to follow.

If we can determine these then we should be able to uncover the organization's ideology, the dominant set of interrelated ideas that explains how the important assumptions that we share fit together and make sense. It is the ideology that gives a meaning to the content of the organization's culture.

14.2.2 A typology of organizational culture

Harrison (1972) identified four types of organizational culture named according to their predominant 'orientation'. These are: Power, Role, Task and Person. Frame 14.3 gives a brief summary of their characteristics. No particular culture is more 'right' than any other, though some seem to suit certain types of organization better than others. Organizations go through various stages of development, and at any given stage one particular culture might be more applicable than another. For in-

Organizational culture ──────────── Frame 14.3 ──

	Power	*Role*
'God'	**Zeus**	**Apollo**
Location of power and influence	Centre (and power rings)	Top (rules and procedures)
Power base	Resource (some person at centre)	Position (sometimes expert) (never person)
Typical examples of where found	Small entrepreneurial companies Investment banks Brokerage houses	Civil Service Oil industry Commercial banks Insurance companies
Conditions in which it thrives	Entrepreneurial situations	Steady state, predictable or controllable markets Long product life
Efficiency depends on	Selection of key indivuals	Rational allocation of work and responsibility
Strengths	Can move quickly in response to threat or danger	Economies of scale Depth of expertise Functional specialisms
Weaknesses	Dependent on person at centre Limited in size	Slow to see change Slow to change
Characteristic type of activity	Policy, Crisis (breakdown)	Steady State
Typical features of psychological contract	Suits those who are: Power orientated, 'Politically' minded, Risk takers Low security	Good security Chance to acquire expertise Predictable and satisficing environment No autonomy
Other comments	Effectivenes relies on trust, empathy and a bit of telepathy!	

'God'	Task **Athena**	Person **Dionysus**
Location of power and influence	At the 'knots' (control of resources)	Individual people
Power base	Expert (position and person have some effect)	Expert (if needed)
Typical examples of where found	Management consultancies High technology firms Accounts groups of advertising agencies	Barristers' chambers Architects partnerships R & D departments
Conditions in which it thrives	Competitive market Short product life Anything requiring sensitivity, creativity or integration	
Efficiency depends on	The right people at the right level	'Autonomous Teamwork'?
Strengths	Extremely adaptable Speed of reaction Ideal for creativity or integration	
Weaknesses	Difficult to control Inherently unstable Limited in size	Control virtually impossible
Characteristic type of activity*	Innovation	
Typical features of psychological contract	Team spirit Considerable work autonomy Judgement by results Respect based on contribution	Organization (if any) subordinate to the individual Work autonomy
Other	Preferred by many as place to work in	The organization eventually takes over

stance, Plant (1987) offers a three-stage development sequence, autocratic, bureaucratic and democratic, which he relates to role, power and task cultures respectively. He stresses the importance of going through all the stages no matter how desirable the democratic stage appears to be: 'It is no use having a highly competent, forward looking, participative management team in place without a firm infrastructure of policies and procedures to bring about co-ordination and progress. People need to be clear about their responsibilities, what is expected of them and the parameters within which they can work. These are all "bureaucratic" processes.'

A family business may start out as a power culture, an entrepreneurial organization driven by a single central figure. As it grows larger or the central figure ceases to be the main driving force then the organization may evolve into a role culture based on functional specialisms. New companies at the forefront of the application of technological research, however, have a tendency to (too quickly?) adopt a task culture orientated towards individual jobs or projects, and a matrix structure providing the flexibility and speed of response demanded by that environment. In times of dire resource limitation, the internal conflict likely to develop within such a culture may force it to change or revert to a role or power culture. Within larger organizations certain departments, for example, marketing, may have a different culture (say, a task culture) from the majority of the rest of the organization (possibly a role culture). The most appropriate culture seems to be related to the principal activity type of the organization or department. These types have been categorized by Handy (1985) as Steady State, Innovation, Crisis and Policy.

It would be extremely difficult to initiate joint problem solving and teamwork in a power culture, which actively encourages competition between its members. Likewise, the people who are drawn towards organizations with role cultures tend to be those less tolerant of change, preferring a predictable environment, and this could well be the reason why this type of culture is generally antipathetic to change. Thus we need to take into consideration both the nature of the culture and its implications in terms of psychological contracts, when planning to effect a change.

All except the role culture are believed to be limited by size. Problems can occur when organizations become so large as to place a strain on these other cultures. One solution to this dilemma, being tried by Apple Computer, a company with a strong culture, is to allow and encourage parts of the organization to split off from the 'mother' company to form separate and virtually autonomous entities, but which still retain close links. A network of smaller companies is achieved; this permits the development of new ideas and business directions, whilst at the same time preserving the 'youth' and small size of the companies that constitute the network. John Sculley (1988), the CEO of Apple Computer, warns of the down-side of culture: 'culture limits us by its emphasis on tradition, on yesterday's heroes, on myths and rituals whose sole value is that they derive from an earlier time.' He believes that this makes us look forever backwards, and suggests that a better way of preserving the best aspects of culture and of passing them on is to think of them as a 'genetic code'. This could be seen as imprinting notions of identity and values as culture does, but in so doing it suggests a sense of forward-looking, a sense that everything done today is an investment in the future, not an expression of the past.

Sculley recommends that we forget all the myths, rituals, symbols, stories and traditions, all the trappings of culture. Organizational meta-phors, such as 'software artist' and 'hardware wizard', should replace myths because metaphors focus on 'relationships of ideas, images, sym-bols, and create tension collision of ideas, fusion . . . get you dreaming in two worlds.' This is creativity! Any 'heroes' should personify a pro-cess, for example, 'gatekeeping' or teamworking, and not any particular set of achievements. The values (which are after all the essence of cul-ture) are held on to but even these are not seen as immutable, and to this we should add visions that embody directions and not goals, and an identity that makes the organization recognizable without tightly defining what it is (or has) to be. The individual is free to develop in his/her own way rather than always having to conform rigidly to the 'tribal' customs more usually associated with culture. And although the basic 'hereditary characteristics' are transmitted down through the generations, they manifest themselves in different ways. This would seem to be a possible way of getting many of the benefits of a strong culture, without encumbering ourselves with a straight-jacket that will hinder future changes.

Now that we know a little more of what culture is, how do we go about dealing with it and changing it?

14.3   Initiating and implementing change

Following from our comments about culture we can predict that the ease or difficulty with which we can achieve any change is dependent on whether it can be accomplished within the existing organizational cul-ture by modifying it, or through a more drastic cultural change which must be led at least partially from outside. A 'major change' is likely to involve considerable change in the culture. What can realistically be achieved depends on our standing or status within the organization, which ultimately reduces to how much power we have *or* have access to, of whatever form. If a major change is being considered – as would probably be the case when trying to instil a flexible and systematic ap-proach to problem solving/decision making throughout an organization, then many **organizational development** specialists would insist that

Diagram 14.1   'Change Map'

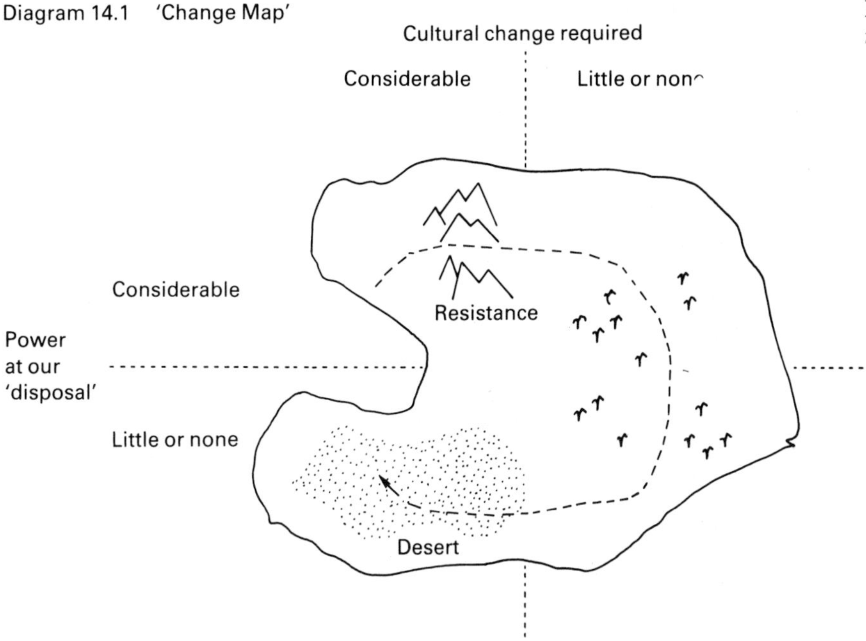

Figure 14.1 *A 'change map'.*

Figure 14.1 *A 'change map'.*

changes of this type *must* come from 'the top'. For example, Deming is adamant that the attitudinal changes needed to bring about his management philosophy of Total Quality Management *have* to be embraced from the top down. And Reddin (1977) has likened the attempt to implement a 'bottom-up' change to mutiny.

We shall approach our discussion of change from the two dimensions of 'amount of cultural change required' and 'amount of power we have at our disposal' shown in Figure 14.1. On the way we will look at how to deal with resistance, remembering that real-life situations do not fall into neat partitions like this. We must first, however, examine the determinant factors or 'lifelines' that ought to be present if we are to be successful in promoting change.

14.3.1   *Status, credibility and acceptance*

Effecting change, particularly if it involves major modifications to the culture, means we will need to have considerable **status** in the organization. Sathe believes (1985) that status is a function of our credibility and acceptance and that high status is achieved with a high level of either credibility or acceptance and at least a moderate level of the other.

Credibility gives others assurance that we have 'the ability and intention to deliver valued results', and we gain credibility by the act of

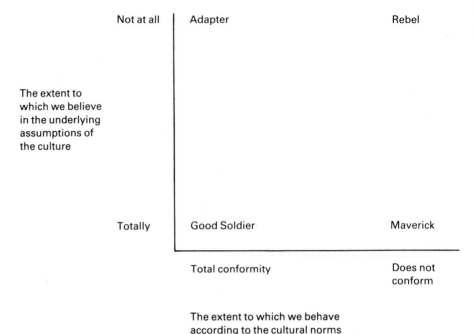

Figure 14.2 *Cultural caricatures (adapted from Sathe, 1985).*

delivering them, however credibility does not come from delivering results that the individual personally values or those one thinks the organization should value, or even those that others say are valued. It comes from results that are actually valued. This depends on the (content of the) organization's culture.

Acceptance implies that we are perceived as part of the community. The cultural caricatures shown in Figure 14.2 suggest that the further from being a 'good soldier' we are, the less acceptance we have and the more difficult will be our task of changing things. In fact all of the 'types' can have acceptability based on what they contribute to the organization and the extent to which they transgress cultural norms. The 'adapter' may work hard for extrinsic rewards, the 'maverick' may supply creative energy and ideas and the 'rebel' may provide useful critique of organizational processes as well as being a negative role model for the 'good soldiers'.

Sathe maintains that **high credibility** requires a high level of either power or trust accompanied by at least a moderate level of the other and sees **trust** as being based on our perception of another's character and competence:

Character:
• Integrity – how others perceive one's basic honesty.
• Motives – how others perceive one's intentions.

Types of 'power' ——————————————— Frame 14.4 ——

According to Sathe, Power is one person's capacity to affect the behaviour and thinking of another. Influence is the process of using power. The basis of this capacity was classified by French and Raven (1959) into Reward, Coercive, Legitimate, Referent and Expert power. Plant (1987) replaces referent power (having that which makes others want to identify with us) with Connection power, which we possess due to our access to and contacts with other people and groups. Handy (1985) draws particular attention to Resource power, but Sathe (1985) in the list below draws all of this together very concisely. He groups legitimate power (being perceived as having some right to give orders) with reward and coercive power (being perceived as having the ability to reward and punish), and together refers to them as Positional power; and he groups referent and expert power as Personal power.

Positional power
The power we have due to our position within the organization that permits us:

- to structure another person's tasks or formal organizational relationships;
- to reward (financially, or with promotions, recognition, etc.) and punish the other people;
- to allocate or control resources valued by another person (including his or her access to others and to information);
- to direct and organize the other people.

Personal power
The power we have due to our:

- ability to create a perception of common goals;
- charismatic appeal in the eyes of the other person;
- creating a sense of obligation in the other person;
- building a reputation as an expert in the eyes of the other person;
- fostering the other person's conscious or subconscious identification with us;
- affecting another's perception of dependence on us for resources and help;
- ability to persuade the other person;
- possession of personal information and resources valued by the other person;
- ability to reduce the uncertainty felt by the other person.

- Consistency – the sense others have of how reliable and predictable one's behavior is.
- Openness – the sense that one is levelling with the other in discussing problems.
- Discretion – the assurance that one will not violate confidences or carelessly divulge sensitive information.

Competence:
- Specific competence – one's competence in the specialized knowledge and skill required to do the job.
- Interpersonal competence.
- Business sense.

Power and trust are not qualities that we as individuals have or can acquire, they are attributes of the relationships we have with others. There are thought to be different types of power, as shown in Frame 14.4, some of which (reward and coercion) are not considered compatible with a trusting relationship.

14.3.2　When is change necessary?

Buchanan and Huczynski (1985) suggested the three main reasons for change are:

- the need to introduce internal changes to cope with developments occurring outside the organization;
- the desire to modify the attitudes, motives, behaviour, knowledge, skills and relationships of the organization's members in the interests of performance;
- the desire to anticipate future developments and to find in advance ways of coping with them.

There would appear to be little to argue over here, unless we raise the question of whether we have any right to try to change other people's beliefs and values, even if it is 'for their own good'. However, when discussing *major* cultural changes, Terence Deal and Allen Kennedy (1982) identified five situations in which top management should consider the reshaping of the organization's culture to be something 'close to its most important mission'. These are:

- When the environment is undergoing fundamental change, and the company has always been highly value-driven (has a strong culture).
- When the industry is highly competitive and the environment changes quickly.
- When the company is mediocre, or worse.
- When the company is truly at the threshold of becoming a large corporation.
- When companies are growing very rapidly.

Interestingly, they go on to say that, in most other situations, large-scale cultural change should simply not be undertaken.

The implication from the above, and from Harrison's typology of cultures (p. 279 above), would seem to be that major cultural change should only be contemplated or attempted at certain stages in the development of an organization: when there is a potentially devastating change taking place in its environment, or as a last resort when things are about to fall apart internally. At other times we should perhaps be content with more modest modifications to culture.

14.3.3   Changing the culture

Organizational culture is maintained by inculcating beliefs and values into newcomers when they join, and through the organization's recruitment process, by appointing only those who possess the right (same) values, attitudes, goals, etc. and/or would, or want to, fit in. Put simply, to effect a major cultural change, one has to do one or both of two things:

- Encourage people to accept the new beliefs and values by persuading them that the new way is better, or at least mutually beneficial.
- Appoint/promote people with the appropriate new values and beliefs, whilst removing or rendering powerless those who are hanging on to the old ones and offering resistance.

Possibly the most critical issue facing organizations today which might well involve a cultural change is in the case of large organizations which seek to regain a flexibility of response to environmental changes which has been lost, possibly due to cumbersome bureaucratic structures. For a smaller organization the issue is often maintaining the flexibility that it presently has, whilst continuing to grow. Central to this will be a culture that encourages and enables everyone to participate in problem solving and decision making. Such a culture will need to encourage the behaviours marked with an asterisk in Frame 14.2, and will have a positive attitude to the use of the systematic problem solving strategies illustrated in this book.

Let us suppose that we are trying to implement such a major cultural change within a large bureaucratic organization, with many levels of hierarchy, discrete areas of functional specialism, a maze-like communication 'system' and tightly defined areas of responsibility and spans of control: an organization where cultural attitudes like 'Your job is to look after the stock cupboard, you're not paid to think, let alone use your initiative!' are endemic. To instil a culture of joint problem solving/decision making, teamwork, etc. into such an organization is going to involve a great deal of structural and procedural change, and correspondingly major attitudinal changes. Some people seem to like the security and order bureaucracy affords. So given that we have the necessary status, how do we go about making this change?

14.3.4   Managing change

Deal and Kennedy (1982) admit that engineering a cultural change is still a 'black art' but offer the following tips:

- Recognize that peer group consensus will be the major influence on acceptance or willingness to change.
- Convey and emphasize two-way trust in all matters (and especially communications) related to change.
- Think of change as skill-building and concentrate on training as part of the change process.
- Allow enough time for the change to take hold.
- Encourage people to adapt the basic idea for the change to fit the real world around them.

A complementary set of key activities for successful implementation is offered by Plant (1987):

- Communicate like never before.
- Turn perceptions of 'threat' into opportunity.
- Ensure early involvement.
- Work at gaining commitment.
- Provide help to face up to change.
- Avoid over-organizing.

Between them, these two lists cover most relevant factors; the importance of good communications and training is emphasized, along with the new idea, captured in the last item in both lists, that what we want is for everyone to 'arrive safely' at the change destination, the route taken being less important than actually getting there. When it comes down to the practicalities of changing the culture's content, there are basically only five ways we can go. We can reorder (the importance of), modify, or remove existing beliefs and values, add new ones, or attempt any combination of these things. The only guideline as to how we should do this is to accomplish the desired change with the minimum amount of disruption to the existing culture. The five options are presented roughly in order of increasing disruptive potential, except that it will probably be easier to add a new belief or value than to remove an old one.

Just because there is an external need for change, for example, changes in an organization's markets, in technology, in legislation or in society generally, we should not assume that this will guarantee or facilitate corresponding internal change. Similarly, the perceived desirability for internal changes due to factors such as organizational growth, acquisi-

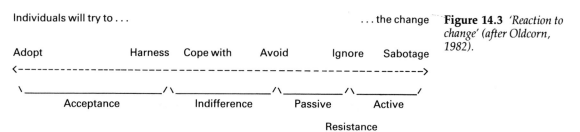

Figure 14.3 *'Reaction to change' (after Oldcorn, 1982).*

tions and mergers, internationalization or a desire to change the organization's mission, no matter how obvious their merits, may not be enough on their own to ensure that changes will be successfully carried through. Change *is* more likely, however, when there is both an internal and an external need present.

14.3.5   Overcoming resistance

No matter how mutually beneficial some changes may be, or how altruistic the motives of the change agent(s), there will be resistance. We need practical methods of analysing resistance so that effective countermeasures can be devised and applied. First, we could attempt to classify people according to the amount of resistance we think they are likely to offer. This should reveal the extent of our problem and clarify where we most need to direct our attention. Figure 14.3 offers a possible classification scheme. There is a danger in rigidly pigeon-holing people, so apply any such classification loosely. A person may hold different positions depending on which aspects of the change being addressed. And a person hostile to one particular change may not necessarily be against change *per se*, and could actually be a change agent with regard to developments elsewhere.

Another useful tool is the often cited **Force-field Analysis** devised by Kurt Lewin, (see Figure 14.4.) The idea here is that at any particular time a situation is held in equilibrium by forces in favour of (driving-forces) and against (resistance) change. The length of the arrows represents the magnitude of these forces, and they can be annotated with what we perceive the cause of the force to be, and from which group of people it is coming. When we try to implement change we are attempting to move this equilibrium point, and in order to do this, we have to increase or add driving-forces and/or reduce or remove resisting forces. Increasing driving-forces may simply increase the intensity of resistance. A better policy is to try to reduce resistance.

But how do we actually do this? Sathe (1985) claimed that resistance to change is overcome when people feel a sufficient incentive to change (they are motivated), when they know what new behaviour is expected

Figure 14.4 *Kurt Lewin's 'Force field analysis'.*

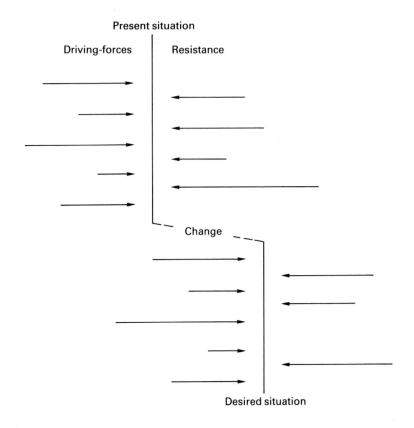

from them (the new model is clear), and when the change process is appropriate to the needs of the situation (the method used is suited to prevailing conditions). For anyone who perceives a problem situation or an opportunity and is about to look for some way of resolving or exploiting it, the key-words must be **motivation, involvement** and **commitment**. To gain commitment from others to an idea, a project or a change, we must ensure that those likely to be affected by it are involved in its development right from its conception, and have the opportunity to take part in the planning, problem solving and decision making that must go on. The only thing we can do when presented with a well-formed idea or a carefully planned set of changes is to accept it or reject it. We need to feel part of any idea or solution, to feel that our contributions were not only wanted, but have been recognized and duly incorporated into it: participation is the only effective way to ensure maximum commitment.

Allowing participation should be just common courtesy – a demonstration of our respect for others, as well as an obvious means of gaining their support and commitment. Its effectiveness unfortunately means that participation is abused by unscrupulous change agents as a tactical ploy to neutralize leaders of resistance. After the real planning and decision making has taken place they are involved in the implementation of the change process by playing on their morality ('You know, the best way you can ensure that what we are saying is the truth, and that your people won't be any the worse off after this, is to help us get these changes through') or by appealing to baser motives, for example by offering to promote them 'after all this is over'.

Other methods of overcoming resistance include the deliberate use of misinformation, for example – 'forgetting' to mention the disadvantages of the change. Another aspect of the 'divide and conquer' ploy above is the disclosure of selected information intended to appeal to specific key parties. There is always explicit and implicit coercion. These methods tend only to work in the short term, can easily misfire and are alien to the 'spirit' of this book.

The other way to overcome resistance is to try to find out its true cause and attempt to understand why people are resisting. If we can discover the cause and there is something we can do about it, then we do it. If not, we should explain why we cannot, and offer some form of compensation.

Making change permanent

Permanent change can only be guaranteed if people genuinely believe and value their new way of doing things. For this we need change in both culture and behaviour, but it does not follow that a change in one means a change in the other. We could change the culture in so much that individuals may change one or more of their beliefs and values, but find that due to, for example, ingrained habit or insufficient intrinsic motivation, they are unable to modify the corresponding behaviour. Similarly, people may pretend to adopt a new behaviour because they perceive they have to (usually only when being observed) although they have not accepted the new beliefs and values. Compliance can only ever be a short-term measure; for cultural change to stick people must identify with the new order, and ultimately internalize the new beliefs and values.

A corollary of the above is that we may be able to achieve desired changes in behaviour without a correspondingly major cultural change. Alternatively, there may be scope within the existing culture creatively to utilize existing beliefs and values to effect attitude change. We can do this by making minor changes to the content of a culture, perhaps by a change in emphasis accomplished by a reordering of cultural assumptions.

If the changes we want to make are compatible with the prevailing culture, we can make the culture work for us. First, we should develop

────── *Frame 14.5   Consultants' Roles (Steele, 1975)* ──────

Teacher	imparting knowledge by seminars, experiential learning sessions, etc.
Student	modelling a learning behaviour that we would like to encourage in the client.
Detective	trying to discover hard and soft data so as to develop an accurate picture of the system, its problems and strengths.
Barbarian	violating comfortable but limiting norms, taboons, etc. that are preventing the system for being as effective as it might be. (A counter measure against 'tunnel vision'.)
Clock	stimulating the client into getting some thinking, experimenting, etc. done by acting as a regular 'time signal'.
Monitor	providing an independent view of how the client is performing in connection with some mutually agreed task relevant to his/her problem.
Talisman	providing a sense of security and legitimacy by our mere presence, thus allowing the client to feel comfortable enough to experiment in areas he or she might not, if we were not actually there.
Advocate	advocating certain decent, non-exploitive, personally satisfying and productive principles or values pertaining to the relationship between an individual and the organization.
Ritual Pig	inadvertently serving as an 'outside' threat that, through having to be dealt with, develops a sufficient sense of solidarity and potency within the client organization that it is able to begin some difficult self-change. (A role that is usually realized retrospectively!)

our ability to decipher culture as outlined earlier, to ascertain which things *are* actually valued. Second, we should ensure the views we express are in keeping with the most important and widely held cultural values; there are benefits in being seen to be a cultural standard-bearer. The degree of acceptance this bestows upon us should ensure that even unorthodox ideas will be seen in the best possible light. We should be careful not to criticize any of these higher values as we need to demonstrate actively that our idea or change fits in with, supports and even enhances the existing culture.

In lowering our sights to more modest changes, we should be aware that a relatively minor change may have far reaching results. For example, a company may attempt to replace a 'tea trolley service' to individual offices with a central provision where people can 'get together'. Those

Ways of exerting influence ——————————— *Frame 14.6* ——

Assertive Persuasion
   The persistent, energetic and ingenious use of logic, facts and opinions to support the ideas and suggestions (often freely donated by themselves).

Reward and Punishment
   The overt and covert use of pressures and incentives to accomplish a clearly defined objective. (Psychologists believe that to be effective this style should involve considerably more praise and rewards than criticism and punishment.)

Common Vision
   The use of a shared vision of what could be a common future for everyone involved that appeals to their hopes, values and aspirations thus releasing the 'energy' of their commitment made available by their feelings of belonging.

Participation and Trust
   The use of an atmosphere of mutual trust, positive support, encouragement, cooperation and openness (in fact, all of the conditions that we believe to be prerequisites of creativity), so as to gain people's total commitment through their feelings of being involved in and having contributed to the outcome.

providing the service may resent the change because the social aspect of going around and meeting people was a satisfying part of their job; the recipients may see the imposition of a central provision as a loss of a status symbol, an inconvenience, or a waste of time. Just these few issues alone could be quite emotive and destructive.

But what do we do if we wish to bring about some change, even a fairly minor one, but our low hierarchical rank leaves us with little positional power?

Fritz Steele (1975) has described a number of 'consultant's roles' which can be adopted by an outside consultant to encourage others to do things differently (see Frame 14.5). Roles similar to those of the Advocate, Barbarian and Student are very relevant to a person trying to make changes from within an organization. I shall discuss these shortly under the headings of being an Evangelist, a Maverick or a Guerilla, respectively. Remember, if you believe that an idea or change is more important than your own well-being within the organization you could be so much of a Rebel that you end up becoming a Ritual Pig, though you may not be around to see the results or get the credit when the organization eventually adopts the ideas you were suggesting!

Whatever we can achieve relies heavily on our personal power (see Frame 14.4) and whatever credibility we can derive from this. If we are short on positional power, then even if we possess some expert power (and it is this expertise we are promoting) it may not be valued any more than that of our peers, and any success we have will be determined by our ability to *influence* others and our ability to use what power we have effectively. According to Lippitt (1982), this is founded in trust, both our trust in others and their trust in us. His notion of what brings about trust is different from but complementary to that noted earlier:

- Integrity – sound and honest in character and moral principles.
- Justice – possessing a sense of right and equity.
- Ability – capable of performing well in the task or relationship involved.
- Intention – determined to achieve some desirable action or result.
- Reliability – dependable in carrying out a commitment.

Beyond this Harrison has identified four ways of influencing others (Frame 14.6): Assertive Persuasion, Reward and Punishment, Common Vision, and Participation and Trust. Each of us apparently feels more at ease using some of these styles than others. The last should be most effective in the long run, as it encourages involvement which is the only sure way of gaining commitment. But Plant believes (1987) that the broader the spread of styles you can use, the more likely you are to be able to influence effectively in different situations. However, many consider the Assertive Persuasion style, like Reward and Punishment, to be totally incompatible with the qualities required to create a situation of 'participation and trust'.

The Evangelist

We ought to be able to use the phenomenon of the self-fulfilling prophecy positively (see Chapter 4) in effecting change by adopting the **Evangelist** approach. Raising expectations and fostering a mind set in others in favour of whatever is being advocated will draw people's attention to its good points and make them more likely to accept it. This can be particularly effective if we can demonstrate its benefits and how this innovation fits in with and enhances the existing organizational culture. This is especially true if we can incorporate appropriate cultural language and symbols, designed to evoke strong positive emotional reactions, in its packaging. We need credibility to make this approach work because the new idea or change we are extolling will be perceived in the same light as we are. Another down-side to this approach is the danger that if we promote an idea too much we will put people off it. Others may not share our enthusiasm, because they are not familiar with it, have not been part of its creation or see it as an implied criticism. Nolan (1981) comments that 'it's no use trying to "sell" your ideas. By all means present them clearly and attractively, explaining the benefits and rationale behind them (once you have established you have a willing audience for them). But no amount of eloquence, persuasion, logic or pressure will make him accept an idea that isn't on target for what he perceives his needs to be.'

The Maverick

Another ploy is to take on the role of **maverick**, a person who despite holding with the beliefs and values of a culture does not conform to organizational norms *just* because they are there, but only if they are perceived as having some inherent sense. Some organizations believe it 'healthy' to have people like this around and are prepared to tolerate their non-conformist behaviour. Mavericks are prepared to stick their necks out on behalf of new concepts, constructively draw attention to deficiencies or injustices and generally fight against complacency. To survive in this role the maverick needs to be well nigh perfect in every other aspect of his dealings with the organization as he is essentially attacking the prevailing culture on the basis of his credibility and acceptance in that culture and/or the support he has from others of high status. Both of these could alter over time; the maverick needs to check periodically that his position is still secure.

If we as maverick persist with this role long enough, we may get the chance to try out one of our ideas on the basis of 'OK, you do something better', or just to shut us up. Alternatively, if such an opportunity does not become available, we could deliberately challenge other people to let us try. Such a challenge is often ignored on the basis that 'If it's that good a way of doing things, why hasn't he done something about it himself?' Being a maverick is by no means a guaranteed way of initiating change.

The Guerilla

We could ignore Reddin's warning that initiating change from the bottom up is tantamount to mutiny and try a **guerilla** action, by infiltrating the organization with bits of the new idea or method we are advocating, starting first on our home ground where we possess the power to do something. Depending on the power and authority we command this may restrict us to changing only our own behaviour or method of working in the first instance. The hope is that wider acceptance of the innovation will be assisted by its own merits rather than our blandishments. Even if we are not suspected or accused of mutiny, trying to convince by example in this way can be a frustrating or even totally demotivating task. Building up the critical mass to ensure the eventual success of a change like this can take a very long time. However, this policy of 'discreetly' applying new methods ourselves and demonstrating their effectiveness by example may be one of the few viable alternatives open to us.

Acquiring a champion

If we feel there is little we can do personally to bring about change, or we feel that we could accomplish more if we had support from others, it is suggested that we should find a **champion** for our cause. Ideally this should be one of the organization's current 'heroes'. A champion is someone in a position of power (see Frame 14.4) and authority, who controls the allocation of resources our cause might need. Having a champion increases our credibility, and helps overcome minor difficulties and obstacles. Also, those not fully committed to our proposals are less likely to resist and risk upsetting the champion. Failing this, we may add to our credibility, by seeking the support of 'good soldiers' (see Figure 14.2).

Having a champion can be effective, but is fraught with danger as a champion's reasons for supporting us may be politically expedient rather than altruistic; our champion may withdraw their favour when their hidden agenda is satisfied and we have served their purpose. If the only reason we have been able to proceed with our idea is because of other people's obeisance to the champion, then when this support is removed, we will be attacked by those people, Choice of champion is also crucial; if our champion does not have the necessary support and respect then getting support may effectively destroy our chances. Remember: to attempt to change other people in a direction they do not want to go themselves is counter-productive. Even if they comply on the surface, out of fear or subservience or even in deference to superior wisdom, their underlying resentment switches off commitment and motivation.

14.3.6   Gaining acceptance and support

Suppose that we do have a wonderful new concept we are trying to introduce, and that we have developed it quite fully without involving others, for whatever reason. What can we do to ensure that it is accepted, either by all concerned or just our potential champion? The following 'Implementation Planning' checklist is intended to help plan the acceptance-gaining process for an idea or solution that we have.

- Acceptance – In what ways might I gain acceptance? What advantages can I show for the idea and how might I dramatize these advantages? (Remember, each of us observes through different eyes. Avoid assuming that the other person will see your idea as you do.)
- Assistance – In what ways might other persons or groups be of help to me in applying my idea?

- Location – What places or locations might be advantageous for putting my idea into practice?
- Anticipation – How might I anticipate objections to my idea and thus be better prepared to overcome them?
- Timing – In what ways might I take advantage of special times, days, dates, etc. for implementing my idea?
- Precautions – What ways might I use to pretest my chosen idea, to safeguard or fortify it, to ensure its effectiveness?

Frame 14.7   Ways to deal with new ideas

- Ignore it. Dead silence intimidates all but the most enthusiastic.
- See it coming and change the subject.
- Scorn it: Get your thrust in before the idea is fully explained or it may prove practicable after all.
- Laugh it off: 'Ho, ho, ho! That's a good one, Joe. You must have sat up all night thinking that up.' If he has, this makes it even funnier.
- Praise it to death. By the time you have expounded its merits for five minutes everyone else will hate it. The proposer will be wondering what is wrong with it himself.
- Mention that it has never been tried. If it is new this will be true.
- 'Oh, we've tried that before.' Particularly effective if the originator is a newcomer. It makes him realize what an outsider he is.
- Find a competitive idea. This is a dangerous one unless you are experienced. You might still get left with an idea.
- Produce 20 good reasons why it won't work. The one good reason why it will is then lost.
- Modify it out of existence. This is elegant. You seem to be helping the idea along, just changing it a little here and there. By the time the originator wakes up, it is dead.
- Try to chip bits off it. If you fiddle with an idea long enough it may come to pieces.
- Make a personal attack on the originator. By the time he has recovered, he will have forgotten he had an idea.
- Score a technical knock-out; for instance, refer to some obscure rule.
- Let a committee sit on the idea.
- Encourage the author to look for a better idea. Usually a discouraging quest. If he finds one, start him looking for a better job.
- Accept it, but do nothing about it . . . it prevents the originator taking it to somebody else.

Nolan (1981)

--- *Frame 14.8   Killed any good ideas, lately?* ---

That's not our problem, the hole is at the other end of the ship!

- 'You can't save half a person.'
- 'It isn't in the budget.'
- 'We haven't got the staff to do it.'
- 'The savings wouldn't come to this division.'
- 'The intangible risks would be too great.'
- 'We're not ready for that yet, but in the fullness of time . . . (let's not rush into things).'
- 'This is the long-term solution . . . we're interested in the here and now.'
- 'This is the short-term solution . . . we're in this for the long pull.'
- 'This is a radical departure from company practice.'
- 'Business Legal/Practices would never agree to it.'
- 'There is already a procedure in place to deal with this.'
- 'We've tried that before.'
- 'If it's that good why hasn't somebody tried it before?'

Answering these questions and acting upon them is a good place to start, and perhaps Potential Problem Analysis applied to 'Anticipation' (Where is my idea vulnerable? What specific points might someone argue/disagree with?) would be a useful exercise as well. Frames 14.7 and 14.8 list typical 'reactions' to new ideas and serve as a warning of what can be in store for a potential change agent about to embark on this stage.

What we can actually achieve depends on how successfully the ploys above can be implemented. If we find ourselves totally stranded with little or no support, our only hope is a lucky break that allows us to demonstrate that our way of doing things will benefit everyone. If we find the culture so alien that only a major change can make it right for us, then our efforts are best spent finding another organization that has a culture we can survive in.

14.4   Encouraging and managing creativity

Let us suppose that we have a culture that values our flexible, systematic approaches to problem solving (particularly the CPS strategies). Is there anything we should do as a team leader in order to encourage creativity? Nolan (1981, pp. 89–90) says that 'when faced with a clear and overwhelming threat to survival, people respond with ingenuity, resourcefulness and energy that previously they did not know they had'. It is ironic that at times of crisis we can be far more creative and amenable to change than when conditions are stable: yet we might benefit more from innovation and creativity when things are running smoothly. One answer might be to set people demanding, apparently impossible tasks and objectives. This seems to work so long as there is no fear connected with failing to achieve these 'impossible' missions. Nolan advises that the manager who wants more innovation, more newness, must give a lead by doing new things himself. By showing he is willing to make changes in what he does, and how he does it, he demonstrates that he himself is open to learning. He is prepared to take the risks of coming unstuck, making a fool of himself, getting it wrong. These are the risks of new action, and the price of new knowledge and understanding, which only comes from experience.

And having accomplished this, how then do we 'manage' all these creative thinking people? John Sculley (1988, pp. 253–61), who at Apple Computer has led some of the most creative people in any organization offers the following suggestions on managing creativity.

> The task is to get them to work at the highest level of creativity, not just productivity.

> The safer you can make a situation, the higher you can raise the challenge. (Tim Gallwey, 'the Inner Game of Tennis')

> Don't give people goals; give them directions. We want to lead people to ideas they haven't dreamed of yet.

> Encourage contrarian thinking. There should be a level of tension between discipline and dissent . . . a little bit of anarchy in the organization.

> Build a textured environment to extend not just people's aspirations but their sensibilities. You can't buy creativity. You have to inspire it. Creative people require the tools and environment which foster their success. Above all, they require an atmosphere conducive to fun and to thinking in non-standard ways. The work environment needs to be informal and relaxed, it needs to remove the symbols of management . . .

> Build emotion into the system. Defensiveness is the bain of all passion-filled creative work. We keep defences down . . .

> Encourage accountability over responsibility. We don't give creative people traditional responsibilities . . . instead they are made accountable for the results of their work.

14.5   The future of organizational problem solving

Three attributes regarded as being essential for the continued survival and success of a modern organization must be:

- Greater flexibility in every thing it does;

- Enhanced performance from its members;
- Innovation in its products, processes and/or services.

And as we have seen in the earlier chapters, the two key factors that contribute to this are:

- high motivation, such as can be achieved through autonomy, participation/involvement, mutual trust, etc.;
- effective problem solving and decision-making skills, allied to which are things like teamwork and open communications.

The dilemma here is that the relationships we need to build between process leader and followers in order to create an effective problem solving group, are very different from, and possibly incompatible with, those required for supervision. We could be asking managers to hold down an untenable position, being a supervisor at one moment and a transformational leader the next. There are no simple answers to this, but in simplistic terms two possible solutions would seem to exist: remove the leadership element from management, or remove the supervision element from management. Neither is entirely feasible, but partial attempts are possible.

We could use an independent process leader to run meetings, particularly those involving problem solving/decision making. This could alleviate some inhibitions and reduce the amount of game-playing during meetings. Such a suggestion might cause anxiety in some managers, especially if the outsider runs successful meetings while they are left with the less charismatic role of supervisor. Alternatively we could reduce the amount of supervision required from managers by the use of autonomous work groups (Frame 14.9) which are to an extent self-supervising. Wall *et al.* (1986) give evidence that both reductions in supervision and increases in intrinsic job satisfaction are the main benefits derived from such 'systems'. What we need is a partial synthesis of these two solutions, because there will be times when our leader wishes to get his hands dirty on the problem content, and needs to step down from process leadership to do this.

Moves towards autonomous working are hampered by the legacy of Scientific Management, that still influence techniques of managerial control. However, sophisticated modern job enrichment techniques, which have superseded earlier attempts at alleviating the effects of scientific management by job rotation and job enlargement, have made improvements in this area. Even so, Buchanan and Huczynski (1985) argue that these measures only combat the dehumanization of work in a fairly superficial way, and do not tackle the root problem of management control. They may make an *individual's* work more satisfying, but still miss important social aspects of work, first, that people like working together, and second, that people like to have a say in their future.

┌─ *Autonomous work groups* ────────────────────────── *Frame 14.9* ─┐

Autonomous work groups were born out of the Tavistock Institute
of Human Relations' open systems approach to the study of organizations. The best known of many attempts to institute autonomous
group working into 'mass production line' environments was in the
Volvo car plant in Kalmar, Sweden. Autonomous work groups were
intended to bring back into work such things as discretion, self-
esteem, the quality assurance that comes from pride in workmanship
and many of the essential social aspects of work, for example, emotional support and a sense of belonging. They sought to achieve this
through letting people collaborate in the production of a 'meaningful'
entity, a 'whole' something that they could associate with.

A substantial task, such as assembling a complete car engine,
would be assigned to a small group of workers. The group was left
to perform this task (with a minimum of outside constraint) in their
own mutually agreed way, rather than as individuals locked into
repetitive tasks. They would decide how they should organize and
coordinate themselves, their skills and the time allotted, etc. in order
to accomplish this task.

Since most existing mass production lines would have to be re-
designed for this style of working, such initiatives have to come from
the top down. Many autonomous work group schemes have been
successful, and where some have subsequently degenerated to the
pre-existing state of affairs, it has usually been because the prerequisites of this type of work organization, such as trust, devolved
responsibilities, appropriate leader–follower relationships and the
consequent level of motivation have ceased to exist.

└──┘

14.5.1   Industrial Democracy

People are nowadays less prepared to accept faceless members of the
organizational hierarchy having total freedom to make decisions that
affect their working lives. They would like access to such people, to
know what is happening and to feel that their opinions have been considered, and ideally they want some say in determining their futures.
Such attitudes and desires are linked to the acceptability of power bases,
for as Handy (1985) says, it is only expert or personal power that is
effective and, these forms of power have to be earned. It is virtually
impossible to do this without interpersonal contact.

One of the arguments put forward against moves toward more demo-
cratic/participative styles of management has been that whilst such a
style is fine for professionals, it is not appropriate for shop floor workers.
The latter are assumed to have neither the desire nor the ability to parti-

_____ Frame 14.10   *Quality circles* _____

A quality circle is a small group of employees who meet on a regular and voluntary basis, in working time, to put forward ideas and suggestions and to solve problems relating primarily to improving the quality of the organization's products and services, but which can also involve related issues such as productivity, safety, cost reduction, etc. Apart from suggesting improvements, the group also participates in planning and implementing any of their ideas given 'the go ahead' by management. Quality circles and Total Quality Management originated in the United States in the 1950s but were largely ignored in the West until the 1980s. Meanwhile they have proved most successful in Japan.

To be effective, quality circles must be initiated, encouraged and supported by top management, and members of the circle need training in problem solving/decision-making strategies and statistical methods like Statistical Process Control. Ideas put forward by the group to senior management must be discussed by the latter; either the ideas are passed back for implementation, or constructive feedback is returned to the group. It is common to have a full-time facilitator/coordinator dealing with the overall running of the quality circles and maintaining a high profile for them and their results, making it easier for them to meet their objectives.

Other benefits claimed to result from the use of quality circles include, increased staff awareness of quality, greater job satisfaction, improved motivation, better communications and better utilization of the intellectual skills of the workforce.

cipate. The number of success stories connected with the introduction of quality circles (see Frame 14.10) within organizations shows that this point of view is fallacious. As Handy (1985) puts it, a quality circle is a practical example of a creative autonomous group.

14.5.2   Internationalization of competition and labour

As international communications and transport improve, more organizations face the problem of operating within differing national/ethnic cultures. In 1992, with the 'single European market' any citizen of any EEC country can work in any other EEC country and free trading relationships between these countries should increase the number of international mergers and takeovers. National cultures vary more than organizational ones, which means that if we are to benefit from potential opportunities, we need to be proficient in deciphering and operating *within* other cultures. Hofstede (1980) collected data about national

Table 14.1 *Cultural dimension scores of the EEC member states (excluding Luxembourg), some Far Eastern countries and the USA (higher scores indicate a greater tendency towards a particular cultural dimension)*

Country	PD	UA	I	M
USA	40	46	<u>91</u>	62
Britain	35	35	89	66
Belgium	65	94	75	54
Denmark	<u>18</u>	23	74	16
France	68	86	71	43
W. Germany	35	65	67	66
Greece	60	<u>112</u>	35	57
Ireland	28	35	70	68
Italy	50	75	76	70
Netherlands	38	53	80	14
Portugal	63	104	27	31
Spain	57	86	51	42
Hong Kong	68	29	25	57
Japan	54	92	46	95
Singapore	74	*8*	20	48
Taiwan	58	69	17	45

Key: PD, Power distance; UA, Uncertainty Avoidance; I, Individualism; M, Masculinity.
Source: Hofstede (1980), p. 315.
Note: The scores underlined, along with Phillippines PD = 94, Venezuela I = 12, Sweden M = 5, are the highest/lowest of the 40 countries whose returns were analysed.

culture from 67 countries throughout the world. From an analysis of 40 of these, he identified four 'dimensions' along which cultural difference could be expressed (Table 14.1). These are:

- **Power distance** – a measure of the extent of human inequality, e.g. the distribution of prestige, wealth and power. In organizations it relates to the difference in the extent to which a leader can influence the behaviour of followers/subordinates and vice versa.
- **Uncertainty avoidance** – a measure of tolerance for uncertainty and the consequent need to take action. It is ascertained from an individual's preference for rules, employment stability and level of stress.
- **Individualism (v. collectivism)** – a measure of individuals' emotional dependence on others and the organizations to which they belong, and the way others respond to this. It is reflected in the way we live together, for example in nuclear families, extended families or tribes.
- **Masculinity v. femininity** – a measure of societal preference for

things thought to be important predominantly by males (tasks and things, performance and growth, achievement, etc.) or females (interpersonal relationships, quality of life, a sense of service, etc.).

Although Hofstede's work was conducted solely within IBM, so the effects of IBM's culture cannot be eliminated from his results, there are apparently substantial differences revealed between countries, even those in the same part of the world such as Europe or the Far East. We ignore such cultural differences at our peril!

14.5.3   Organizational development and training

To gear ourselves and our organizations up for challenges like those above, and to facilitate cultural changes within organizations, including the development of problem solving and decision-making skills, requires carefully planned, professionally and systematically implemented, directly relevant training for everybody involved. This provision is essential.

Once the strategic decisions have been taken to embark on some major organizational development, programmes of training for managers and other personnel will need to be initiated: it is not good enough to expect the necessary training to occur naturally, or be effective if it is performed in an ad hoc way. If such training is not to be seen as indoctrination it needs to occur throughout all levels of the organization, senior management included.

The quality of training provided is an important factor in its success. Educational principles suggest that it should be interactive and participative, involve practice of the knowledge/skills being imparted and provide ample feedback. Above all, it should be flexible enough in content, approach and delivery to satisfy the needs of all trainees and be presented in such a way that the knowledge and skills learnt are transferable to other situations, and enjoyable. When the training is intended to bring about a change in outlook, attitudes or behaviour, an *external* trainer is virtually essential. Rightly or wrongly they tend to have more credibility than anyone from inside the organization.

14.5.4   The role of information technology

Information technology (IT) can be effectively used in delivering much of this training requirement through the use of computer-based training (CBT) packages and interactive video (IV). Being self-paced and private, offering immediate and individual feedback, these techniques provide the advantages of individualized instruction, and are available at times to suit the trainee, whilst being standardized (instructor-independent) and offered at any location where appropriate equipment is available.

The IT factor permits the simulation of complex, expensive or dangerous situations, and can provide unbiased monitoring of performance and diagnosis of problem areas. Although custom made CBT can be very expensive, if appropriate off-the-shelf packages are not available it may still be cost-effective to commission a training package rather than put on repeat performances of training courses for large numbers of people. It should be remembered, however, that these methods, even IV, are not substitutes for real experiential learning, especially in regard to areas such as interpersonal skill development (except possibly as an introduction or as a refresher).

The desire for technology, in particular IT, is one of the main protagonists of change, and the impact of technology on members of an organization is mostly determined by managerial policy decisions. The purpose of its introduction is to give managers more control over those they manage, to eliminate human intervention and error, to increase productivity and reliability and/or to provide vital information for strategic and operational decisions affecting the organization's future. Plant's argument that all organizations need to go through a bureaucratic phase in their development also predicts that IT will assist this process by providing the necessary infrastructure required of a modern organization, 'taking much of the rigidity and work volume out of bureaucracy – if used sensibly'. Certainly IT can provide us with quicker, more versatile and efficient communications. It can reduce the tedium of the 'number crunching' required in business, and provide us with up-to-date and relevant management information. But the computer systems that are designed to perform these processes must be designed around *the way we wish to work*. We should not allow designers and implementers to enforce unnatural ways of working upon us just to fit in with the computer's requirements.

14.5.5   The future of organizations

It was thought that the introduction of IT would result in more centralization within organizations: everyone would huddle around the company's massive mainframe computer installation. However, even though some large international companies still require large mainframe super-computers, this still does not guarantee centralization. Deal and Kennedy (1982) argue that IT will not foster centralization because:

- the environment is becoming more complex;
- the rate of change is accelerating;
- competition is intensifying and becoming more global.

They claim that these factors demand quicker response and more effectiveness and productivity, especially from knowledge workers. This can only be achieved through small work units.

The current technological revolution is more to do with communications than computers: over the next decade we will in all probability have quicker and easier access to much greater amounts of data and information. We will also have 'intelligent' hardware/software combinations to help us cope with and utilize this. How is this communications revolutions affecting organizations and problem solving?

Coinciding with the realization of the inadequacies of large bureaucracies in dealing with a changing environment, the communications revolution is having a dramatic impact on the structure of our organizations. Ten years ago, Deal and Kennedy (1982) were talking of 'the increasing use of distributed processing as companies discover that networks of mini- and micro-computers better serve their international and communications needs than large centralized computer installations', and were predicting the advent of 'highly decentralized organizations in which the work of the coporation will be done in small, autonomous units linked to the mega-corporation by new telecommunications and computer technologies'. We are now on course towards the realization of this; large companies are breaking up, and franchising continues to flourish. Dead and Kennedy's view of the future is rapidly becoming a reality with the move towards small, task-focused work units, which are both economically and managerially autonomous, linked by benign computers and communications links and held together by strong cultural bonds.

14.5.6   Computer-enhanced meetings

In the area of group problem solving, computers are being increasingly used to enhance the proceedings of local meetings, where everyone concerned is gathered physically in the same room. The portrayal of data and information, previously written on whiteboards and flipcharts, is now accomplished via overhead projectors and TV monitors connected to computers. These give us the facility of instant call back of any material, as well as enhancing it, for example by rearranging its order, and subsequently publishing it. The implications for creative problem solving groups depend on whether the keyboard operator simply acts as a scribe, typing in the meeting's proceedings, providing reviews, etc. when requested, or whether the meeting's leader is the one operating the computer. If it is considered desirable and efficient for the meeting leader to operate the computer, then training courses which link the skills of process leading with those of using IT will be needed. However, the process leader has a lot to do already; being relieved of writing up group responses, may permit them to run the session better.

A potentially more serious problem is that it is getting more common for geographically separated people to communicate with each other via computers, fax machines, telephone conferencing, etc. for the purpose of 'group' problem solving: this means losing the all-important face-to-face human interactions that contribute to creativity. The relative anonymity that these media offer can also be abused.

It would be useful to devise a protocol in keeping with the spirit of CPS, that we could adopt for group problem solving at a distance even though it would be difficult to ensure adherence to this. Perhaps video telephones and one day live holographic images will be the answer to this problem. By seeing our fellow group problem solving participants, we can pick up their body language and regain some of the sense of being in the same room.

14.6   In conclusion

There is no need to be fearful of change. If we apply the problem solving strategies described in this book, we can not only find ways of coping with it, but also ways of turning it to our advantage. Problems should be seen as opportunities. Resolving these problems can be exhilarating. What would life be like if nothing ever changed and there were no fresh stimuli to exercise our imaginations; no new things to learn about or challenges to fulfil? As Nolan (1981) said: 'We live in a changing world, and the rate of change is accelerating. How to live with change is perhaps the most important single challenge of our time.'

Appendices: Possible solutions to selected exercises

Having offered Exercises in the text, I feel obliged to provide some 'answers. In all these cases, of course, there will be no one 'right' or 'correct' answer. Instead, there will be many different possible solutions of varying merit. I have tried here to provide an indication of what might constitute an answer or solution but your answers, although likely to be different, may well be equally acceptable, if not better.

Appendix 1   Lost at Sea (Chapter 5)

In order to assess the quality of the group consensus decision compared with any ranking obtained from an individual or by averaging the group's individual responses, a 'correct' answer is needed (see below).

The consensus score is almost invariably better than the group average. What is more, unless you do have an 'expert' in the group capable of convincing the other members of his or her expertise, the group consensus score is often better than any one individual's score.

Individual and group scores are computed simply by calculating the difference in rank between the individual/group rank and the 'correct' rank for each of the 15 items and then adding up the sum (ignoring positive and negative values) of these 15 differences. The smallest number wins.

	Rank
sextant	15
shaving mirror	1
5-gallon can of water	3
mosquito netting	14
one case of US Army C rations	4

map of the Pacific Ocean	13
seat cushion (a Coast Guard approved buoyancy aid)	9
small transistor radio	12
shark repellent	10
20 square feet of opaque plastic sheeting	5
one quart of 160° proof Puerto Rican rum	11
15 feet of nylon rope	8
two boxes of chocolate bars	6
fishing kit	7
2-gallon can of petrol/oil mixture	2

This expert opinion is believed to be that of a group of US Marines Officers. It is based on the 'fact' that something like 90 per cent of rescues of people in this sort of predicament are effected within 36 hours. This ranking is based on the rationale that our priorities should:

- make sure that when the time comes (note the positive thinking here) you will be able to make yourself seen ... shaving mirror, smoke from burning petrol/oil mixture;
- keep essential food and water to survive in the short term;
- collect things for long-term survival ... plastic sheet for collecting water, fishing kit.

One bone of contention is usually the sextant, an emminently useful piece of equipment you might think. To use a sextant to find your position you need to know the time of day/date and (unless you have a very good memory) a set of tables to go with it. However, what is the point of knowing your exact position when you cannot tell anyone, and there is no way you are going to row/sail to the nearest land quickly. You might as well just drift ... and hope!

Appendix 2   Northcliffe Sands (Chapter 7)

Backward/forward planning

Task Headline: How to increase revenue from tourism without 'spoiling' the location?

Backwards
If we had now managed to solve this problem, what other higher level problems would it solve. What would it allow you to do?

> Increased funds would mean that we could get on with some long overdue and much needed improvements to the town's amenities etc., and be able to do it in a more flexible way.

(i)   I wish we could speed up the implementation of the long overdue and much needed improvements.

(ii)   I wish we had more flexibility in the way we can handle the town's development.

If you were able to get on with the 'implementation of . . . the improvements', what could you do then?

> By improving some of the town's facilities, we would be able to lessen some of the fears that the local residents have about their environment being 'destroyed', and at the same time, the 'breathing space' that this would bring us, would allow us time to think things through – we wouldn't always be in a near crisis situation.

(iii)   How to reassure the local population about the possible future development of the area?

(iv)   How to find time to think in the middle of a crisis?

Forwards

If we had now 'increased our revenue from tourism without "spoiling" the locations' what benefits would we get from this?

> It would stabilize our local economy, and enable us to do some long-term planning and development. It would improve the general environment and increase the standard of living of the indigenous population.

(v)   How to bring more stability (less seasonality) to our local economy.

(vi)   How to improve the quality of life of the indigenous population?

What is stopping you doing all this?

> We can't seem to reach any agreement on what actions to take.

(vii)   I wish we could stop arguing and make a few decisions.

Itemized Response

Itemized Response on 'I wish we had a multiscreen cinema.'

Positive features
- It would keep a fair number of tourists 'hidden' away from sight and concentrated in one place for several hours a day. This would be really useful on rainy days.
- We would be generating more revenue (for somebody!).
- It should improve this facility for the indigenous population at the same time, even more so if it has an alternative 'off season' use.

Concerns
The major concern might be . . .

> the cost of converting our single screen cinema into a multiple one, and the additional running costs.

An idea to overcome the concern:

> Offer the owners help with the cost of conversion, in exchange for multiple use of the facility, for example, the local arts centre theatre group presentations, conferences, etc.

or

> The general decline in cinema attendance.

An idea to overcome the concern:

> Since we have a large, transient and changing 'captive' audience coupled with the fact that they are 'on holiday' (people tend to do things on holiday that they do not do otherwise, or do things more often than they normally do) we are more likely to be able to buck this national trend. We should also be able to adopt the policy of going for volume ticket sales at low prices if necessary.

Ideas to satisfy Peter Frith's concern

Since planning permission will be required by potential 'fringe' retailers, Peter Frith will be forewarned of possible competition. He and the other retailers could either:

- offer to supply a 'fringe' retailer with any goods that he/she wishes to sell at competitive 'trade' prices; or
- offer to run the 'fringe' retail operation as an extension of their own businesses, paying rent and/or a small commission to the land-owner, or whoever manages the camp site, hill-walking/nature centre, etc.

Little can be done about the sale of 'home produced' products except to secure from the Council an assurance that all health, hygiene and trading laws are observed.

Appendix 3   The Engineers problem: abstraction (Chapter 8)

Figure 8.1 on page 156 contains all the information that we have been told about the situation. By taking the subtotals that we have away from the grand total, we can easily find the 'missing' subtotals 11 and 7. By bringing the 3 into play we can similarly deduce what numbers should be in the other 'gaps' in the table and hence the required information.

Figure 8.2 attempts to represent the (overlapping sets of) previous work experience of the engineers as two circles. Whilst not so immediately helpful in this instance (with the same basic problem but with different information 'known' and 'unknown' the diagram can be more explicit than the table), we can (relatively) easily determine that there must be 2 engineers who have petro-chemical and civil engineering experience. If there are 3 with neither experience there must be 14 within the two overlapping circles. But 6 engineers with petro-chemical experience have to be placed in the left circle, and 10 in the right civil experience circle, and $10 + 6 = 16$, therefore $(16 - 14 =) 2$ engineers have to be in both circles.

The algebraic proof is as follows:

Let p be the number of engineers with only petro-chemical experience

$\quad\quad c$ be the number of engineers with only civil experience

$\quad\quad b$ be the number of engineers with both types of experience

$\quad\quad n$ be the number of engineers with neither experience

then $p + c + b + n = 17$	(1)
$p + b = 6$	(2)
$c + b = 10$	(3)
$n = 3$	(4)

one possible solution method is . . .

from (1) − (4) we get	$p + c + b\ \ = 14$	(5)
from (2) + (3) we get	$p + c + 2b = 16$	(6)
and from (6) − (5) we get	$b = 2$	

The cognoscenti will realize that all these approaches are mathematical in one form or another – the diagram method being a Venn diagram taken from Set Theory. However, there might have been a totally non-mathematical way of abstracting this problem.

Appendix 4   Decision alternatives: MUST and WANTS (Chapter 10)

New marina development

MUSTS
- Capacity for 500 by 10m berths
- Deep non-tidal moorings
- Freehold site
- Outline planning permission

WANTS
- Proximity of other marinas
- Low cost of land purchase
- Low development costs
- Space for residential accommodation
- Good transport facilities nearby (motorway, airport, railway)
- Local acceptance
- Sheltered moorings (against tidal extremes/storms)
- Local amenities (cinemas, restaurants)

Site for new hotel

MUST
- Outline planning permission for at least 200-bedroom hotel
- Projected Net Present Value of investment > ?%
- Development area

WANTS
- Good long-term investment
- Expansion possibilities
- Good position
- Local amenities (cinemas, restaurants, etc.)
- Proximity of similar establishments
- Condition of local tourism industry
- Future demand
- Availability and quality of local staff
- Weather profile

Note: It could be important to know whether the situation is within a developing area. Gaining some form of government development grant may be more important than long-term investment.

Bibliography

Suggested further readings are indicated by an asterisk and a chapter reference.

Ackoff, Russell L. (1957) 'Towards a Behavioural Theory of Communication', in W. Buckey (ed.), *Modern Systems Research for the Behavioural Scientist*, Aldine, Chicago.

Ackoff, Russell L. (1978) *The Art of Problem Solving*, John Wiley, Chichester.

Ackoff, Russell L. (1981) 'The Art and Science of Mess Management' *Interfaces*, vol. 11, no. 1, Feb. 1981 (The Institute of Management Sciences).

Ackoff, Russell L. (1983) 'An Interactive View of Rationality', *Journal of the Operational Research Society*, vol. 34, no. 8.

*Adams, James L. (1979) *Conceptual Blockbusting* 2nd edition, W. W. Norton, New York (Chapter 4)

Alexander, John (1979) 'Synectics: Creativity, Problem-solving and Interpersonal Skills', *Bacie Journal*, Jan. 1979.

Allen, M. S. (1962) *Morphological Creativity*, Prentice-Hall, Englewood Cliffs, New Jersey.

Ansoff, H. Igor (1968) *Corporate Strategy: An Analytic Approach to Business Policy for Growth and Expansion*, Penguin, London.

Avolio, Bruce J. and Bass, Bernard M. (1988) 'Transformational Leadership, Charisma, and Beyond', in James Hunt, B. Baliga, H. Dachler, Chester A. Schriesheim (eds), *Emerging Leadership Vistas*, Lexington Books, D. C. Heath and Co., Lexington, Mass., pp. 29–49.

Bales, Robert F. and Slater, Philip E. (1956) 'Role Differentiation in Small Decision-Making Groups', in Talcott Parsons, Robert F. Bales *et al.*, *Family Socialization and Interaction Process*, Routledge and Kegan Paul, London.

Bass, Bernard, M. (1985) *Leadership, Psychology and Organizational Behaviour*, Free Press, New York.

Beishon, John and Peters, Geoff (eds) (1981) *Systems Behaviour*, 3rd edn, Harper and Row, London (first published 1972).

Belbin, R. M. (1981) *Management Teams*, Heinemann.

Boal, Kimberley B. and Bryson, John M. (1988) 'Charismatic Leadership: A Phenomenological and Structural Approach', in James Hunt, B. Baliga, H. Dachler, Chester A. Schriesheim (eds), *Emerging Leadership Vistas*, Lexington Books, D. C. Heath and Co., Lexington, Mass., pp. 11–28.

Buchanan, David A. and Huczynski, Andrzej A. (1985) *Organizational Behaviour: An Introductory Text*, Prentice Hall International, London.

Burns, James MacGregor (1978) *Leadership*, Harper and Row, New York.

Buzan, Tony (1974) *Use Your Head*, BBC Publications, London.

*Checkland, Peter B. (1981) *Systems Thinking, Systems Practice*, John Wiley, Chichester. (Chapter 12)

Checkland, Peter B. (1983) OR and the Systems Movement: Mapping and Conflicts. *Journal of Operations Research*, **34**(8).

*Checkland, Peter B. (1985) 'From Optimizing to Learning: A Development of Systems Thinking for the 1990s' *Journal of the Operational Research Society*, vol. 36, no. 9.

*Checkland, Peter B. (1986) 'The Politics of Practice', International Roundtable on The Art and Science of Systems Practice, IIASA, November 1986.

Checkland, Peter B. (1987a) 'Images of Systems and the Systems Image', Presidential Address to the International Society for General Systems Research, Budapest, June 1987.

Checkland, Peter B. (1987b) 'Soft Systems Methodology: An Overview', a paper given at a plenary session of the 31st Annual Meeting of the International Society for General Systems Research, Budapest.

Checkland, Peter B. and Scholes, J. (1990) *Soft Systems Methodology in Action*, John Wiley, Chichester. (Chapter 12)

Checkland, Peter B. and Wilson, B. (1980) '"Primary Task" and "Issue based" Root Definition', *Journal of Applied Systems Analysis*, vol. 7.

Cutts, Geoff (1987) *Structured Systems Analysis and Design Methodology*, Paradigm, London.

Cyert, R. M., Simon, H. A. and Trow, D. B. (1956) 'Observation of a Business Decison', *Journal of Business*, vol. 29.

Deal, Terrence E. and Kennedy, Allen A. (1982) *Corporate Cultures: The Rites and Rituals of Corporate Life*, Addison-Wesley, Reading, Mass.

Diesing, Paul (1958) 'Socioeconomic Decisions', *Ethics*, vol. 69.

Drucker, Peter F. (1955) *The Practice of Management*, Heinemann, London.

*Eden, Colin, Jones, Sue and Sims, David (1983) *Messing About in Problems: An Informal Structured Approach to their Identification and Management*, Pergamon Press, Oxford. (Chapter 7)

Eldridge J. E. T. and Crombie A. D. (1974) *A Sociology of Organizations*, George Allen and Unwin, London.

Forrester, Jay (1961) *Industrial Dynamics*, The MIT Press, Boston, Mass. and Wiley, Chichester. Reported in George H. Rice, 'But How DO Managers Make Decisions?' *Management Decision*, vol. 18, no. 4, p. 197.

French, J. R. P. and Raven, B. H. (1959) 'The bases of social power', in D. Cartwright (ed.), *Studies in Social Power*, University of Michigan Press.

Georgopoulos, Basil S, Mahoney, Gerald M. and Jones, Nyle W. (1957) 'A Path-Goal Approach to Productivity' *Journal of Applied Psychology*, vol. 41, pp. 345–53; and in Vroom (1964), p. 239.

*Gordon, William J. J. (1961). *Synectics*, Harper and Row, New York. (Chapters 4, 7)

Graham, J. (1988) in Hunt *et al.* (1988)

Graves, Desmond (1986) *Corporate Culture – Diagnosis and Change: Auditing and Changing the Culture of Organizations*, Frances Pinter, London.

Grogono, Peter and Nelson, Sharon H. (1982) Problem Solving and Computer Programming', Addison-Wesley, Reading, Mass. (The first 80 pages discuss problem solving methods.)

Guilford, J. P. (1962) 'Creativity: Its Measurement and Development', in Parnes and Harding, pp. 156–68.

Hall, A. D. (1962) *A Methodology for Systems Engineering*, Van Nostrand, Princeton, NJ.

Hall, Jay (1971) 'Decisions, decisions, decisions', *Psychology Today*, November

Handy, Charles B. (1978) *Gods of Management*, Pan Books, London.

Handy, Charles B. (1985) *Understanding Organizations*, 3rd edn, Penguin Books, London.

Harrison, Roger (1972) 'Understanding Your Organization's Character', *Harvard Business Review*, May–June.

Hastings, Colin *et al.* (1986) *Superteams: A Blueprint for Organisational Success*, Fontana, Glasgow.

Hofstede, Geert (1980) *Cultures Consequences: International Differences in Work-Related Values*, Sage Publications, London.

Hosking, Dian-Marie and Morley, Ian E. (1988) 'The Skills of Leadership', in James Hunt, B. Baliga, H. Dachler and Chester A. Schriesheim (eds), *Emerging Leadership Vistas*, Lexington Books, D. C. Heath and Co., Lexington, Mass., pp. 89–106.

House, Rober J. (1988) 'Leadership Research: Some Forgotten, Ignored, or Overlooked Findings', in James Hunt, B. Baliga, H. Dachler, Chester A. Schriesheim (eds), *Emerging Leadership Vistas*, Lexington Books, D. C. Heath and Co., Lexington, Mass, pp. 245–60.

Hunt, J., Baliga, B., Dachler, H. and Schriesheim, C. (eds) (1988) *Emerging Leadership Vistas*. Lexington Books, Lexington, Mass.

Janis, Irving L. (1982) *Groupthink*, Harcourt Brace, Boston, Mass.

Katz, Daniel and Kahn, Robert L. (1966) *The Social Psychology of Organizations*, John Wiley, New York.

Kelly, Joe (1969) *Organizational Behaviour*, Richard D. Irwin Inc. and the Dorsey Press, Illinois.

*Kepner, Charles H. and Tregoe, Benjamin, B. (1981) *The New Rational Manager*, John Martin Publishing, London (first edition published as *The Rational Manager* by McGraw-Hill, 1965). (Chapter 10)

Kobery, D. and Bagnall, J. (1974) *The Universal Traveller. A Soft Systems Guidebook to: creativity, problem solving, and the process of design*, William Kaufmann, Los Altos. (Chapters 4, 9)

Kolb, D. A. (1976) 'Management and the Learning Process', *California Management Review*, XVIII, no. 3.

Lawler, Edward E. (1969) 'Job Design and Employee Motivation', *Personnel Psychology*, vol. 22, pp. 426–35, reprinted in Vroom and Deci (1970, 1989), pp. 160–9.

Leavitt, Harold J. (1978) *Managerial Psychology*, 4th edn, University of Chicago Press, Chicago.

Lindblom, C. E. (1959) 'The Science of "Muddling Through"', *Public Administration Review*, vol. 19, no. 2, and in Pugh (1984) p. 238–55.

Lippitt, Gordon L. (1982) *Organization Renewal: A Holistic Approach to Organizational Development*, 2nd edn, Prentice Hall, Englewood Cliffs, NJ.

March J. G. (1976) 'The Technology of Foolishness', Chapter 5 in J. G. March and J. P. Olsen, 'Ambiguity and Choice in Organizations', *Universitetsforlaget*. Also in Pugh (1984), pp. 232, 236–7.

Maslow, Abraham H. (1943) 'A Theory of Human Motivation', *Psychological Review*, vol. 30, pp. 370–96. An abridged version can be found in Vroom and Deci (1970, 1989).

Maslow, Abraham H. (1962) *Emotional Blocks to Creativity* in Parnes and Harding.

McGregor, Douglas M. (1957) 'The Human Side of Enterprise', in 'Adventures in Thought and Action', *Proceedings of the Fifth Anniversary Convocation of the School of Industrial Management*, MIT, Boston, Mass. and also in Vroom and Deci (1970, 1989).

Mintzberg H. (1975) 'The Manager's Job: Folklore and Fact', *Harvard Business Review*, July–August, and in Pugh (1984), pp. 424–5.

Moore, Carol-Lynne (1982) *Executives in Action*, 2nd edn, Macdonald and Evans, Plymouth (originally called *Action Profiling*, 1978) A brief account of Action Profiling also occurs in Nolan (1989).

Morgan, Gareth (1989) *Creative Organization Theory: A Resourcebook*, Sage Publications, London.

Nolan, Vincent (1981) 'Open to Change: How to Initiate, Cope with and Benefit from Change at Work', *Management Decision*, vol. 2, no. 1.

*Nolan, Vincent (1989) *The Innovator's Handbook: The Skills of Innovative*

Management, Sphere Books, London. (Chapter 7)

Noon, J. (1985) *A Time*, Van Nostrand Reinhold (International), London.

Oldcorn, Roger (1982) *Management. A Fresh Approach*, Pan Books, London.

*Osborn, Alex F. (1957) *Applied Imagination*, rev. edn, Charles Scribner's Sons, New York (originally published 1953). (Chapter 6)

Parnes, Sidney J. (1972) *Creativity: Unblocking human potential*. DOK Pub. Inc. (Creative Education Foundation)

Parnes, Sidney J. and Harding, Harold F. (eds) (1962) *A Source Book for Creative Thinking*, Charles Scribner's Sons, New York.

Plant, Roger (1987) *Managing Change and Making It Stick*, Fontana/Collins, London.

Polya, G. (1957) *How to Solve It: A New Aspect of Mathematical Method*, Doubleday Anchor Books, New York (originally published by Princeton University Press, 1945).

*Prince, George M. (1970) *The Practice of Creativity*, Collier Books (Macmillan Publishing), New York. (Chapter 4)

Prince, George M. (1976) 'Mindspring', *Chemtech*, May 1976.

Prince, George M. (1980) 'Problem Solving Strategies: The Synectics Approach', a management training video produced by McGraw-Hill International Training Systems.

Pugh, D. S. (1984) *Organization Theory*, Penguin Books, London.

Rogers, Carl R. (1954) 'Toward a Theory of Creativity' etc: a Review of General Semantics, vol. XI, no. 4, and, in Parnes and Harding (1962), pp. 63–72.

Reddin, W. J. (1977) 'Confessions of an Organizational Change Agent' Group and Organisational, Studies, *International Journal of Group Facilitators*, vol. 2, no. 1, March.

Rhodes, D. J. (1985) 'Root Definitions and Reality in Manufacturing Systems', *Journal of Applied Systems Analysis*, vol. 12.

Rickards, Tudor (1974) *Problem Solving through Creative Analysis*, Gower Press, London.

Sathe, V. (1985) *Culture and Related Corporate Realities*, Richard D. Urwin, Homewood, Illinois.

Sculley, John with Byrne, John A. (1988) *Odyssey – Pepsi to Apple*, Fontana/Collins, Glasgow.

Simon, Herbert A. (1955) 'A Behavioral Model of Rational Choice', *Quarterly Journal of Economics*, vol. 64, no. 1.

Simon, Herbert A. (1957) *Models of Man*, John Wiley and Sons.

Simon, Herbert A. (1960a) 'The executive as decision maker', in *The New Science of Management Decision*, Harper and Row, New York and also 'Decision Making and Organizational Design' in D. S. Pugh (1984), pp. 202–8.

Simon, Herbert A. (1960b) 'Organizational design: man–machine systems for decision making' in *The New Science of Management Decision*, Harper and Row, New York, and also 'Decision Making and Organizational Design', in Pugh (1984), p. 209.

Smyth, D. S. and Checkland, P. B. (1976) Using a systems approach: the structure of root definitions. *Journal of Applied Systems Analysis*, **5**(1).

Steele, Fritz (1975) 'Consulting for Organizational Change', University of Massachussetts Press, Amherst, also in Sathe (1985) pp. 355–7.

Steinberg, Rhona and Shapiro, Stanley (1982) 'Sex Differences in Personality Traits of Female and Male Masters of Business Administration Students', *Journal of Applied Psychology*, vol. 67, no. 3, pp. 306–10. Also cited in Buchanan and Huczynski (1985), pp. 386–7.

Stevens, M. (1989) British Institute of Management.

Taylor, Calvin W. (1962) 'Tentative Description of the Creative Individual', in Parnes and Harding (1962).

*Van Gundy Jr., Arthur B. (1988) *Techniques of Structured Problem Solving*, 2nd edn, Van Nostrand Reinhold, New York (first published 1981). (Chapter 4)

Vickers, Geoffrey (1961) Judgement, The Sixth Elbourne Memorial Lectures, The Manager, pp. 31–9.

Vickers, Geoffrey (1965) *The Art of Judgement: A Study of Policy Making*, Chapman and Hall, London.

Vickers, Geoffrey (1970) *Freedom in a Rocking Boat*, Allen Lane, London (also Penguin, 1972).

Vickers, Geoffrey (1981) *Some implications of systems thinking*, in Beishan and Peters (1981), pp. 19–25.

Vickers, Geoffrey (1983) *Human Systems are Different*, Harper and Row, London.

Vroom, Victor H. (1964) *Work and Motivation*, Wiley, Chichester.

Vroom, Victor H. and Deci, Edward L. (eds) (1970, 1989) *Management and Motivation*, Penguin Books, London.

Wall, T. Kemp, N.J., Lackson, P. R. and Clegg, C. W. (1986) 'Outcomes of Autonomous Workgroups: A Long-Term Field Experiment', *Academy of Management Journal*.

Wild, R. (1972) *Management and Production*, Penguin Books, London.

Woodburn, Ian (1985) 'Some Developments in the Building of Conceptural Models', *Journal of Applied Systems Analysis*, vol. 12.

Zwicky, F. (1969) *Discovery, Invention, Research through the Morphological Approach*, MacMillan, New York.

Author Index

Subject Index